Sixth Grade Homeschooling

(Includes Social Science, Math and Science)

By Thomas Bell, Greg Sherman, and Terri Raymond

Home School Brew Press

www.HomeSchoolBrew.com

© 2014. All Rights Reserved.

Cove Image © aboikis - Fotolia.com

Table of Contents

- Sixth Grade Science 9
  - Chapter 1: The Scientific Process 10
    - The Scientific Process: Activities and Experiments 14
    - The Scientific Process: Quiz 17
  - Chapter 2: Properties of Matter 19
    - Properties of Matter: Activities and Experiments 25
    - Properties of Matter: Quiz 29
  - Chapter 3: The Human Body 31
    - The Human Body: Activities and Experiments 38
    - The Human Body: Quiz 42
  - Chapter 4: Earth / Moon / Sun 46
    - Earth / Moon / Sun: Activities and Experiments 51
    - Earth / Moon / Sun: Quiz 55
  - Chapter 5: Characteristics of Plants 57
    - Characteristics of Plants: Activities and Experiments 64
    - Characteristics of Plants: Quiz 67
  - Chapter 6: Energy, Force, & Motion 70
    - Energy, Force, & Motion: Activities and Experiments 76
    - Energy, Force, & Motion: Quiz 80
  - Chapter 7: Electricity & Magnetism 83
    - Electricity & Magnetism: Activities and Experiments 90
    - Electricity & Magnetism: Quiz 94
  - Chapter 8: Periodic Table 97
    - Periodic Table: Activities and Experiments 105
    - Periodic Table: Quiz 108
  - Chapter 9: Photosynthesis 111
    - Photosynthesis: Activities and Experiments 117
    - Photosynthesis: Quiz 121
  - Chapter 10: Weather 122
    - Weather: Activities and Experiments 131
    - Weather: Quiz 135
  - Answer Key 139
    - Chapter 1 140

- Chapter 2 140
- Chapter 3 140
- Chapter 4 141
- Chapter 5 142
- Chapter 6 143
- Chapter 7 143
- Chapter 8 144
- Chapter 9 145
- Chapter 10 145

Sixth Grade Math 147
- Whole Numbers 148
  - Addition 148
  - Subtraction 149
  - Multiplication 150
  - Division 150
  - Factor Families 151
  - Whole Numbers – Practice Sheet 152
  - Whole Numbers – Quiz 154
- Operations with Whole Numbers 155
  - Multiplication 158
  - Division 158
  - Order of Operations 160
  - Operations with Whole Numbers – Practice Sheet 161
  - Operations with Whole Numbers – Quiz 163
- Decimals 164
  - Adding and Subtracting Decimals 166
  - Decimals – Practice Sheet 169
  - Decimals – Quiz 171
- Integers 172
  - Subtraction 174
  - Integers – Quiz 178
- Graphing 180
  - Interpreting Graphed Data 180
  - Creating Graphs 184
  - Graphing – Practice Sheet 190
- Fractions 194

- Multiplying Fractions 195
- Dividing Fractions 196
- Fractions – Practice Sheet 198
- Fractions – Quiz 200

Ratios / Proportions / Percents 201
- Ratios 201
- Comparing Ratios 202
- Proportions 202
- Completing / Solving Proportions 203
- Percents 204
- Ratios / Proportions / Percent's - Practice Sheet 206
- Ratios / Proportions / Percent's - Quiz 209

Measurements 210
- Converting Standard Units 211
- Metric Units of Measurement 212
- Measurements – Practice Sheet 215
- Measurements – Quiz 218

Functions and Probability 220
- Functions 220
- Functions and Probability – Practice Sheet 225
- Functions and Probability – Quiz 228

Geometry 229
- Perimeter 231
- Area 232
- Angles of Polygons 234
- Geometry – Practice Sheet 235
- Geometry – Quiz 238

Answer Key 239
- Whole Numbers – Practice Sheet 240
- Whole Numbers – Quiz 242
- Operations with Whole Numbers – Practice Sheet 243
- Operations with Whole Numbers – Quiz 244
- Decimals – Practice Sheet 246
- Decimals – Quiz 248
- Integers – Practice Sheet 249
- Integers – Quiz 251

    Graphing – Practice Sheet 253

    Interpret the following Data/Graph 254

    Graphing - Quiz 255

    Fractions – Practice Sheet..256

    Fractions – Quiz 258

    Ratios / Proportions / Percent's – Practice Sheet..260

    Ratios / Proportions / Percent's – Quiz...263

    Measurements – Practice Sheet 264

    Measurements – Quiz..267

    Functions and Probability – Practice Sheet 268

    Functions and Probability – Quiz 271

    Geometry – Practice Sheet...272

    Geometry – Quiz 275

Sixth Grade Social Science 276

Chapter 1: Paleolithic-Agricultural Revolution 277

    Paleolithic-Agricultural Revolution Discussion Questions 281

    Paleolithic-Agricultural Revolution Activities 282

    Paleolithic-Agricultural: For Further Reading..284

    Paleolithic-Agricultural Revolution: Quiz...285

    Paleolithic-Agricultural Revolution: Works Cited 289

Chapter 2: Mesopotamia, Egypt, and Kush 291

    Mesopotamia, Egypt, and Kush: Discussion Questions 296

    Mesopotamia, Egypt, and Kush: Activities 297

    Mesopotamia, Egypt, and Kush: For Further Reading 298

    Mesopotamia, Egypt, and Kush: Quiz 300

    Mesopotamia, Egypt, and Kush: Works Cited 304

Chapter 3: Ancient Hebrews...305

    Ancient Hebrews: Discussion Questions..309

    Ancient Hebrews: Activities...310

    Ancient Hebrews: For Further Reading..312

    Ancient Hebrews: Quiz...314

    Ancient Hebrews: Works Cited 318

Chapter 4: Ancient Greece..319

    Ancient Greece: Discussion Questions...324

    Ancient Greece: Activities..325

    Ancient Greece: For Further Reading...327

- Ancient Greece: Quiz 329
- Ancient Greece: Works Cited 333
- Chapter 5: Ancient India 334
  - Ancient India: Discussion Questions 337
  - Ancient India: Activities 338
  - Ancient India: For Further Reading 339
  - Ancient India: Quiz 340
  - Ancient India: Works Cited 344
- Chapter 6: Ancient China 345
  - Ancient China: Discussion Questions 349
  - Ancient China: Activities 350
  - Ancient China: For Further Reading 352
  - Ancient China: Quiz 354
  - Ancient China: Works Cited 358
- Chapter 7: Ancient Rome 359
  - Ancient Rome: Discussion Questions 364
  - Ancient Rome: Activities 365
  - Ancient Rome: For Further Reading 367
  - Ancient Rome: Quiz 369
  - Ancient Rome: Works Cited 373

Disclaimer

This book was developed for parents and students of no particular state; while it is based on common core standards, it is always best to check with your state board to see what will be included on testing.

About Us

Homeschool Brew was started for one simple reason: to make affordable Homeschooling books! When we began looking into homeschooling our own children, we were astonished at the cost of curriculum. Nobody ever said homeschool was easy, but we didn't know that the cost to get materials would leave us broke.

We began partnering with educators and parents to start producing the same kind of quality content that you expect in expensive books...but at a price anyone can afford.

We are still in our infancy stages, but we will be adding more books every month. We value your feedback, so if you have any comments about what you like or how we can do better, then please let us know!

To add your name to our mailing list, go here: http://www.homeschoolbrew.com/mailing-list.html

Sixth Grade Science
(For Homeschool or Extra Practice)

By Thomas Bell

Chapter 1: The Scientific Process

The world around us is a fascinating and exciting place to live. To fully understand why and how our world and universe are the way they are, we humans carry out all kinds of scientific research. This gives us insight into many facets of life, as well as into the nature of the universe. We base many of our important ideas on scientific discoveries, and it's thanks to science that we have all of the technologies and medicines that help us in our day-to-day lives. All of these things require research. When researchers carry out scientific research there are many things they have to take into consideration. Because science gets more and more complicated the deeper you get into it, scientists have developed a process that they like to follow. This keeps them on track, and allows them to practice science while carrying out experiments in a good and controlled setting. Once we understand how scientists perform science, we can move on to specific subtopics of science, in the later units.

There are 4 main components to the scientific process:

1. PLANNING- 2. CONDUCTING- 3. PROCESSING- 4. EVALUATING

Some components have sub-components, which will be highlighted in the same color below.

Pretend for a minute you have discovered a new species of plant on a scientific expedition into a deep jungle, and you bring back some cuttings to your lab. You want to find out, using the scientific process, how often you should water these cuttings in order for them to grow.

We will start with the planning phase. First you need to develop a **title and aim**. They give a brief indication of what you are investigating, and your aims

Example:

- Title- Investigations into watering frequency and growth rates of a newly discovered jungle plant
- Aim- The aim of this study is to determine the frequency* of watering needed for optimal growth of this newly discovered plant species.

*here frequency means how often you do something

Then, once you have your title and aim, you need to form your **hypothesis**. Your hypothesis will usually explain what you are going to do, and what you expect to happen in response. It is your most educated and best guess as to what you expect to happen when you carry out the experiment.

Example:

- Hypothesis- Due to the high frequency of rain in the area where the plant was discovered, we hypothesize that the more often we water the plant, the faster the plant will grow.

In this hypothesis we said lots a few things, so lets take a closer look. The most important thing, and the thing you absolutely need for the formation of your hypothesis, is what you expect to happen. Since the plant was found in a forest where there is lots of rain, we can hypothesize that frequent watering must be the best way for this plant to thrive, since that is the closest thing to its natural habitat.

The next thing you need to determine is your set of **variables**. A variable is anything that can vary in a measureable way. For example, your height may vary, since you get taller. Your height can be measured. That means height is a variable. Other examples are time, temperature, and weight. Science is all about cause and effect. When one thing changes, something else responds. All these changing and responding parts are called variables. You have 3 kinds of variables:

- **Independent variables**: These are variables that the scientist controls. Most experiments will have just 1 independent variable per experiment. For us in our pretend plant scenario, our independent variable is the frequency of watering. It is called the independent variable because it does not depend on anything except you, the scientist. It is the variable you change to see what happens.
- **Dependent variables**: Dependent variables are the variables that change in response to the independent variable, and they are the ones that the scientist wishes to observe and measure. In our example, since we want to measure how fast the plant will grow, the height of the plant is our dependent variable. It is the responder variable, or rather, the one that changes because of the experimental manipulation.
- **Controlled variables**: When you carry out an experiment you also have controlled variables. For example, if you were to carry out your imaginary plant experiment, you would have to be very careful to keep all the plants in the same amount of sunlight, and you would have to make sure that you always water them the same amount, otherwise this will affect the results of the experiment. Therefore, sunlight levels and watering dosages are called controlled variables. If you keep some of the plants in less light, or if you give them different amounts of water each time, you cannot know if the changes that happen are because of one variable or the other. That is why you have to try to keep every single other thing as controlled and constant as possible, and that is also why you only have 1 independent variable at a time. Controlled variables should be observed and measured, the same as dependent variables, to ensure that they remain constant.

Once you understand all of your variables, you must determine your **materials and methods**.

Your materials are a list of items and consumables you need in order to carry out your experiment. It should include everything you need for your own safety, for the proper carrying out of the experiment, and for recording the data.

For us it may include the following:

Water

Plant samples (the number we would need would depend on how many conditions you want to have and how many trials you want to have)

Measuring cup (for giving the plants the same amount of water each time)

Ruler (for measuring the growth of the plant)

Pencil & notebook (for recording watering times and dates, and for recording plant height)

The methods that you use are step-by-step processes that you will follow, kind of like following a recipe.

CHALLENGE: Try to write out a method for our plant watering experiment. You have to write a numbered step-by-step guide that should be followed to determine if the plant grows faster if it is watered once every day, two days, three days, or four days. Don't forget to include how much and when to water them, when and how to measure the height of the plants, and how to keep all controlled variables such as light and temperature constant for all the plants. (*It is ok if the light and temperature change, as long as this change is the same for all plants*)

Now that we have understood the planning phase, we can move onto the **conducting phase**. In the conducting phase we carry out the experiment. For each and every type of experiment there are different things to take into consideration, but there are also some general rules that you should always follow. The first and most important thing to do is to work safely! **Safety** should always come first, and you must be aware and prepared for all risks involved. For example, be careful when working with sharp objects, and wear gloves and glasses around chemicals. Any security precautions should always be presented to you by the person who teaches you how to work in that particular kind of lab, or for that particular kind of experiment you are doing. If they do not, be sure to ask what precautions you should take, and what risks are involved. Since we would not work with any dangerous chemicals in our plant experiment, there would be no special safety precautions.

When you are going to carry out your experiment, make sure that you have read and fully understood the entire material and methods section. Sometimes you will be the person that writes the materials and methods, and then you will understand them already. Sometimes, however, they will be given to you, and in this case, you must make sure you understand everything **before** you start the experiment, or you will run into problems later. **Recording data** is the next most import step in the conducting phase. You must make sure to fully label and neatly record all data. This should include the use of tables. Raw data should be recorded in your lab book (which should also be used for all notes pertaining to your whole research topic and all of your experiments. Your lab book is important because it has all the information inside of it. That way you cannot lose your data, and if you ever get confused about something you can always check your lab book). Later it can transferred, for example, to an excel worksheet on a computer. All of your data should also include the unit of measurement, for example centimeters (cm).

After you conduct the experiment and record the data the next step is processing. **Processing** the data starts with the act of taking your data, and turning into something that you can use in a lab report, like a graph. A **graph** should always have a title, and it should be properly labeled. This means that both the x and y axes should be labeled, the unit should be written, and appropriate intervals should be marked. Always use a ruler when drawing graphs. After you have done this you move on to the **discussion.** In the discussion phase you must outline what the investigation tells you. All of the data, and the graphs you got from the data, must be discussed and interpreted. You should be able to explain the specific effects of the independent variable in the experiment, and try to answer the following questions:

- Are there any trends?
- Was the test accurate?
- Are there any theories that support your observations?

After the processing phase, where you make graphs and discuss, comes the last phase: evaluation. In the evaluation phase you The evaluation is a task on its own, but also included in the evaluation phase is the conclusion. When you write a conclusion you should provide a brief summary, explaining if your hypothesis was supported or not. Be sure to include the independent and dependent variable. After concluding you must evaluate. In the evaluation you should talk about what worked well, what didn't work well, if the results are reliable or not, and what you would do differently if you did it again.

All scientists follow a process just like or very similar to this one, and if you understand this process then you have already taken the first step into the world of science.

The Scientific Process: Activities and Experiments

1. Observing and recording

What you need:

- Pencil
- Paper
- Ruler
- A scale
- An object from your room

What you do:

- Take the object and lay it on the table.
- Using your pencil and paper, draw the object as best you can. If the object has straight edges, use a ruler.
- Measure the dimensions of the object, and label the drawing appropriately.
- Write down additional characteristics of the object, such as the color, texture, and weight.

What you should learn:

- This exercise should teach you how to properly observe something, as well as record data in a scientific way.

Question:

- In what phase of the scientific process do you normally observe and record?

2. Writing materials and methods

What you need:

- Pencil
- Paper
- All the materials that you choose to include for the method you write
- A friend, teacher, or parent

What you do:

- Write a materials and methods guide for making a peanut butter and jelly sandwich.
- Include all details needed, as if the person reading your materials and methods has no idea about sandwich making.
- Give the materials and methods to the other person.
- The second person should follow the methods EXACTLY, using ONLY things that are on the materials list.

What you should learn:

- This should show you how important it is to be precise and detailed when writing materials and methods.

Questions:

- Did everything go according to plan?
- Was everything you need on the materials list?
- Is there any possibility that your methods could have accidentally been interpreted in the wrong way?

3. Forming your hypothesis

- Pencil
- Paper
- Empty plastic water bottle
- Full plastic water bottle
- Wine cork
- Penny
- Pencil
- Paperclip
- Anything else you would like to test that can go in water

What you do:

- Hypothesize, for each object, whether it will float or sink.
- Fill a bucket or bathtub with water.
- Check whether each object floats or sinks
- Record your data

What you should learn:

- How to try to form a hypothesis

Question:

- How accurate were your hypotheses?

4. Identifying variables

What you need:

- Pencil
- Paper
- Bouncy ball
- Measuring tape

What you do:

- Take the ball to different locations and drop it from the same height.
- Measure how high the ball bounces on different surfaces.
- Measure the height of the bouncing and record your data.
- Identify in your results which variable is your independent variable, which is your dependent variable, and what your controlled variables are.

What you should learn:

- How to identify which variables are which, and how important it is to control them.

Questions:

- What is your independent variable?
- What is your dependent variable?
- What are your control variables?

5. Drawing graphs

What you need:

- Pencil
- Paper
- Ruler

What you do:

- Go around the house or room and count how many objects you see that are green and record your data
- Go around the house or room and count how many objects you see that are red and record your data
- Go around the house or room and count how many objects you see that are yellow and record your data
- Repeat for as many colors as you like
- After you have counted your objects and recorded your data, carefully draw a bar graph with a ruler that shows your results. Make sure to label your axes properly.
- Calculate how many objects you counted on average per color

What you should learn:

- How to draw a graph, and how to process your data

Questions

- How does looking at a graph change your perception of your data?
- Is a graph useful for interpretation of the data?
- How many objects did you count on average?

The Scientific Process: Quiz

1. Arrange the following parts of the scientific process in the order they are carried out:

    Processing, Evaluating, Planning, Conducting

    _____

True or false:

2. After you do an experiment you should form a hypothesis. _____

3. When you process your data you often have to make a graph. _____

4. Controlled variables should be measured. _____

5. Dependent variables are ones that are altered by the scientist. _____

6. Most experiments only have 1 dependent variable. _____

7. Safety is very important to consider when carrying out experiments. _____

8. A variable is anything that can vary in a measureable way. _____

9. You should state if your hypothesis was correct in the processing phase. _____

10. When carrying out experiments you don't always have to follow the scientific process. _____

11. Recording data is part of the conducting phase. _____

12. Explain why control variables are important.

_____

_____

_____

What do the following words mean in the context of the scientific process?

13. Materials

_____

14. Methods

_____

15. Explain why it is important to keep a lab journal.

_____

_____

_____

Link the following phrases on the left with their counterparts on the right by drawing lines

16. Dependent…   hypothesis

17. Materials and…   recording data

18. Title and…   variable

19. Planning phase   methods

20. Conducting phase   aim

Chapter 2: Properties of Matter

Matter is the word we use to describe all of the 'stuff' that our world is made out of. All substances in the universe are made out of matter. You are matter, food is matter, and air is matter. The study of matter, like the study of anything, has rules (they also follow the scientific process you learned before!). The branch of science that investigates matter is called **chemistry**. Matter takes up space, meaning that a group of matter will have a certain **volume**; it refers to the amount of 3-dimensional space that the matter will fill. Volume is often measured in cubic meters, abbreviated as m^3. If a cube has a volume of $1m^3$, it means its measurements are as follows:

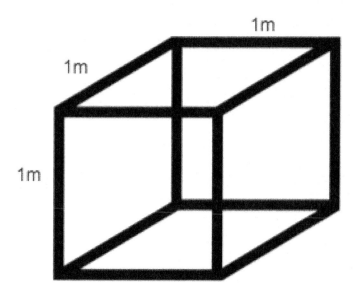

Matter also contains a certain amount of material, meaning that it also has properties of **mass** and **inertia.** Mass refers to the amount of material in the matter, and is measured in units of kilograms (kg). Note that mass is not the same as weight! Weight requires a force of gravity. Of course, objects in space also have mass. Gravity has an effect based on the mass of the material, but mass is independent of gravity. A good way to think about it is to imagine you are on the moon. On the moon and on the earth you will have the same mass, but your weight will be different. If you were on the moon, because of a different gravitational pull, you would only weigh $1/6^{th}$ of what you weigh on earth. Your mass, however, would stay the same.

Inertia is a bit more complicated. It refers to the tendency of an object to resist a change in its motion. An easy way to understand this is to think of how it feels when you stand on the bus or on a train. When you are standing there and the bus or train begins to slow down, your body feels like it wants to keep going forward. This is you experiencing inertia. **Aristotle**, a scientist and philosopher who died in 322 BC, was one of the first to wonder about force and movement. He mistakenly thought that all matter would come to a complete stop if there would not be constant input of energy. This makes sense on the surface of course, since when you throw a ball the energy does not carry it forever, right?! The ball falls of course. What Aristotle did not take into account was that the ball falls down due to the force of gravity (since it had not yet been described and understood), and because of friction with the air. Much later **Isaac Newton** came along (1642- 1727), and revolutionized science as we know it. He discovered gravity, and he also was responsible for determining the laws of motion. His first law of motion, in fact, was about inertia.

Isaac's **first law of motion** states that an object will either stay at rest or continue to move at a constant velocity, unless acted upon by an external force. This means that if you would throw a ball in the vacuum of space, where this is no gravity or friction with air to slow it down, the ball would continue to fly onwards in the same direction at the same speed. This is due to inertia. This is why you feel pushed forward when the bus slows down.

In previous years, you may have learned that matter has both **physical and chemical properties.** The more properties we can attribute to the matter we investigate, the more we can learn about that particular type of matter. This helps us understand how this matter will act under various conditions. Here we will learn how different types of matter can be classified by these properties.

Physical properties:

Physical properties are properties that do not change the chemical composition of that matter when you assess them. In other words, measuring these properties will not alter the basic state of the matter. Examples of physical properties:

1. **Odor-** how does it smell?

This is a very subjective property, which means that things may smell different to different people. This means that it may not be the best physical property to describe a substance. Some substances, however, do have very distinct odors. Sulfur, for example, smells like rotten eggs!

2. **Texture/ hardness-** how does it feel to the touch?

This is another physical property that you can describe just by using your senses. Is it hard or soft, lumpy or smooth?

3. **Color-** what color is it?

4. **Melting point-** at what temperature does it become a liquid?

5. **Boiling point-** at what temperature does it become a gas?

6. **Solubility-** can it dissolve in another substance?

An example of solubility is salt in water. When you dissolve one substance in another, one is called the solute, and one is called the solvent. In this case, the salt is the solute and the water is the solvent.

7. **Conductivity-** does it conduct electricity, heat, or sound?

A material that is very good and conducting is called a conductor, while a material that is very bad at conducting is called an insulator.

These are just a few physical properties. There are many more! To be sure if a property is physical property, ask yourself the following question: Does observing or measuring this property change the chemical composition of the substance? If the answer is no, then it is a physical property.

Chemical properties:

While physical properties do not change the chemical composition of the substance, chemical properties do. They include any properties that allow any change the inherent nature of the matter. Here are some examples:

1. **Combustibility-** Does the substance react with heat and oxygen to create fire?
An example of a substance showing a chemical property of combustibility is a burning piece of paper. The paper is ignited and burns in response to oxygen and heat. Since this changes the chemical composition of the paper it is said to be a chemical property.

2. **Reactivity to water-** Does the substance react on a chemical level in response to another water?
A good example of reactivity is with water. Some substances, such as alkali metals, will react when they come into contact with water. An example is sodium, which when dropped in cold water produces a vigorous and even explosive reaction!

3. **Rust-** Does the substance rust?
A good example of rust is when iron rusts. Rusting is similar to the process of combustion, in that it requires a reaction with oxygen. The difference is that rust takes a lot longer to form than fire. You can imagine fire and combustion as an extremely fast and vigorous reaction of oxygen with the fuel (wood, paper, coal, etc.), while rust is a slower paced reaction with oxygen.

Anything that causes a chemical change in the substance can be called a chemical change. The property that allows this change is the chemical property. You can see all kinds of chemical changes in the world around you, if you take a look. When you fry an egg, or burn a piece of paper, it is a chemical change. When the milk in the fridge gets old and turns sour, it is also a chemical change. There are also many kinds of tiny chemical change happening inside your body. This happens all the time for your whole life!

States of matter:

All matter may exist in any of the 4 possible states: **Gas, liquid, solid, or plasma**. The state of matter is one of its physical properties.

For the first 3 states, we can use the example of H_2O:

Solid state → ice

Liquid state → water

Gas state → steam

These 3 states of matter are commonly encountered, and you probably already knew about them. Plasma, however, is a more rare state of matter. You can see it and observe it from time to time, when you come across a neon sign, or when you see a lightning strike.

Plasma is essentially a gas, but it has been **ionized**. When a substance is ionized, it means that the atom or the molecule has acquired a negative or a positive charge, via the gain or loss of electrons.

To scientifically understand matter is an enormous task, and in the next years more and more concepts will be introduced to you that show you that matter is very complex in the way it behaves and interacts with other matter. For these reasons it is important to be able to describe matter in terms of **chemical and physical properties**. These properties give rise to different **physical and chemical changes**, as well as different **states of matter**.

Properties of Matter: Activities and Experiments

1. Making naked eggs

What you need:

- Eggs
- Transparent vinegar
- Large container
- Spoon
- Pencil and lab book

What you do:

- Put several eggs in the container
- Cover the eggs with vinegar completely, and notice how small bubbles begin to form.
- Put the eggs on the bench and leave them overnight
- The next day carefully and gently take the eggs out with a spoon and feel them.
- Record your observations.

What you should learn:

- The eggs become soft because the vinegar is an acid, called acetic acid. The acid reacts with the calcium carbonate in the shell, which causes small carbon dioxide bubbles to form. The carbon floats away in the bubbles, leaving a soft egg behind.

Question:

- Is this a physical change or a chemical change?

2. Making Sugar crystals

What you need:

- Sugar
- Stove
- Water
- String
- Scissor
- Button
- Pencil
- Pot
- Spoon
- Glass
- Lab book

What you do:

- Boil some water in the pot on the stove.
- Once it is boiling turn off the stove.

- Put sugar in the water spoon by spoon.
- Continue adding sugar until no more sugar can be dissolve.
- Let the water cool.
- In the meantime, tie a string that is the same height as the glass to a pencil in the middle.
- Tie a button to the other end of the string.
- Place the pencil across the top of the glass, letting the button fall to the bottom.
- Fill the glass with the now cold sugar water solution.
- Put the glass in a warm place and leave it undisturbed for a few days, checking on it from time to time.
- When the water has fully evaporated, you can see the sugar crystals hanging on the string. You can even eat these sugar crystals!

What you should learn:

- Students should grasp the concepts of solutions and evaporation.

Question:

- Where did the water go?
- How did the sugar crystals taste?

3. Baking soda and vinegar reaction

What you need:

- Baking soda (not baking powder)
- Transparent vinegar
- Glass
- Pencil and lab book

What you do:

- Put the glass in the sink, since you will make a mess
- Pour some of the baking powder in the bottom of the glass
- Pour some of the vinegar into the glass
- Record your observations

What you should learn:

- Vinegar, as you learned in a previous experiment, is a kind of acid called acetic acid. Baking soda is sodium bicarbonate, which is a base. The acid reacts with the base, causing a chemical reaction. Together they form carbonic acid, which is very unstable. It breaks apart into water and carbon dioxide, which is what you see happening in the glass.

Question:

- Is this a physical change or a chemical change?

4. Air pressure can crush

What you need:

- An empty and washed soda can
- Stove

- Cooking tongs
- Cold water
- Bowl

What you do:

- Fill the bowl with cold water. The colder the water is the better it will be for the experiment.
- Add a full tablespoon of water to the contents of the can.
- Place the can on the stove and turn it on
- Once the water starts bubbling and you see some vapor rising from the can, then you know the water is evaporating. Wait 1 more minute.
- This step is the important step. After the can has been sitting for 1 more minute, use the tongs to grab the can. Quickly flip the can over and plunge it top-down into the cold water. It is important to not hesitate when you carry out this step.
- Record your observations

What you should learn:

- Before you heated the can, it was filled with water and air. When you turned on the stove to boil the water, it changed from a liquid to a gas. When water is in a gas state, the molecules are much further apart from one another, and it takes up more space. Because of this the water vapor pushes some of the air out of the can. When you flip the can over and put it in the water, it returns to its liquid state, and takes up less space. Because it takes up less space, there is now less pressure inside the can, and the pressure outside the can is great enough to crush the can.

Question:

- Is this a chemical change or a physical change?

5. Magic Milk

What you need:

- A bowl
- Milk
- Liquid dish detergent
- Various shades of food coloring
- Pencil and lab book

What you do:

- Pour milk into the bowl
- Add several drops of food coloring to the center of the bowl, all in the same spot.
- Repeat for several different colors.
- Carefully drop a single drop of detergent into the center of the milk where the colored spot is.
- Record your observations.

What you should learn:

- Milk is mostly just made of water, but it also contains protein and fat. The important component in this experiment, however, is the soap. Dish soap molecules have 2 very differently behaving ends. One end of the molecule wants to dissolves in water. The other end does not like water and is repelled away from it; instead, it wants to grab onto fat molecules. For this reason, the soap moves throughout the plate, grabbing onto loose fat molecules. Because of this, the food coloring in the milk is pushed all around. Without the food coloring this would still occur, but you would not be able to see it.

Question:
- What will happen if you add more dish soap after the first drop? Try it in different areas of the bowl and find out for yourself!

Properties of Matter: Quiz

1. What is the branch of science that investigates matter and states of matter?

_____

Are the following properties chemical or physical properties? Write a 'C' for chemical, or a 'P' for physical.

2. Conductivity _____

3. Flexibility _____

4. Freezing temperature _____

4. Ability to rust _____

5. Reactivity to water _____

6. Hardness _____

7. Combustibility _____

8. Color _____

10. Solubility _____

True or false:

11. Volume is measured in kg. _____

12. Mass is measured in kg. _____

13. Your mass is the same on earth and on the moon. _____

14. Your weight is the same on earth and on the moon. _____

15. Aristotle discovered the laws of gravity. _____

16. Inertia is a concept first understood by Isaac Newton. _____

17. Physical changes alter the chemical nature of the matter. _____

18. Chemical changes occur because of chemical properties. _____

19. Name and describe the 4 states of matter below. Give examples of each state of matter, or describe where we might see those states of matter in the world around us.

_____
_____
_____
_____
_____
_____
_____

20. Give an example of an object and name some of its physical properties.

_____
_____
_____

Chapter 3: The Human Body

Your body: the thing that you use to walk, eat, sleep, and everything else that allows you to live. Even your thoughts and your feelings are functions of your body! You use it all the time, so understanding a little bit about how it works is very important, not to mention interesting.

We will separate our understanding of the body into the following components:

1. Functions- 2. Parts- 3.Systems

1. Functions

Your body carries out many important functions and processes every single minute of every single day. Some good examples are your 5 senses.

- Sight
- Smell
- Touch
- Taste
- Hearing

When you are asleep, then your body does not consciously carry out these functions, but of course, sleeping is a function of the body too!

Not all of the functions of the body are things that you can feel happening to you. Your body also performs many functions it doesn't feel, such as the growing of your hair, and the digestion of your food (sometimes you can feel that!).

Challenge: Can you name any more functions that your body carries out?

2. Parts

The body is composed of many parts, called organs. All organs have a certain function. They need each other to perform their own functions, and cannot survive on their own. Below is a picture that shows some of the body's organs.

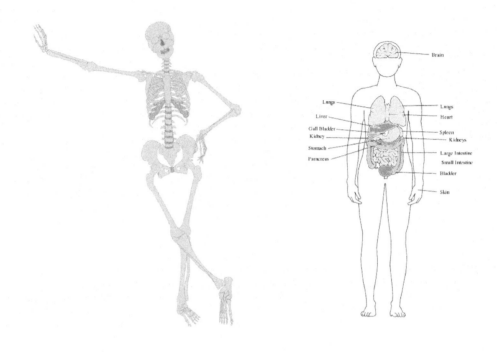

Shown here are some of the organs your body is composed of. Your bones are organs, all of the small squishy compartments in your torso are organs, your skin is an organ, and all of your muscles are organs too!

Bladder – It is a muscular organ that gathers urine until you expel it via urination.

Bones - The bones in your body serve multiple functions. They protect other organs. An example would be ribs protecting the lungs and heart, or the skull protecting the brain. They also keep the body in its position, since they are attached to muscles. The forces that the muscles pull with, and the rigidity of the skeleton, are what keep the body in its upright position. Bones also produce bone marrow.

Central Nervous system

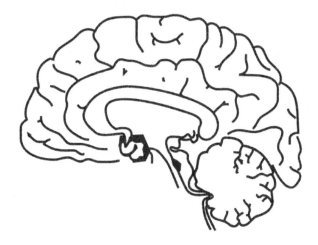

– The central nervous system includes the brain and the spinal cord. The brain and the spinal cord are the control center of the entire body. They receive all the information from the inside of your body, and also some from outside the body, in the form of your senses. The brain then looks at all this information, and sends messages to the body via nerves that control all future functions. The brain specifically is what gives you a personality, a memory, and your feelings. It also controls many internal functions of the body.

Ears - The ear converts vibrations that enter the ear canal into electrical signals, which it then sends to the brain. The ear also has another interesting function of helping us with our balance! Inside the inner ear there is a series of tubes that contain fluid, and the movement of this fluid helps us keep our balance.

Eyes – The eyes receive light; aided by so-called 'photoreceptor' cells, they convert light into electrical signals, which then travels to the brain.

Below you can see a visual representation of the eyes and ears, and the areas of the brain they send their information to.

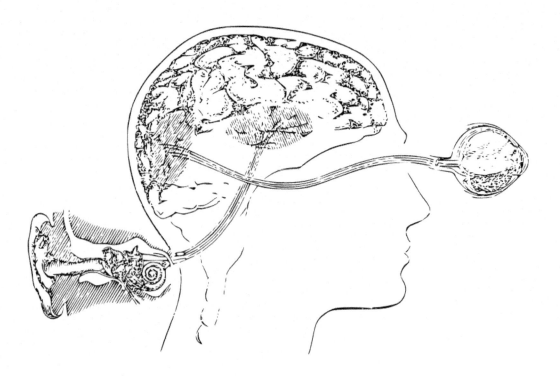

Epithelial Tissue –This is a membranous tissue that covers most internal organs.

Gallbladder -A small cavity located underneath one of the lobes of the liver, the gall bladder collects bile that is produced by the liver ,and stores it until it is needed for digestion.

Heart –The heart is essentially a big piece of muscle. It contracts and pumps blood around the whole body. Since the heart is a muscle. The heart has 4 chambers: the right ventricle, left ventricle, right atrium, and left atrium. The heart receives deoxygenated blood via **veins**. The heart then sends the blood to the lungs, where it is oxygenated. The blood is then returned to the heart, where it is pumped out in **arteries**.

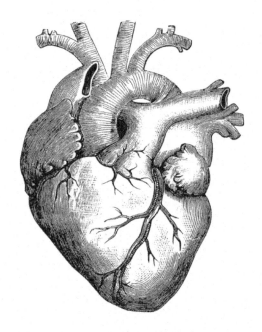

Kidneys –The kidneys are a pair of organs- you have two of them! You can live without one and live a mostly normal life, but you need at least 1 to survive. Kidneys regulate water and salt concentrations in the body, and also act as filtration device for the blood, getting rid of metabolic waste, which is released as urine.

Large and small intestines – The small intestine is the first part of the intestine, and it consists of 3 smaller parts: the duodenum, jejunum, and the ileum. This is where food is partially digested, before it is fed to the large intestine. The large intestine is also separated into 3 smaller parts: the cecum, colon, and rectum. The large intestine extracts water from semi-digested food, which is later excreted as feces.

Liver –The liver is a large organ that secretes bile, which is used for digestion. It also takes care of many metabolic functions.

Lungs –The lungs are two big spongy lobes that collect air and replace deoxygenated blood with oxygenated blood. The air is sucked into them when you expand your chest. The oxygen in the air is then exchanged for carbon dioxide. This process gets rid of deoxygenated blood and by oxygenating it again. The newly oxygenated blood travels back to the heart, and is then pumped around the body for use.

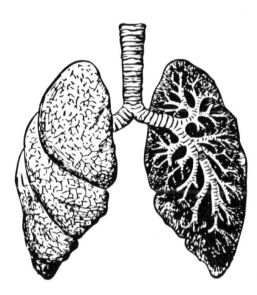

Muscles - A tissue composed of fibers capable of contracting to move the body around and control internal processes, such as the pumping of the heart, and the digestion of food.

Pancreas -A long glandular organ that sits behind the stomach, the pancreas is in charge of secreting a variety of enzymes, into the small intestine. Together these enzymes are called pancreas juice, and they help digestion. The pancreas also secretes insulin and glucagon into the bloodstream, which are important for maintaining sugar blood levels.

Skin –Skin, as you know, is the tissue that forms our external covering. It is made of lots of layers of so-called 'ectodermal tissue'. It contains sweat pores, hair follicles, and it has lots of sensory nerve endings embedded in it, which allow us to feel things on our skin.

Spleen- The Spleen is an organ that resides under the left lung. It is important for filtering out old red blood cells, and it also plays important roles in the immune system.

Challenge: Above are some of the organs of your body, but this list is far from complete! Try to name some more organs of the body, and find out their functions. Some research with a computer will be helpful for this challenge.

3. Systems

The body has many systems in place that perform certain functions. The often involve multiple organs working together to achieve a common goal. Below are some of the systems your body has.

The Circulatory System

This is the body's blood transport system. It is made up of several organs, including the heart, and pumps blood via the body's **veins** and **arteries**. Arteries carry oxygenated blood to the tissues, and veins carry the deoxygenated blood back to the heart. On its way to the tissues, it enters the smallest type of blood vessels, known as **capillaries**. The blood's purpose in this system is to carry oxygen and nutrients to the tissues all over the body.

Digestive System

The digestive system breaks down food into carbohydrates, proteins, fats, vitamins, and minerals. The body needs all of these to grow and survive. First, food is broken down by powerful acid in the stomach. From there, the food travels into the small intestine. This is where nutrients are absorbed, through the walls of the intestines. From here the food travels to the large intestine, where the water is removed. All that is left is waste, which is excreted as feces.

Challenge: Can you remember the sections of the small and large intestine?

Endocrine System

The endocrine system is a group of organs that release **hormones**. There are many of them in the body, as hormones are an important part of signaling processes. A hormone is a molecule that is used as a long distance messenger from one area of the body to another, telling it what to do. An example would be adrenaline, a hormone that tells your body that it is time to get ready to use lots of energy, often stimulated by fight-or-flight situations.

Immune System

The immune system is our body's way of defending against infectious diseases. Many parts of the body work together to respond to dangerous threats, such as viruses and certain bacteria.

Nervous System

The nervous system a system that is composed by your brain, spinal cord, and all of the other nerves in your body. It has the huge responsibility of coordinating the whole body to work together. It does this by using cells called **neurons**, which use electrical signals to send messages all over the body.

Reproductive System

The reproductive system is what we use to make new children. Sperm from the male travels to the woman's fallopian tube, where it fertilizes the egg. The fertilized egg then travels to the uterus, where the fetus will grow. This period takes nine months.

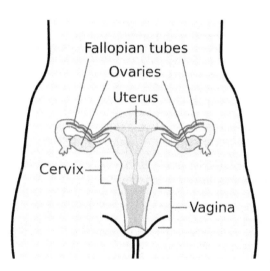

Urinary System

The urinary system gets rid of waste in the form of urine. First, the kidneys remove the waste from your blood. From the kidneys, the waste (in urine) travels to the bladder. When the bladder is full, it empties via urination.

These are some of the functions, parts, and systems of the human body. Our bodies carry out so many important functions, and it works in such complicated ways, that if you would try to learn everything we know about it right now, it would take years and years! There is always more to learn, and scientists learn more about the body and the details of its functioning every day.

The Human Body: Activities and Experiments

1. Heart rate investigations

What you need:

- A watch with a seconds hand
- A pencil
- Paper

What you do:

- Sit in a relaxed place, and try not to do anything strenuous for a few minutes. Just breathe normally and try to relax.
- Using your first two fingers, feel your neck, just to the side of your windpipe. Search around with your fingers until you find your pulse.
- Look at your watch and count the how many times your heart beats in a ten second period.
- Multiply this number by 6, and now you have the number of beats per minute.
- Record your result
- Now, find an area to safely run around, and run for 5 minutes. Work hard so that you get tired.
- Repeat the process of counting and multiplying your heartbeats.
- Record your data.

What you should learn:

- When you check your pulse in this area what you can feel is your carotid artery. The pulse indicates the beating of your heart, which is important for carrying blood around the body. When you exercise, your body needs more oxygen, which means your body needs more blood circulation. Your heart compensates for this by pumping harder and faster.

Question:

- Why does your body need more oxygen when you exercise? To answer this question, you might need to do some research with a computer.

2. Investigating your bladder capacity

What you need:

- A large measuring cup
- Paper
- Pencil and lab book

What you do:

- Wait until you feel the need to urinate.
- Go to the bathroom and carefully collect your urine in the measuring cup.
- Record how much urine you released.
- Pour your urine in the toilet and rinse the measuring cup.
- Repeat the process several times, always waiting until you need to go, and always recording your data.

- Average all of your data.

What you should learn:

- Everyone will have a different average urine capacity. This is due to the size of the bladder. Females will have a lower bladder capacity on average, since they have smaller bladders. This is because they also need space in their abdomens for the uterus, which men do not have.

Questions:

- Does your pee gross you out? Don't worry! It may smell bad, but it's completely sterile!

3. Measuring lung capacity

What you need:

- Large empty plastic bottle
- Large and deep bowl
- Water
- Measuring cup
- 30 cm flexible plastic tubing, such as aquarium tubing
- Marker
- Pencil and lab book

What you do:

- Using the measuring cup, measure out 100 ml of water. Pour the 100 ml into the bottle
- Using the marker, label the water level of the bottle.
- Add 100 ml more, and mark the new level as well.
- Repeat until the whole bottle is marked.
- Put water in the large and deep bowl, until there is a good layer of about 10 cm covering the bottom.
- Fill the bottle with water until it is completely full.
- Cover the opening of the bottle with you hand so that no water can get out, and flip it upside down with the top in the bowl. Make sure not to remove your fingers until the mouth of the bottle is completely in the water.
- Without letting any air into it, insert one end of the plastic tubing into the bottle.
- Inhale deeply, and exhale all the air into the tube.
- Measure how much air is in the bottle and calculate your lung capacity.
- Record your data.

What you should learn:

- Lung capacity is usually measured with a tool called a spirometer, but in this do-it-yourself setup, we can easily measure our lung capacity. We use displacement in this experiment. This means that we displace the water in the bottle with the air from our lungs. This lets us see exactly how much we exhaled in ml, since we marked the bottle.

Questions:

- Compare your results with those of an adult and a friend. Is your lung capacity larger or smaller than theirs?
- Why do you think this is?

4. Depth perception test

What you need

- 2 pencils and lab book

What you do:

- Hold the two pencils sideways and at arms length, with the erasers facing inwards
- Close one eye and bring the two pencils closer together in front of you.
- Try to touch the eraser tips together. If you miss, extend your hands to the side and try again.
- Repeat this 5 times, and record how many times you successfully touched the eraser tips together.
- Repeat the experiment, but this time with both of your eyes open.
- Record the data.

What you should learn:

- It is much easier to touch the ends of the pencils together when both of your eyes are open. This is because of depth perception. Two eyes are better than one because they work together as a team. Because the two eyes will see things from different angles depending on the object's distance from the eyes, the brain can use this information and determine how far away the object is.

Question:

- When is depth perception important to have?
- Are there any other factors you can think of that help with depth perception? Hint: look at things that are far away, and try to ask yourself the following question: How do I know it is far away?

5. Reaction time test

What you need:

- A ruler
- A partner
- Pencil and lab book

What you do:

- Have your partner hold the ruler at the end, near the largest number
- Your partner should then let the ruler hang down
- Put your hand at the bottom of the ruler, but do not touch it. Get ready to grab it.
- The partner should then drop the ruler after a random interval of time. This is important because you should not be able to guess when the ruler will drop.
- When the ruler is dropped you should catch it between your thumb and forefinger.
- Record the markings at which your fingers grabbed the ruler.
- Repeat 5 times and make an average of the distance the ruler fell.

What you should learn:

- When you do this task your body is doing many things at once. First, your eyes will receive visual information about the ruler dropping. Then, your eyes will send this information to the brain, which will process the information and send signals to the muscles. Your muscles will then contract and move your body, allowing you to catch the ruler.

Question:

- Using the distance that the ruler fell, calculate how long your reaction time was. For this you can use the following formula:

- $t = \sqrt{\dfrac{2y}{g}}$
- In this formula, t is time, y is the distance in cm that the ruler fell, and g is 980 cm/sec², due to gravity. Get a teacher or parent to check your work.

The Human Body: Quiz

Name the following organs:

1.

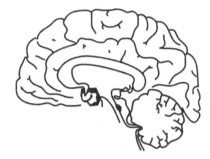

_____

2.

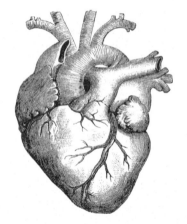

_____

3.

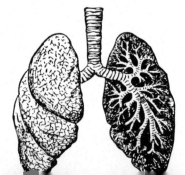

_____

True or false:

4. Muscles are only important for moving around. _____

5. Your body has parts, functions, and systems. _____

6. The liver is important for metabolic functions. _____

7. The small intestine is divided into 5 sub-sections. _____

8. The large intestine is before the small intestine. _____

9. The stomach secretes bile. _____

10. You have 2 kidneys. _____

11. Your eyes turn light into electrical signals that get sent to the brain. _____

12. Give an example of a body part. _____

13. Give and example of a body function. _____

14. Give an example of 2 body parts that work together to perform a certain function, and name that function.

What are the following body systems important for?

15. Endocrine system

16. Circulatory system

17. Immune system

18. Female reproductive system

19. What is the primary function of the bladder?

20. What are the 5 senses?

Chapter 4: Earth / Moon / Sun

We live on the earth. Every day we can look up and see the sun, and every night we can look up and see the moon. Did you ever wonder how all of these celestial bodies relate to one another?

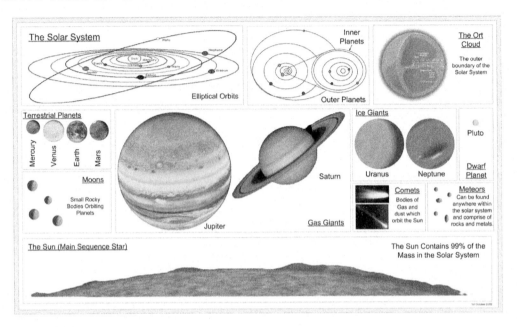

Properties of the sun:

The sun is the biggest body in our solar system. It is 100 times bigger than the earth. The sun is a star, just like the stars you can see in the night sky. The difference is that our sun is close to us. Each solar system has its own star at the center. One amazing thing about stars is that many chemical elements were made inside of them, including carbon, nitrogen, and oxygen. When the stars die and explode, they release all of these elements. The matter that we are made also would have come from a star, and so in a way, we are all made of stardust!

The sun is our star, and it gives organisms all the energy they have to survive. Plants, which are at the bottom of the food chain, use photosynthesis to generate food. This process uses light. That means that all of the energy in the food chain system came from the sun. Without it there would be no life on earth.

Our sun formed 4.6 billion years ago, and has 330,000 times the amount of mass the earth has. It contains mostly hydrogen and helium, but around 1.7% is made up of other elements too. The surface of the sun has a temperature of is 5778 Kelvin, which is equal to 5505 degrees Celsius, or 9940 degrees Fahrenheit. At the core of the sun, however, immense pressure and temperatures exist, with temperatures soaring to an estimated 15 million degrees Celsius, or 27 million degrees Fahrenheit!

Properties of the earth

The earth rotates around the sun in a circular path. This path is known as the earth's orbit around the sun. The earth takes 365.25 days to completely orbit the sun. This period defines what we call 1 year. While the earth is moving around the sun, it is also spinning all the time, just like a basketball on a basketball player's finger. The spinning of the earth is what gives us day and night. It takes 24 hours for the earth to spin all the way around once. Because the earth is a big sphere, when light is on one part of the earth, the other side is in darkness. That means while you are awake, somebody on the other side of the earth is asleep, and vice versa.

While earth takes 24 hours to spin once around its axis, other planets spin faster. Jupiter, for example, spins so fast that its day would be less than 10 hours!

The axis of the earth is tilted, however, giving rise to one of earth's most striking features: our seasons. If the earth were on a straight axis, the seasons would always stay the same, since all year round the different parts of the earth would receive the same amount of sunlight. Since the earth is on a tilt, however, the amount of sunlight that reaches a certain area will vary over the course of a year.

An easy way to think about it: Since the earth is tilted, sometimes the northern hemisphere will be facing towards the sun. When this is happening, the northern hemisphere will get more sun, and it will be winter. In the southern hemisphere, we would get less sun, and so it will be winter. When the earth is on the other side of the moon, then the southern hemisphere is facing the sun, and the seasons would be reversed.

Properties of the moon

Similarly to the earth, the moon also travels a circular path, or around an orbit. It travels, not around the sun like the earth does, but around the earth itself. It does not spin on its own axis like the earth does, and so we always see the same features when we look at it. Until we managed to take pictures of the other half with satellites, we only knew what half of it looked like. The moon takes 29 days to travel around the earth, and this is the period of time we have roughly come to associate with 1 month.

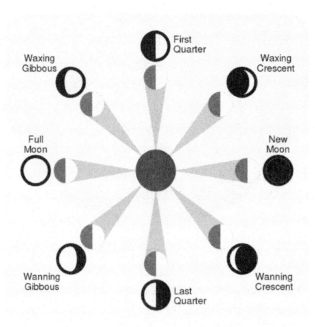

This revolution of the moon around the earth is what makes the moon appear different at different times of the month. Firstly, the sun lights it up. The light of the sun hitting the moon is being reflected towards us, and this is why we see it as glowing during the night. It is kind of like a mirror. The different shapes of the moon, or so-called phases, are caused by the position of the moon as it travels on its orbit around the earth. As the moon travels on its path, we get to see the side that is lit up by the sun from different angles, and this is what causes the different phases.

Here you can see these different phases. The blue dot represents the earth. It shows how the phase of the moon changes depending on the moon's position around the earth. Each month you see the moon go through theses phases, until it completes the cycle. We call this a month.

The tide

The moon and sun are also responsible for another common phenomenon on earth: the tide. The tide is created because of the gravitational pull that the earth, sun, and moon exert on each other. Because the oceans are liquid, they are easier for gravity to manipulate. The tide is very important to the history and existence of earth. Some have theorized that evolution owes a lot of thanks to the tide, and that we would not be here today if it was not for this interaction of huge bodies that pull on each other with gravity. The idea is that because of the tide, there were areas of the earth that were exposed to both wet and dry conditions. This interface and switching between wet and dry allowed some organisms to experience both on land and off land conditions, helping them make the transition from one state of being to the other.

Space objects/ debris

Of course, there are a number of objects in space that are close to our earth, moon, and sun. Not to mention all of the other plants in our solar system of course, there are many smaller objects such as satellites, comets, asteroids, meteors, meteorites, and meteoroids. What is the difference between all of these!? Lets check:

Comet: A comet is a small celestial body in the solar system. A comet orbits around the sun, just like earth. The difference is that they are relatively smaller. A comet will show a **coma** or a tail when it is close enough to the sun. (A coma is a fuzzy outline that you can see when you look at a comet. It is usually made of ice and dust)

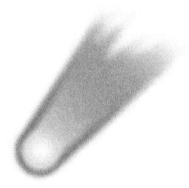

Asteroids: An asteroid is very similar to a comet, but an asteroid will not have a coma or a tail. Asteroids can range from 10 meters in size, to over 1000 km wide.

Meteoroid: A meteoroid is similar to an asteroid, but is usually of a much smaller size (up to 10 meters).

Meteor: A meteor is a meteoroid that has entered the earth's atmosphere. When you look up at the sky at night, if you are lucky enough to see a shooting star, what you are really seeing is a meteor. Most meteors burn up upon entry.

Meteorite: A meteorite is a meteor that has managed to reach and make contact with the earth's surface.

Satellite: A satellite is a man made, artificial object, that has been intentionally shot into orbit. Over 6000 satellites have been launched into space by mankind!

Earth / Moon / Sun: Activities and Experiments

1. Calculate how long it would take you to reach the moon

What you need:

- Pencil
- Paper
- Calculator

What you do:

- Consider the following pieces of information: You are travelling down the highway at 70 miles per hour.
- Imagine the highway could take you all the way to the moon. How long do you think it will take you to get there at this speed? Guess, and record your guess.
- How long will it take you to travel 70 miles at this speed?
- Now calculate how long will it take you to travel 100 miles. If you need help, ask a parent or teacher.
- Now consider how far away the moon is: 238,900 miles!
- Calculate how many hours it will take you to travel to the moon at this speed.
- Calculate how many days this is.

What you learn:

- The moon is far away, and now you should have an idea of how far away it really is. You may also have learned some more about how to calculate speeds and distances.

Questions:

- How long would it take?
- How close was your guess?
- Does it take more or less time than you expected?

2. Calculate how long it would take you to reach the sun

What you need:

- Pencil
- Paper
- Calculator

What you do:

- Just as in the previous experiment, we are going to calculate how long it will take to reach a certain distance
- Imagine we are still going 70 mph, but this time the highway stretches all the way to the surface of the sun!
- Again, guess how long it would take, and record your answer.
- Now consider that the sun is very far away. It is 92,960,000 miles away!
- How many hours would it take you to get to the sun from earth?
- How many days does this equal?
- How many years does this equal?

What you should learn:

- The sun is very, very far away! At this speed, you would not even make it there in your lifetime. This shows just how far away it really is.

Questions:

- How long would it take?
- How close was your guess?

3. Calculate how long it takes light to reach the earth from the sun

What you need:

- Pencil
- Paper
- Calculator

What you do:

- First, guess how long it takes for light to travel from the sun to the earth.
- Record your guess
- Then, use the following information to calculate the proper answer.
- As previously mentioned, the sun is 92,960,000 miles away.
- Light travels very fast. It goes 670,616,629 miles per hour!
- How many hours does it take for light from the sun to reach the earth?
- Calculate how many minutes this is.

What you should learn:

- Although the sun is very far away from the earth, light travels very quickly. That's why it takes just a matter of minutes for light to reach us here on earth.

Questions:

- How long did you calculate would it take?
- How close was your guess?

4. Making a sundial

What you need:

- A paper plate
- Markers
- A straw
- Ruler
- Pins
- Pencil and lab book
- Sticky tack

What you do:

- Start this activity on a sunny day, at around 11 am.
- Turn the paper plate onto its back.
- Use a ruler to find the center of the paper plate, and poke a hole through the center with the pencil.
- Use the markers to draw the numbers 1-12 on the plate, just like they are on a clock. Draw the numbers 12, 3, 6, and 9 first, to make it easier.

- Just before 12 o'clock, go outside and take the plate, pins, and straw with you. Put the plate in a sunny place on the ground, and put the straw inside push the straw down through the hole. Keep the straw facing up, and keep it as straight as possible. You can use sticky tack to keep the straw in place if need be.
- Now, at exactly 12, take the plate and rotate it so that the shadow of the straw points towards 12.
- Pin the plate in place to the ground, on a flat surface. Do not allow the plate to move.
- Come back in 1 hour and look at the clock. Record the location of the shadow and the number it points to.

What you should learn:

- You can use the position of the sun to determine the time. This is an old technique that has been used for a long time. This works because of the sun's shifting position in the sky during the earth's rotation.

5. Simulating the phases of the moon.

What you need:

- Small flashlight
- Shoebox with a lid
- Scissors
- Black thread
- Transparent tape
- White polystyrene ball, about the size of a golf ball
- Black paint
- Paint brush
- Black paper
- Pencil and lab book

What you do:

- Paint the inside of the box and the inside of the lid with black paint and let it dry.
- Cut 8 holes in the box, 3 on each long side, and 1 on each short side, as in the picture below. You can use a hole punch to make this easier, if you have one. Also cut a larger hole for your flashlight, as illustrated.

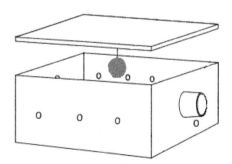

- Next, hang the polystyrene ball from the lid of the box, using the black thread and the tape.
- Tape a small flap of black paper over each hole.
- Shine the flashlight through the large hole, and look through each small hole, 1 at a time.
- Record your observations in the form of descriptions and drawings.

What you should learn:

- When you look through the small holes in the box, this is like a simulation of the phases of the moon. Looking through each hole is like seeing the moon from a different angle, as we do during the different times of the month. The flashlight represents the sun.

Questions:

- What are the names of the different phases of the moon? Can you correlate those phases with the different angles you see through your box?

Earth / Moon / Sun: Quiz

Use the following words to complete the sentences below. Each word is used only once.

Meteor, Satellite, Meteorite, Comet, Meteoroid, Asteroid

1. A/an _____ is a small celestial body in the solar system. They orbit around the sun, just like earth. They have a visible tail, sometimes called a coma.

2. A/an _____ is very similar to a/an (answer to number 1), but will not have a coma or a tail. They can range from 10 meters in size, to over 1000 km wide.

3. A/an _____ is similar to a/an (answer to number 2), but is usually of a much smaller size (up to 10 meters).

4. A/an _____ is a/an (answer to number 3) that has entered the earth's atmosphere. They burn up upon entry.

5. A/an _____ is a (answer to number 4) that has managed to reach and make contact with the earth's surface.

6. A/an _____ is a man made, artificial object that has been intentionally shot into orbit.

7. What effect do the gravitational pull of the sun and moon have on the earth's oceans? Bonus points: What effect may this have played in the evolution of animals on earth?

_____
_____
_____

_____

_____

_____

_____

8. What causes the phases of the moon?

_____

_____

_____

True or false:

9. The earth takes 465 days to orbit the sun. _____

10. The earth is constantly spinning. _____

11. The seasons of earth are due to earth being on a tilted axis. _____

12. 1 day on Jupiter would be longer than 1 day on earth. _____

13. The earth orbits the moon. _____

14. The moon is the same size as the earth. _____

15. The moon does not rotate the same way the earth does. _____

16. The moon is responsible for gravity on earth. _____

17. The sun is 100 times bigger than the earth. _____

18. The surface temperature of the sun is cooler than the temperature of the core. _____

19. The sun is over 10 billion years old. _____

20. The sun is made up of mostly hydrogen and helium. _____

Chapter 5: Characteristics of Plants

Before animals existed on our planet, it was only covered with plants. We all know what plants are, but what is it exactly that separates plants from animals? First of all, lets look at the way plants and animals gather their energy.

All plants and animals need food, oxygen, and water to survive. They both use these things to growing and repair injured parts. Although they both need all of these things to survive, they way they obtain them is very different. There are two types of food obtainment that we need to compare here: autotrophic and heterotrophic.

Autotrophs: Autotrophs provide their own food, via a biological mechanism known as **photosynthesis**. You will learn more about that in a later unit, but all you need to know now is that autotrophs use photosynthesis to make their own energy. A plant is autotrophic.

Heterotrophs: Heterotrophs need to provide their own food, as they cannot produce their own. This requires hunting, grazing, scavenging, or any other form of food procurement that gets the food from an external source.

You may remember from previous years that organisms have been classified based on a taxonomical hierarchy, or a series of groups designed to segment and arrange the organisms. The order is as follows:

Kingdom→Phylum→Class→Order→Family→Genus→Species

These categories range from broad to specific, but already at the first level, plants and animals are separated. All plants belong exclusively to the kingdom known as **Plantae**.

All plants belong to this group, and they are then sorted based on different characteristics. Some of these characteristics include:

- How they absorb and circulate the fluids inside of them- Are they vascular or non-vascular?

- How do they reproduce- do they use spores or do they use seeds?

- How do they produce seeds- via cones or via flowers?

Lets start with distinguishing **vascular plants** from **non-vascular plants.**

Vascular plants:

These plants are the best developed, and they are also the largest group of plants. They have true roots, stems and leaves, which they use for transporting nutrients and water throughout the whole plant.

These plants have **xylem** and **phloem**. Xylem and phloem are like the circulatory system of the human body, but in plants. Xylem are tubes that carry water and minerals up from the roots of the plant, where the water and minerals get absorbed. The phloem, on the other hand, are responsible for carrying food down from the leaves of the plant, where the photosynthesis is carried out and the sugar is produced.

Examples of vascular plants include all plants with wood stems, like trees, as well as many others.

Non-vascular plants:

These plants are far less developed than vascular plants. They do not have a good circulatory system for transporting sugars and water and minerals. They do not have true roots, stems, or leaves. These cells have to obtain their nutrients from the environment, and then directly diffuse these nutrients throughout the whole plant in a cell-by-cell manner. This means that non-vascular plants usually cannot grow to be very large, since they lack the proper methods of transport that a big tree has, for example.

Examples of non-vascular plants include moss and algae.

We can also make the distinction between **seed-growing plants** and **spore-growing plants.**

Seed growing plants:

Seed growing plants are plants that use seeds to reproduce. A seed is a complete embryo for a plant. That means that inside is everything needed for the plant to grow. It has the beginnings of roots, stems, leaves, and it has a store of food for the initial spurt of growth. They are usually surrounded by a seed coat. Examples of seeds can be seen in many places. A great example would be corn, or beans! Above we can see a picture of a maple seed.

Spore growing plants: Another type of plant reproduction uses spores, and doesn't even involve seeds. Spores are similar to seeds, but they are much smaller. Some examples of plants that use spores would be mosses and ferns.

Within seed growing plants there can be another subdivision: Does the plant produce seeds via cones, or via flowers? Flowering plants differ all cone producing plants in that they grow their seeds inside an ovary, which is inside of the flower. Examples include all plants that have flowers and fruits.

When the plant is a cone producing plant, it can also be called a **conifer**. They never produce flowers, but rather produce seeds inside of structures known as cones. An example would be pinecone trees, and spruces.

Seeds can be separated into two groups:

Monocot: Monocot seeds have only a single compartment, and give rise to plants that have a less defined vasculature, such as grass.

Dicot: Dicot seeds have 2 food storage areas, and produce plants that have their vascular tubes in more specific structures.

Specialized plant structures

Since plants have to stay in the same place all the time, they have to be equipped to deal with many kinds of difficult scenarios. Where a human or animal would be able to run away, a plant just has to sit in the same spot and hope to survive. For this reason plants have developed many specialized structures that can aid in this survival.

Leaves: Leaves function as a site for many processes. Photosynthesis is carried out in leaves, as well as respiration (the exchange of oxygen and carbon dioxide).

Stems: Function as a storage site, or a structure to keep the plant ridged. They also serve as a structure to push the leaves up to the light.

Roots: Roots are the primary method for water absorption in plants. They also perform the mechanical function of anchoring the plant in place. They absorb nutrients as well. There are two types of roots: **fibrous roots**, and **taproots**.

- Fibrous roots have long branching segments that break off and branch out in all directions.
- Taproots are singular, long, thick roots, with very few smaller roots branching off.

All roots have root hairs. Root hairs have the responsibility of increasing surface area of the roots that is in contact with the soil. This allows for faster absorption of water and minerals.

Cells: Plants have special cells that look different to cells of animals. One of the main differences is the **cell wall**. Both animals and plants have cells, and both types of cells have cell membranes, however plants have an additional, hard outer layer to their cells. This additional later is known as the cell wall, and gives the cells rigidity.

Structures for reproduction

All plants have specialized structures that aid them in their reproduction.

Flowers are one of the most prominent. They produce seeds, and often have both male and female parts, needed to produce new flowers. The smell and color of their flowers is used to attract animals. This is because many animals are absolutely instrumental to the reproduction of plants. They will carry pollen from plant to plant, pollinating them. This is often done by bees. They also carry seeds around. This is usually done by the animal ingesting the seed, and passing it as waste later in a different place, where hopefully the seed can grow.

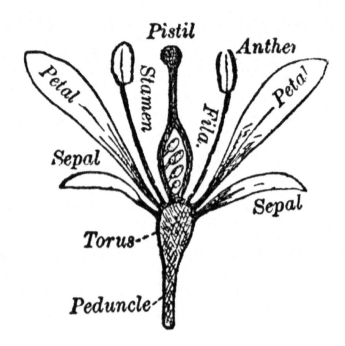

In addition to flowers, they may have a **stamen** and a **pistil.** A stamen is the male reproductive organ of the plant, while a pistil is the female reproductive organ. At the tip of the stamen is an **anther.** The anther is the bulb that releases the pollen. The pollen lands on the **stigma**, which resides at the top of the pistil.

Defense and response mechanisms

There are actually many ways that plants respond to the environment. They are also not so bad at protecting themselves as well. Some plants, for example, have thorns that act as a deterrent against animals that may want to eat them otherwise. Some plants have poisonous fruits or leaves that prevent animals from eating them as well.

Some plants are also able to open or close their leaves in response to being touched. While they cannot move like we can, plants still have many ways to respond to stimuli in their environment. An example would be **dormancy**. Plants are often able to sense changes in temperature or water availability, and sometimes this triggers periods of dormancy, where the plant will not grow, and will lower all levels of activity. A good example of this is the winter-time, when plants shed their leaves and do not grow them until the spring.

There are also several types of **–tropism.**

- **Phototropism-** The act of moving/ growing towards the light source

- **Gravitropism**- The act of movin/ growing against the force of gravity

- **Hydrotropism**- The act of moving/ growing towards water sources- this is usually carried out by the roots of the plant

- **Thigmotropism**- The example that was given before- moving in response to touch. A good example of this is the Venus flytrap. (Interestingly, this is one of the few examples of an organism that has both heterotrophic and autotrophic functions)

Plants may seem as if they are simpler than animals, but in many ways they are much more complex! Here we only got a chance to cover a few characteristics of plants. In a later unit we will learn more about how plants are able to use photosynthesis to grow their own food.

Characteristics of Plants: Activities and Experiments

1. Coloring flowers

What you need:

- 5 glasses or plastic cups.
- 5 different food coloring colors
- 7 or 8 white freshly cut daises
- Pencil and lab book

What you do:

- Fill the glasses half way with lukewarm water.
- Add 20-30 drops of food coloring, until the color is nice and visible in the water.
- Put a daisy in each glass.
- Return in 1 hour to observe and record your results. Come back every hour and record your results again. Sometimes the process will take up to a whole day, and sometimes it will be very fast.

What you should learn:

- The daisies become colored because the stem sucks up the colored water. Usually roots of the plant deliver the water to the stems, but water can be taken up by stems alone.

Questions:

- What is the name of the structure that sucks up the water?
- What do you think will happen if you slit the stem up the middle and put each half into a different colored solution? Give it a try with your last couple of flowers!

2. Make pressed flower specimens

What you need:

- 5 freshly picked flowers. Go outside and find your favorite types and colors!
- White sheets of paper
- Some heavy books
- Pencil and lab book
- White paper

What you do:

- Line the inside of a heavy books pages with sheets of white paper
- Lay the flowers, one in between each page.
- Close the book and lay many heavy books on top
- Leave the books undisturbed for at least 3 weeks. The longer you leave them the better they will be pressed.
- Identify each species in your lab book and paste the samples inside, labeling and describing each plant type. You might need the help of a parent, teacher, or the Internet to find it all out.

What you should learn:

- You may have had to do a bit of research to find out which plants were the ones you picked flowers from. You learned how to collect and document botanical samples as well.

Questions:

- What is the function of a flower?
- Why do flowers have interesting appearances and smells?

3. Investigating gravitropism

What you need:

- Shoe box with lid
- Small square flower pot with young radish plant

What you do:

- Put the plant inside the shoebox on its side.
- Close the box and leave it on the bench for 24 hours.
- Open the box and observe/ record the results.

What you should learn:

- Since radish plants grow quickly it should be possible for you to see the change in direction of growth after 24 hours. This is due to gravitropism, where the plants tend to grow against the force of gravity.

Questions:

- Why do we put the plant in the shoebox? If you don't know the answer, try to answer it again after the next experiment. If it is still hard to answer you should review the different types of variables in chapter 1.

4. Investigating phototropism

- Taller cardboard box.
- Small flower pot with young radish plant
- Pencil and lab book
- Scissors
- Adjustable table lamp
- Camera (optional)

What you do:

- Cut a hole in the side of the box.
- Put the plant inside the box.
- Adjust the table lamp so that it shines in the hole in the side of the box.
- Record your observations every 24 hours for a few days, taking pictures if possible, for your lab book.

What you should learn:

- Plants do not only display the ability to grow against gravity, but they also have the ability to grow towards the light. This is called phototropism.

Question:

- Why is it better to use the box with a hole, instead of just the table lamp, next to the plant? Do you think the plant grow differently? Try it if you like!

5. Investigating effects of fertilizers

What you need:

- 3 pots
- Bag of soil; enough for 3 pots
- Seeds of your choice, all from the same plant.
- Organic fertilizer
- Chemical fertilizer
- Ruler
- Pencil and Lab book
- Water

What you do:

- Fill pots with soil and plant 3 seeds.
- Keep all three pots in the same conditions, and water them at the same time and with the same amount of water.
- Following instructions on the container or bag, use the organic fertilizer for 1 plant, chemical fertilizer for another plant, and no fertilizer for the third plant.
  Measure the growth of the plants every day for 2 weeks.
- Observe and record the results.

What you should learn:

- Different types of fertilizer will affect each plant slightly differently, so in this case we cannot generalize. This just allows you to design a small experiment, see the effects of different fertilizers, and try to interpret the results.

Questions:

- Which fertilizer worked better for your plant?
- Were there any problems with the growth of the plants? If so, why do you think this may be?
- What is your dependent variable?
- What is your independent variable?
- What are your control variables?

Characteristics of Plants: Quiz

1. Arrange the taxanomical hierarchy from most broad to most specific:

Phylum-Genus-Class-Kingdom-Order-Species -Family

_____

2. Which Kingdom do plants belong to?

_____

3. Explain the difference between autotrophs and heterotrophs. Give an example of each.

_____
_____
_____
_____

True or false:

4. Non-vascular plants have xylem and phloem. _____

5. Non-vascular plants do not grow to be very large. _____

6. All plants use seeds to reproduce. _____

7. Plants that produce cones are called conifers. _____

8. Conifers contain spores. _____

9. All roots have small hairs on them to increase surface area. _____

10. Animals are important for plants to reproduce. _____

11-13. Give a description of the purpose of **leaves**, **stems**, and **roots**. Explain what they are, and more importantly, what use they have for the plant.

_____
_____
_____
_____
_____
_____
_____
_____

14. Do plants have any way of protecting themselves? If so, please give an example.

_____
_____

Define the following words:

15. Hydrotropism _____

_____

16. Gravitropism _____

_____

17. Phototropism _____

_____

Link the following words on the left with their counterparts on the right.

18. Monocot					Pistil

19. Seeds					Dicot

20. Stamen					Spores

Chapter 6: Energy, Force, & Motion

In a previous section, we learned about the properties of matter. We learned that one important property of matter is its **mass**, and we learned about **Newton's first law**. This was the beginning of introducing you to the world of **energy**, **force**, and **motion**. Now we will learn even more.

There is energy all around us in the world, and it appears in many forms. It is defined as the **ability to cause change**. Energy is what is used to change the temperature, speed, and direction of an object. It takes energy for you to walk around and play, it takes energy for the wind to blow, and countless other things use energy too. Energy is what makes everything happen.

Challenge: Can you name 10 more things that need energy to happen?

Energy can come in many forms.

Electrical energy: This is probably the most obvious form of energy, since we use it all the time every day. Electric energy is created by the movement of electrons. We use it to light our homes, listen to music, and countless other things as well.

Sound energy: All sounds and noises are created by energy. The energy takes the form of vibrations in the air. Vibrations can also travel through some liquids and solids as well. All of this vibration is just very small movement, which of course means that this is energy too!

Solar energy: Light travels as waves from the sun to the earth, and is also created by other sources, such as chemical reactions. Light is a type of energy known as electromagnetic radiation. Light is an especially important for us because it is needed for vision and the growth of plants.

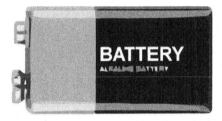

Chemical energy: Chemical energy is used in plants, animals, batteries, and in many other things too. Our bodies use chemical energy that we get from our food. Your pasta is filled with chemical energy!

Heat energy: We need heat to live, to eat, and for everything else that happens as well. Temperature is a way to measure how much heat energy there is in a system. This is called thermal energy. It can be transferred from one body to another, and is caused by movement on a molecular scale. The faster the movement, the higher the temperature

Mechanical energy: A form of energy that is shown through movement.

These are just a few types of energy. There are many more! One interesting fact about these different forms of energy is that many times, when you use the energy to change something, the energy also changes too! A great example would be fireworks. The energy is initially in the form of chemical energy, but is later converted to light and thermal energy.

Kinetic energy and potential energy

When it comes to talking about energy in terms of motion, energy comes in 2 main types: **kinetic energy**, and **potential energy**. Potential energy is energy that is waiting to be used, and kinetic energy is the energy of movement. Potential energy is like stored energy, and kinetic energy is energy being used. An example is a ball at the top of a hill. The ball has the potential to roll down the hill, which would convert the potential energy into kinetic energy. Another example would be a pendulum. If you were to lift it up to one side, you would be creating potential energy. Then, when you drop the pendulum, this energy would be transferred to kinetic energy. The potential energy always becomes kinetic energy when something happens that prompts it to make this change. The more potential energy something has, the more kinetic energy it will have.

Forces and motion

Energy is also used to create **forces**, which allows **motion.** A force can be described as anything that cause push or pull on an object. Force and motion are always around you. When you kick a ball or jump in the air you are using forces to move. Even the food moving through your intestines is pushed by force! Force is measure in Newtons, which is abbreviated to 'N'. This unit of measurement is named after Isaac Newton, and you can measure how many Newtons of force are being exerted by using a device called a spring scale.

When force produces movement, what do we mean by movement? Movement is not only a change in position. There is another component that is very important for movement. That component is called the **reference point.** This is because the motion always has to happen in relation to something else! To say that I moved in this direction or that direction is meaningless without previously known points.

Lets take a look at Isaac Newton's 3 **laws of motion**. In an earlier unit you heard about the first law of motion, which is as follows:

- *An object will either stay at rest or continue to move at a constant velocity, unless acted upon by an external force.*

This means that without forces such as friction and gravity, an object will continue to move along its current path at its current speed. If the object is sitting still, then it will stay sitting still. All of this stays the same until an external force causes it to change. Newton's second law of motion:

- *The acceleration of an object depends on the mass of the object, and the amount of force applied to it.*

What this means is that the more force you apply to an object, the faster you can make it accelerate. This also depends on the mass of the object. There is even a formula for this.

$$F = m * a$$

In this equation F = force, m= mass, and a=acceleration. If you know this equation, you can also rearrange it to the following equations:

$$m = F/a, \text{ as well as } a = F/m$$

A good example of this is a car. The faster you want to accelerate the car, the more force the engine has to generate. Of course, if the car is heavier, then you will need even more force to make the car accelerate.

Newton's third law of motion:

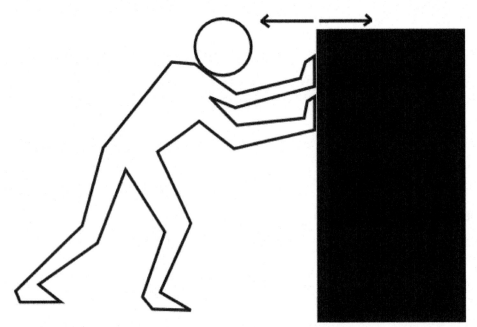

When one object exerts force on another object, the second object will have the equal, yet opposite reaction on the first object.

This law can be observed happening all around you. When you see a bird flying, you may notice that it keeps flapping its wings to push the air down. Because of the effect described by Newton's third law, the air will also push the bird upwards, allowing it to fly.

Another example of Newton's third law is a moving car. The tires grip the ground and push backwards on it. Because there is an equal and opposite reaction, this pushed the car forwards.

A third and final example of Newton's third and final law of motion is that of gun recoil. When a gun is shot, the shooter feels a kick. This is the equal and opposite reaction of the force used to shoot the bullet.

Gravity and Friction

While objects that sit still may appear as if they have no forces exerted upon them, this is incorrect. Don't forget about the force of gravity!

What is gravity?

Gravity is an attracting force that exists between all objects. The force of the gravitational pull depends on the lass of the two objects, as well as the distance between them.

On earth, the acceleration rate of objects being pulled by gravity is **9.8 meters per second per second**.

Friction is another important factor when considering motion and force. It is a force that works against motion between two surfaces that contact one another. Friction can prevent motion from starting, and it can also work against motion in progress. There are 4 different types of friction

- **Sliding friction** → force that comes into play when 2 surfaces slide along each other. An example of sliding friction would be when you scrub things with a sponge.
- **Rolling friction** → a force that slows down the movement of a rolling object. A good example of rolling friction can be seen in cars, skateboards, roller skates, and anything else that moves with wheels!
- **Fluid friction** → When an object moves through fluid or air it encounters a resistance force that slows it down. This is fluid friction. An example of fluid friction is swimming in water, or using a rowboat.
- **Static friction** → when the friction prevents the movement from starting. An example of static friction would be if you tried to push a very big rock, but it didn't move.

In this section about energy, force, and motion, you learned many important concepts. Try to complete the following challenges below to see if you have fully understood the ideas.

Challenge: Describe the effect of gravity.

Challenge: Name 3 different types of energy and describe them.

Challenge: Explain the difference between kinetic and potential energy.

Energy, Force, & Motion: Activities and Experiments

1. Investigating kinetic and potential energy

What you need:

- Thin wooden board
- Wooden block, or a small stack of books
- Toy skateboard
- 3 metal washers
- Rubber band
- Ruler/ meter stick
- Pencil and lab book

What you do:

- Build a small ramp on a smooth surface using the thin wooden board and the block.
- Hold the skateboard at the top of the ramp and let go.
- Allow skateboard to roll down and off the ramp without interrupting it.
- Measure the distance from the starting point.
- Record your results.
- Attach a washer to the skateboard using the rubber band.
- Repeat the measurement with these conditions.
- Record your data.
- Add another washer and repeat.
- Record your data.
- Add the third washer and repeat.
- Record your data.

What you should learn:

- When the skateboard has the washers attached to it, it has more mass. This gives it more potential energy when it sits at the top of the ramp. When you push it down, this potential energy is transferred to kinetic energy. The greater the potential energy, the greater the kinetic energy. That is why the skateboard travels further with the washers attached.

Question:

- Can you think of any other examples of potential energy being converted to kinetic energy?

2. Observing Newton's third law in action

What you need:

- Balloons
- Paper and pencil

What you do:

- This experiment is easy!
- You start by blowing up the balloon, but not tying it.
- Hold the opening downward and let go.

- Repeat several times and record your observations.
- Describe what is happening in terms of the third law of motion.
- To make this one more fun, you can also create a small tube of paper that you tape to the balloon. Then, string a long string through this tube. Tie one end of the string at one end of the room, and one at the other. Then repeat this experiment and see how the balloon flies down your newly created balloon highway!

What you should learn:

- This should give students the chance to revise and refresh their memory of newton's third law. It also gives students a chance to explain a physical phenomenon in terms of a scientific description.

Question:

- What is Newton's third law and what does it mean?

3. Observing Newton's first law in action

What you need:

- Full 2 liter plastic bottle
- Wax paper
- Kitchen table
- Pencil and lab book

What you do:

- Place the wax paper at the edge of the table, with some hanging off the edge.
- Place the full bottle on the paper.
- Quickly and sharply pull the wax paper out from underneath the bottle.
- Record your observations.

What you should learn:

- If you managed to do this properly, the paper should have been removable without tipping the bottle over. This is due to the effect seen in Newton's first law. Because of the heavy bottle's inertia, it did not fall.

Questions:

- What forces were acting on the bottle?
- What forces were acting on the wax paper?
- What would happen if the bottle were much lighter? Why?

4. Friction studies

What you need:

- Board
- Wax paper
- Foil
- Block or stack of books
- Pencil and lab book

- Tape
- Toy skateboard
- Ruler or meter stick

What you do:

- As you did previously in experiment 1, set up the board with the block to make a ramp. Do this on a smooth surface.
- As you performed in experiment 1, allow the skateboard to race down the surface, and measure the distance it traveled.
- Record your data.
- Using tape, attach the wax paper to the board.
- Repeat the measurement and record your results
- Using tape, attach foil to the surface of the board.
- Repeat your measurements and record the results.

What you should learn:

- Friction is one of the variables that determine the movement of an object through space. Different amounts of friction are introduced in this experiment through the different surface materials of the ramp. This shows you that surface that generate less friction allow the skateboard to travel further than the surfaces that generate more friction.

Question:

- What would happen if there was no friction at all?

5. Making a potato powered clock

What you need:

- 2 potatoes
- 2 small pieces of copper wire
- 2 galvanized nails (it is important that they are galvanized)
- 3 clip wire units (clips connected to each other with a wire in between)
- 1 low-voltage clock (uses 1-2 Volt battery)
- Pencil and lab book

What you do:

- Remove the battery from the clock
- Insert the galvanized nails into the potatoes, 1 in each.
- Insert the small lengths of copper wire into the potatoes, 1 in each, at as far a distance from the galvanized nail as possible.
- Use one of the clips to attach the copper wire to the + terminal in the battery compartment.
- Use of the clips to attach the nail in the other potato to the – terminal in the battery compartment.
- Use the remaining clip to attach the remaining nail and copper wire in the adjacent potatoes.
- If everything worked your clock should be on now!
- See how long the potato battery lasts and record your result.

What you should learn:

- A potato in this scenario acts as an electrochemical cell. What this means is that chemical energy is being transferred to electric energy via the potato. The galvanized nails are covered in zinc, which is negatively charged. The copper is positively charged. When the nail comes into contact with a naturally occurring acid inside the potato, called phosphoric acid. This causes a chemical reaction that frees electrons. The copper takes up these electrons, and thus creates a circuit.

Question:

- Can you think of any other examples of one energy type being transferred into another energy type?

Energy, Force, & Motion: Quiz

1. What defines energy?

_____

_____

_____

True or false:

2. When you use energy, often the energy is transformed from one type into another. _____

3. Energy is used to create force. _____

4. Force allows motion. _____

5. Sound energy is generated by the movement of electrons. _____

6. Batteries use chemical energy to create electrical energy. _____

7. Mechanical energy does not involve movement. _____

8. The only natural light comes from the sun. _____

9. Newton discovered 5 laws of motion. _____

10. Gravitational forces exist between all objects. _____

11- 14. Extended question: Describe the 4 types of friction, how they arise, and give an example of where you might find each one.

_____

_____

_____

_____

_____

15. When we talk about energy in terms of motion, we talk about 2 main types of energy. What are these 2 types called?

16. Considering Newton's first law of motion, what would you expect to happen if you threw a ball in outer space, where there is no gravity and no air friction?

17. Considering Newton's second law of motion, what would happen if you tried to drive two cars fast, with the same engine, but one car was heavier than the other?

18. What is Newton's second third law of motion? Give an example of when you can see this happening in the world around us.

19-20. Give an example of energy, and how it is used to create force, which is used to create movement. Explain where the energy comes from and what type of energy it is, explain where the force is applied, and explain how this causes movement.

Chapter 7: Electricity & Magnetism

Most people would agree that electricity is one of the most important things in our day-to-day life. We use it to power all of our technology, all of our lights, and countless things that we rely on. But what exactly is electricity? In the previous chapter we learned that electricity is a form of energy, and that it is created by the movement of electrons.

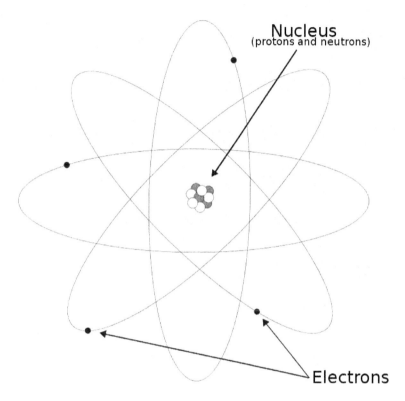

When you look at this simplified picture of an **atom**, you can see a few things. The first thing you can see is that at the center of the atom exists a large group of mass. This is made out of **protons** and **neutrons.** Neutrons have no charge, while protons have a positive charge. An atom also has **electrons,** which move around the nucleus of the atom at a much greater distance. Electrons are negatively charged.

Normal atoms have a net charge of 0, since they have the same amount of positively charged protons, and negatively charged electrons. When an electron moves from one atom to another, this creates **ions**. There are 2 types of ion.

- **Cation-** an ion that has lost electrons, giving it a positive charge
- **Anion-** an ion that has gained electrons, giving it a negative charge

The loss or gain of an electron, which carries a negative charge, will give the atom a net gain or loss in terms of its charge. This charge of ions is called **electrostatic charge**.

Sometimes, we can cause an electrostatic charge. This can happen for a few reasons:

- Friction transfers electrons between 2 objects/ surfaces
- Coming into contact with a charged body, which can cause a transfer of electrons and cause an electrostatic charge
- It can also be caused by a process called induction, which causes a redistribution of charge in a material

Conductors/ insulators

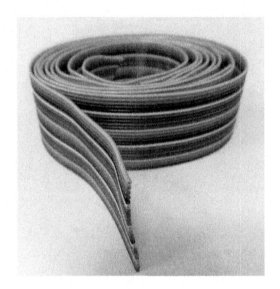

Some materials are very good at taking up electrons, while some materials will not take up any. A material that will take up electrons is called a conductor, while a material that will not take up any electrons is called an insulator. Many metals are good conductors, for example copper, which is the best conductor. Examples of insulators include rubber and wood. That is why when you rip open an electrical cable, the inside is made of metal, while the outside is made of rubber. This is because the inside should be a good conductor, so that electrons can travel through it freely. The outside, however, should be a good insulator; otherwise the electricity would shock you whenever you touch the cable. This would be because the electrons travel from the metal to your body. The rubber stops this, since it is a good insulator.

Measuring electrical charge

Electrical charge can be measured! It is measured in units called **coulombs**. Objects with the same kind of charge repel each other, while objects with opposite charges attract each other. There was French physicist who lived during the late 18th century, who's name was **Charles Augustin de Coulomb**, and he found a way to quantify this attraction or repulsion. That is why the unit of measurement is called coulombs. Notice how similarly to Netwon, Coulomb has a unit of measurement named after him!?

Coulomb's Law is a very important concept, and it is one that is integral to electricity and physics. The law examines the forces created between two charged objects. As the distance between the objects increases, the forces and electric fields between them decrease. The force between two objects will be either positive or negative. This depends on whether the objects are attracted or repelled from one another.

The formula:

$$F = k * q_1 * q_2 / d^2$$

While the formula may look scary and complicated, it is really quite simple!

F= force

K= a constant (a number that is always the same) found by Coulomb

q_1=the electrical charge of object 1

q_2=the electrical charge of object 2

d= the distance between the 2 objects

Once you see that each of these variables has a meaning, then you realize that it's just a question of multiplication and division! In later years you will learn how to use this formula, but for now the important thing you need to know is that it exists, that Coulomb discovered it, and that it is a way for us to measure electric charge.

The existence of an electrical charge around an object also creates an **electrical field.** It is a kind of force field, but it is called an electrical field because it is caused by electric charge of an object. It exerts force on other electrical charges in the field.

One can map an electric field by introducing a positive test charge into the electrical field. Then, **lines of force** are drawn to represent the direction of the electrical field.

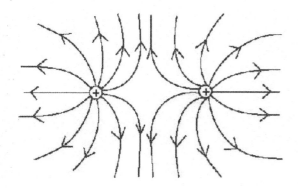
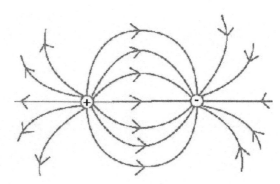

Above we can see some examples of such electric field lines. On the left we can see a positive and a positive charge. The lines of force repel each other, since both charges are positive. On the right we see a positive charge, as well as a negative charge. These charges attract each other, since they are opposites.

Electric current flows similarly to water currents. Electric current is defined as the flow of charge. In biological systems this charge is carried via ions, which if you remember, are entire atoms that are charged. In wire this is achieved by the movement of electrons alone. Imagine it as a kind of river, down which charge flows. Electric current has one very interesting effect, which is the creation of a magnetic field. There are two kinds of current: **alternating current**, and **direct current.** Alternating current has the advantage of being able to transfer over very long distances.

Magnetism

All of us know what a magnet is. In a magnet, we have 2 magnetic poles, namely the North Pole and the South Pole. Poles of opposite types attract each other, while poles of the same type repel each other. When one magnet is moved near another magnet, they will affect each others' magnetic field. A **magnetic field can** be represented by **field lines**, just like an electric field can.

As previously mentioned, the magnetic field is created by the electric field. This has even led to a common understanding of the two phenomena. They are intrinsically linked, and since their relationship is so close, we can even call it by a singular '**electromagnetic field**'. The effect of an electric current inducing a magnetic field was discovered by a scientist named **Hans Christian Ørsted** in 1820. He noticed by chance that the needle of a compass was deflected from North when he turned on a battery powered current. Interestingly, magnetic field lines and electrical field lines lie perpendicular to one another. That is to say that they intersect each other at right angles.

Of course, our earth has a North and a South Pole, just like a magnet. That is because our earth is, in fact, a giant magnet! It is thought that the earth's magnetic field originates from moving charges, since the core of the earth is composed of metals that flow as the earth rotates, which creates electrical currents. These electrical currents then induce a magnetic field, as previously explained.

Magnetoreception & Electroreception

Some animals have the ability to sense the magnetic field of the earth. The same was us humans can perceive all kinds of things like light and sound, some animals can perceive the magnetic field. There are some bacteria, known as **magnetotactic bacteria**, which orient themselves in relation to the earth's magnetic field. This is possible because of a structure known as a **magnetosome.** It is inside the cell, and acts a kind of molecular compass. There are also several species of migratory birds that have the ability for magnetoreception, as well as some smaller invertebrate species.

The same way there are animals that can sense the magnetic field of the earth, there are animals that are able to sense natural electrical stimuli. Since water is a much better conductor than air, this is mostly seen in animals that live in the water. This is not always the case, since we can see electroreception in bees, as well as in cockroaches. In the water however, we see that animals such as sharks, rays, electric eels, and dolphins also have electroreception!

In this section we covered the fundamental aspects of electricity and magnetism. These are new and complicated ideas, and you will probably have to think about it for a while to fully understand it. If you can complete the following challenge, then you have a good idea about electricity and magnetism. This is a hard one!

Challenge: Using the things you learned, describe the relationship between electrical charge, electrical current, and magnetic fields.

Electricity & Magnetism: Activities and Experiments

1. Making a compass

What you need:

- Sewing needle
- Cork
- Bar magnet
- Sticky tack
- Scissors or knife
- Bowl or dish of water
- Compass

What you do:

- Cut a circle of cork using the scissors or knife.
- Magnetize the needle by using 1 end of the bar magnet, and swiping the needle from one end to the other 50 times, always in the same direction. Rubbing in the other direction will demagnetize the sewing needle.
- Use the tack and stick the magnetized needle flat on the center of the cork.
- Put the cork in the water dish and wait for the needle to rotate to show which way is north.
- Check with your compass that this is correct.

What you should learn:

- When you use the magnet to magnetize the needle, it can interact with the magnetic field of the earth. Using cork allows the needle to float, and using water gives a mostly frictionless surface for the needle to rotate on. Over time the needle will lose the magnetic charge.

Question:

- How could this skill be useful?

2. Holding a charge

What you need:

- Paper straw
- Napkin

What you do:

- Do this experiment in a dry area
- Use the napkin and slide it up and down the straw, 20 or 30 times.
- Remove the napkin and put the straw in your open palm to see if it sticks.
- Record your results

What you should learn:

- When you rub the paper on the straw you electrically charge it, making the straw more negatively charged. When you bring it near your palm, it causes the palm to become positively charged, and they attract each other.

Question:

- Can you think of any other time when static electricity causes things to stick to you?

3. Eddy currents

What you need:

- A neodymium magnet
- A pencil and lab book
- 1 meter of copper, brass, or aluminum tubing, larger in diameter than the magnet
- 1 meter of non metallic tubing such as PVC pipe

What you do:

- Hold the metal pipe vertically, and drop your pencil through the pipe.
- Now, drop the magnet through the pipe.
- Try dropping the magnet and the pencil through the PVC pipe as well.
- Record your observations.

What you should learn:

- As the magnet is falling through the tube, the magnetic field around it is constantly changing, and the tube experiences this changing magnetic field. This causes something called eddy currents, which occur in the metal tubing. The eddy currents create a magnetic field that affects the course of the magnet's movement. The force inhibits the magnet's fall, causing it to move more slowly through the tube.

3. Shorting the circuit

What you need:

- 6 volt battery
- Length of copper wire with clips
- A strand of very thin iron wire. E.g. unbraided picture hanging wire

What you do:

- Attach one end of the clip to the battery
- Attach the other end of the clip to the thin iron wire
- Attach the other end of the iron wire to the other battery terminal.
- Slowly move the clip attached to the iron wire closer and closer to the battery along the iron wire.
- Observe what happens and record your results. (Caution: the wire will get very hot!)

What you should learn:

- If it worked properly the iron wire should have gotten hotter and hotter until it melts the wire and breaks the circuit. The thin iron wire has a higher resistance to electrical current compared to the copper wire. The voltage from the battery pushes electrons against the resistance, heating the wire. As you make the wire shorter by moving the clip closer to the battery, the wire gets hotter and hotter. Eventually this causes the wire to melt.

Question:

- How does this relate to the concept of a fuse? (Some research will be required to answer this question)

4. Insulators versus conductors

What you need:

- Several different small pieces of material e.g. wood, plastic, string, foil, etc.
- 6 volt battery
- 3 wire leads with clips
- 6 volt light bulb with leads
- Cutting board

What you do:

- Use the cutting board as the base for your circuit.
- Attach a wire to each terminal of the battery.
- Take the other end of the wire attached to the – end and attach it to one of the light bulb leads.
- Attach the third and yet unattached wire to the second light bulb lead.
- Now you should have 2 loose clips. When you attach them, if you made the circuit correctly, the light bulb should light up.
- Now, introduce your testing materials in between these two clips.
- Look at how this affects the brightness of the light, for each material.
- Observe and record the results.

What you should learn:

- If the material is an insulating material, the light will be more dim, or even completely off. The better the material conducts the brighter the light will shine.

Question:

- Which materials were good insulators?
- Which were good conductors?

5. Levitation with magnets

What you need:

- Paperclip
- A large strong magnet
- Thread
- Pencil and lab book
- Tape

What you do:

- Tape one end of the thread to the table.
- Tie the other end of the thread to the paperclip.
- Use the large magnet to attract the paperclip upward. Keep the magnet higher than the thread allows, suspending the paperclip in the air.
- Use a ruler to measure the distances at which the magnet still attracts the paperclip.

What you should learn:

- You should see how strong your magnet is! Magnets are amazing tools that can be used in all kinds of industrial applications. After seeing what you can do with a single magnet and paperclip, imagine what you could do with all the tools that engineers have available today.

Question:

- Can you think of another kind of technology that uses magnets?

Electricity & Magnetism: Quiz

1. What are the 3 basic components of an atom?

_____
_____

2. Which 2 are located in the nucleus of the atom and which one is in orbit around the nucleus?

_____
_____

3. What is an electrical conductor? Give an example.

_____
_____

4. What is an electrical insulator? Give an example.

_____
_____

True or false:

5. Electrons are positively charged. _____

6. A charged atom is called an ion. _____

7. Coloumb's law is what allows us to measure electrical charge. _____

8. Electricity and magnetism have no effect on each other. _____

9. Some animals can sense magnetic fields. _____

10. There are no animals that can sense electric fields. _____

11. Electrical charge of an object causes an electric field. _____

12. Our earth is a magnet. _____

13. An electric current can affect magnets by creating a magnetic field. _____

14. A scientist named **Hans Christian Ørsted** discovered something about electric currents. What did he discover?

_____

_____

15. What are electric field lines?

_____

_____

16. Draw an example of electric field lines below, between 2 positively charged bodies.

17. What advantage does alternating current have over direct current?

_____

_____

18. What is thought to cause the earth's magnetic field?

_____
_____

19. Give an example of something that uses an electric current. What is the current used for?

_____
_____

20. Give an example of something that uses a magnet. What is the magnet used for?

_____
_____

Chapter 8: Periodic Table

Group →	1	2	3	4	5	6	7	8	9	10	11	12	13	14	15	16	17	18
↓ Period																		
1	1 H																	2 He
2	3 Li	4 Be											5 B	6 C	7 N	8 O	9 F	10 Ne
3	11 Na	12 Mg											13 Al	14 Si	15 P	16 S	17 Cl	18 Ar
4	19 K	20 Ca	21 Sc	22 Ti	23 V	24 Cr	25 Mn	26 Fe	27 Co	28 Ni	29 Cu	30 Zn	31 Ga	32 Ge	33 As	34 Se	35 Br	36 Kr
5	37 Rb	38 Sr	39 Y	40 Zr	41 Nb	42 Mo	43 Tc	44 Ru	45 Rh	46 Pd	47 Ag	48 Cd	49 In	50 Sn	51 Sb	52 Te	53 I	54 Xe
6	55 Cs	56 Ba		72 Hf	73 Ta	74 W	75 Re	76 Os	77 Ir	78 Pt	79 Au	80 Hg	81 Tl	82 Pb	83 Bi	84 Po	85 At	86 Rn
7	87 Fr	88 Ra		104 Rf	105 Db	106 Sg	107 Bh	108 Hs	109 Mt	110 Ds	111 Rg	112 Cn	113 Uut	114 Fl	115 Uup	116 Lv	117 Uus	118 Uuo

Lanthanides	57 La	58 Ce	59 Pr	60 Nd	61 Pm	62 Sm	63 Eu	64 Gd	65 Tb	66 Dy	67 Ho	68 Er	69 Tm	70 Yb	71 Lu
Actinides	89 Ac	90 Th	91 Pa	92 U	93 Np	94 Pu	95 Am	96 Cm	97 Bk	98 Cf	99 Es	100 Fm	101 Md	102 No	103 Lr

In this unit we are going to learn about one of the most important scientific organizational tools- **the periodic table of elements**. Below is the whole periodic table. We are going to learn how it is arranged and how to understand it.

The periodic table was developed by Russian chemist and inventor, Dmitri Mendeleev, in the year 1869. He tried to sort the known elements in a way that they would be somehow grouped by property, which we will take a look at soon.

Most of these elements can be found under natural conditions, but there are also many on this list that could only have been observed under laboratory conditions. Elements 99 – 118 are elements that have only been synthesized in the lab. Some of the elements on the table were found in nature, but only sometime after they had already been synthesized in a lab, due to their rarity.

The periodic table of elements is an arrangement of all the elements. Each of the little blocks represents 1 element, with the abbreviation of the 1 or 2 letters indicating which element it is. They are arranged in this table in general patterns.

In atoms, the electrons are arranged around the nucleus. When there are many electrons, they arrange themselves in regions of orbit called **electron shells**. These shells are also called **energy levels**. Imagine these shells as kind of orbit paths around the atoms' nuclei.

Each energy level has a different number of possible electrons positions.

The maximum number of electrons that can sit at each energy level can be found using the formula:

Electron Capacity = $2n^2$

The variable n represents something called the principle quatum number. This is also the energy level.

Energy Level	Shell	Electron Capacity
1	K	2
2	L	8
3	M	18
4	N	32
5	O	50
6	P	72

It is not necessary for each shell to be completely filled up before electrons occupy the outer shells. The outermost shell is called be **valence shell,** and the electrons that occupy this shell are called **valence electrons**.

In the periodic table of elements, the elements are grouped by several characteristics. One of those characteristics is **valencey**, or rather, the number of valence electrons the atom has.

If you look above the periodic table you see that the elements are arranged in groups. In groups 1 and 2, the number of valence electrons is the same as the group. Groups 3- 12 are composed of the so-called transition metals, and the atoms in these groups do not follow a general rule in regard to valence electrons. In groups 13-18, the number of valence electrons in the atom is always 10 less than the group number the atom is in.

Group 1

Apart from hydrogen, the group 1 elements are known as the most reactive of the bunch! All of them except hydrogen are **alkali metals**. These atoms are not stable and will easily lend some of their valence electrons to other atoms. Because of this, these atoms are never found in an unbound state in nature. A great example would be the element **potassium**. It is abbreviated with the letter K. *(It was originally known as Kalium, and still is in some languages. That is why it is abbreviated with a K!)*

Because potassium is so unstable, and so prone to lending electrons to other atoms, you often see it bound into small molecules, but never alone. A good example would be in bananas! They have lots of potassium, but it is always in a bound form, usually as KCl (potassium chloride).

Group 2

Group 2 is made up of alkaline-earth-metals. These metals are also reactive, but not nearly reactive as the alkali metals from group 1. This is due to the extra valence electron that the atoms have, since it is harder to lend 2 valence electrons than 1. Some examples include **magnesium** (Mg) and **calcium** (Ca). Magnesium is used in construction. It is the third most widely used metal for construction, following iron and aluminum. It is also found in small traces in the body. Calcium is also found in the body, where it plays a role in many important processes. It makes your bones strong, and your brain cells need it for them to form memories!

Groups 3-12

These groups do not have individual names like groups 1 and 2 do, however together they are called the transition metals. These groups are not nearly as reactive as groups 1 and 2, since it is harder for them to lend their valence electrons. Despite the fact that we lump them all together, there are some very important transition metals!

Both **silver** (Ag) and **gold** (Au) are transition metals. We use them for jewelry and as forms of wealth. They also both have other purposes, such as in electronics and dentistry, as well as in other fields of application.

More transition metals include the only 3 elements that can produce a magnetic field, **iron** (Fe), **cobalt** (Co), and **nickel** (Ni), as well as the hugely popular building material **aluminum** (Al). Aluminum is used to build all kinds of things, from cards, to cans. This is probably because of its low density, which makes it light, as well as its resistance to corrosion.

Group 14

This group is the **carbon** (C) group, since it is home to what is probably one of the most important elements on the periodic table. Carbon is often found uncombined in nature, and forms both diamond and charcoal. Not only is in the main ingredient in these two structures, but it is also used by humans to make **graphene**, which is a single monolayer of carbon atoms. It is amazingly strong for its tiny size of just 1 atom thick, since it is 100 times stronger than steel! All of this, however, would not be enough to make carbon the most important atom on the periodic table. The reason why it is so important atom, to humans, is because we are carbon-based life forms. What this means is that all of the molecules needed for life to thrive are based on a carbon backbone. All proteins, all fats, and all carbohydrates are built on a carbon backbone. This is why the human body is actually 18% carbon by weight!

Group 15

This group is home to **nitrogen** (N), which makes up most of the air you breath! (about 80%) Nitrogen is widely used in biological systems, as well as in science. Scientists use liquid nitrogen as a refrigerant, since it stays liquid at very low temperatures. (It actually boils at -195°C!) Doctors also use liquid nitrogen to freeze warts and kill them.

Group 16

Group 16 is home to another very important element, **oxygen** (O). Oxygen makes up 21% of the air you breath, and it also makes up a whopping 65% of your body by weight! Oxygen is what drives many processes in life. Group 16 is also home to **sulfur** (S), which is very important. Sulfur is used to make sulfuric acid, and is also used in many manufacturing of many materials. It is also a component of fertilizer, pesticide, and fungicide. It also has a very important role in wine-making.

Group 17

Group 17 contains halogens, non-metalic elements that are very reactive. They are very reactive because they just need 1 more electron to fill their shell, and so are very good acceptors. An example of a halogen would be **chlorine** (Cl), which has many applications. In its pure form it is a yellow greenish gas. It is commonly used a disinfectant for water that we drink and swim in.

Group 18

Group 18 is home to the so-called noble gases. These are nonreactive gases, since they have full outermost energy levels. This means that they are actually unable to react with other elements. A notable noble gas is **neon** (Ne). We use neon in signs. We electrically charge it, putting it in a state of plasma. (If you recall, we learned about this in the earlier unit, *states of matter*) This causes it to glow, giving the neon sign effect.

These are all 18 groups in the periodic table. There are many elements we did not discuss in this section, but many of the most prominent atoms were mentioned, either because of their importance to nature, or because of their importance in man made productions.

Atomic number

If you refer to the periodic table, you will notice that above every single element there is a number. This number is called the atomic number. It represents the total number of protons in the atom's nucleus. The atomic number is also equal to the number of electrons, assuming that the atom is in an uncharged state. Every chemical element is uniquely identified by its atomic number.

Challenge: Explain why it is important to understand the periodic table, and what the table might be useful for.

Periodic Table: Activities and Experiments

1. Draw your own periodic table

What you need:

- Paper
- Pencil and colored pencils
- Pens
- Ruler

What you do:

- Draw your own periodic table
- Put it in your lab book

What you should learn:

- This should help you become more familiar with the periodic table, and now that you have your own that you drew yourself, you can proudly put it in your ever-filling lab book, or even put it on your wall!

Question:

- How many elements can you name from the top of your head?

2. Create an element information brochure

What you need:

- A computer
- A printer
- Paper

What you do:

- Choose an element from the periodic table
- Include such information as the name, how it got its name, the abbreviation, its atomic number, atomic mass, physical properties, chemical properties, abundance in the earth, places where it is found, what it can be used for, and anything else you can find out about it!
- Print your brochure and put it in your lab book.

What you should learn:

- You should have learned everything there is to know about your element!

Questions:

- Why did you choose the element you chose?
- Was it interesting to study that element? What other elements do you want to know more about?

3. Make a model of an atom

What you need:

- Arts and craft materials

What you do:

- Using whatever arts and crafts materials you like, create your own model of an atom.
- Your atom can be made in any way you like; it can be a 3 dimensional model, or a 2 dimensional model stuck onto cardboard. It can be suspended or sitting. It can be any way you like!
- Make sure that your model has something to represent electrons, protons, and neutrons.

What you should learn:

- This should reinforce your understanding of the atom, and provides a fun activity to transfer theoretical imaginary conceptions into tangible models!

Questions:

- How many electrons does your model atom have?
- Which element would it be?

4. Investigate the elemental composition of the human body

What you need:

- A computer with internet connection
- Pencil
- Lab book

What you do:

- Do some research to find out what kinds of elements are in the human body.
- Find out which elements we contain, and in what amounts.
- Record all of your findings in your lab book, and write down your sources.

What you should learn:

- Science is not always about doing experiments. A lot of the time, being a good scientist means searching for data. There have been so many scientists working on so many topics, finding something out can be as easy as searching with Google! In this activity you should learn what elements are contained within the human body, and maybe a little bit about why the distribution is this way.

Question:

- Which element is the most abundant in the human body?
- Is this abundance by weight, or by number of atoms?
- Is the answer going to be different if you change your criteria? If so, why?

5. Decorating your lab coat

What you need:

- Fresh white lab coat
- Many permanent markers

What you do:

- If you are going to be a scientist, you are going to need a lab coat one day! Now, you have the chance to design and decorate your (perhaps) very first lab coat!
- Using your permanent markers, design and draw a science themed lab coat. You can include scientific symbols, elements, or anything related to science.

What you should learn:

- Designing and drawing your lab coat might just seem like a bit of fun, but keep in mind that safety in science is of the utmost importance. Since it is such an important and personal tool for scientists' safety, you want to like your lab coat, and enjoy wearing it.

Question:

- How do you think a lab coat helps with safety?

Periodic Table: Quiz

1. Who developed the periodic table?

_____

2. Are all elements of the periodic table found in nature? Please explain.

_____
_____
_____
_____

3. What does it mean to say that every atom has an atomic number?

_____
_____
_____
_____

True or false:

4. Bananas contain a lot of potassium. _____

5. Neon is a highly reactive gas. _____

6. Halogens are very reactive. _____

7. Humans are silicon-based life forms. _____

8. Coal is made of carbon. _____

9. Diamonds are made of carbon. _____

10. Oxygen is used to make sulfuric acid. _____

11. Silver and gold are both transition metals. _____

12. The periodic table has 20 groups. _____

13. Each element has its own abbreviation. _____

14. All atoms have the same number of electrons. _____

Name 3 elements that were not mentioned already in this quiz.

15. _____

16. _____

17. _____

18-20. Extended question: Explain the concepts **of electron shells**, **valence shells**, and **valence electrons**.

_____
_____
_____
_____
_____
_____
_____
_____

Chapter 9: Photosynthesis

In an earlier unit when we covered plants, we learned how plants are autotrophs, which means they make their own food. Plants are, by definition, able to use sunlight and water to carry out photosynthesis. So what exactly is photosynthesis, anyway?

Photosynthesis:
$$6CO_2 + 6H_2O \xrightarrow{Light} C_6H_{12}O_6 + 6O_2$$

Above you can see the general formula for the process of photosynthesis. 6 carbon dioxide molecules, plus 6 water molecules, with the addition of energy from light, can be used to give 1 sugar molecule, and 6 molecular oxygen units. The oxygen is then discarded as a waste product and the sugar is used as food. This means that photosynthesis is a way for plants to convert energy in the form of light into chemical energy that can be used later.

Photosynthesis is important because it is the basic chemical formula that allows all life on earth. Even humans benefit from photosynthesis, because without it there would be no plants, and the animals that eat the plants would starve, and the animals that eat those animals would starve, and then soon, there would be no more animals left on the world! Every day the sun feeds energy into the earth's food chain, and this is accomplished only through photosynthesis! Without it, we would be nowhere.

Taking in water

The roots of the plant take up water. The water then travels up the xylem to reach the rest of the plant, and in the meantime, the plant grows its roots even deeper, always probing and checking for more water. The roots will growing in the direction of the water, should it find some.

Taking in CO_2

Carbon dioxide is also taken up by the plant prior to photosynthesis! On the bottom of plants' leaves, there are small holes called **stomata.** These stomata are then used for gas exchange. When the plant wants to photosynthesize, oxygen goes out, and carbon dioxide goes in. The plant can open and close these stomata.

Taking in sunlight

The plant doesn't only absorb water and CO_2. It also absorbs sunlight. This absorption happens in the green leaves of the plant, and in just the same way we learned how plants grow to orient themselves towards more water, they also grows towards more sunlight.

Plants have special cellular structures, called **chloroplasts**. These chloroplasts contain **chlorophyll**, which is what gives them their green color, as well their ability to absorb light. When the plants' leaves wither and turn brown in the autumn, this is because of the lack of chlorophyll. Without the chlorophyll, the leaves would really be those darker shades of brown.

When plants use this method to make food for themselves, they use CO_2 and expel oxygen. This means that for the plants, oxygen is sometimes waste. We are exchanging our waste for theirs! This is one more reason why we must treat our plant friends with respect. Since they help us filter out the carbon dioxide from our air, they also help us stay alive.

Do plants need anything else?

Now that we have covered water, carbon dioxide, and sunlight, (everything needed for photosynthesis) we can ask ourselves the question: Do plants need anything else to survive?

Yes, plants need various minerals to survive, such as potassium, nitrogen, phosphorus, and others. These help the plant in ways that photosynthesis cannot.

After photosynthesis

Some of the sugars that the plant creates will then be stored for later in other forms. The glucose the plants produce can be used to make many other structures. They include starch, fats, and oils. When you go to the store you can see all kinds of oils that were created by plants, like sunflower oil. These high-energy foods will then be used for 2 purposes. The first purpose would be to use them for the seeds, giving them enough energy, to make sure they are able to grow when it comes time to germinate. The second task would be to grow various plant tissues, such as leaves, stems, and wood. (Lots of glucose goes towards building cellulose, which is an integral component of the cell wall.)

When the plant needs to undergo **transpiration**, the stomata of the plant will open. This allows water vapor through. Transpiration is like sweating.

Although during photosynthesis plants use carbon dioxide and release oxygen, when a plant needs to break down the food that it has produced via photosynthesis, it still needs oxygen! That means that sometimes the plant will also absorb oxygen, which is a process called **respiration**. This is important to break down the food.

Respiration is a chemical reaction that must occur in all living cells, since it is needed for the breakdown of sugar. It is the way for both plants and animals to release the chemical energy stored inside the glucose. Through many components, with a lot of enzymatic machinery, plants and animals eventually break down the glucose, and in the process they manage to create some high-energy molecules. The most common high-energy molecule created is called adenosine triphosphate or just ATP. Below is a picture of the chemical structure of ATP.

These two processes (photosynthesis and respiration) are compared below:

- Photosynthesis prepares food, while respiration uses the food
- In other words, energy is stored during photosynthesis, and released during respiration.
- Oxygen is produced in photosynthesis, and used during respiration
- Carbon dioxide is used during photosynthesis, and used during respiration
- Water is used during photosynthesis, but is produced via respiration
- Photosynthesis requires light, while respiration can occur on both the light and the dark

Challenge: Explain the two processes: photosynthesis and respiration. Describe what the plant uses and what the plant generates as a result of these processes.

Only in leaves?

We have learned here that photosynthesis mainly occurs in the leaves of the plants, but is this the only place in the plant where it can be carried out?

The answer is: any cell that has chlorophyll can carry out photosynthesis! In some young plants the stems have cells containing chlorophyll, and there are also algae that have chlorophyll in their cells, allowing them to carry out photosynthesis. In more complicated plants that have more specialized structures, the photosynthesis really does carry out in the leaves. This is because the other structures do not have cells that contain chlorophyll.

Efficiency of photosynthesis

Exactly how efficient do you think photosynthesis is in a percentage?

If you want to look at the efficiency of photosynthesis, the first thing to look at is the amount of light that is in the range for photosynthesis activation. The reason for this is that not all wavelengths of light activate the photosynthesis machinery! If you are talking about normal outdoor lighting conditions, then only 45% of the light is within the effective range! That means 55% of the light energy already cannot be used. Because of this, and because the process is not perfectly conserving all energy, or rather, the process will not convert all energy into a biomass, the maximum theoretical conversion efficiency is as low as 11%!

You might think this is quite low, however, plants do not even absorb all incoming sunlight, so the value will be even lower than that! Because some the light will be reflected away, and because some of the light will be obscured by shadows and other disruptions, the final percentage of efficiency when it comes to converting the energy from light is probably as low as around 5% of the total solar energy.

Fertilizers

If plants get their food via photosynthesis, what is fertilizer for?

Fertilizer is a way for us to give plants more of the minerals they need, to encourage their grown. There are two types of fertilizer: organic, and factory made. It used to be the case that all of the fertilizers being used were organic and natural. Fertilizers like manure were being used. Manure is the waste of an animal, and also a natural fertilizer. There are many people who advocate the use of only natural fertilizers, claiming that using too many factory made fertilizers is bad for the food.

When fertilizing your plants you have to take the needs of your plant into account. Not all plants need the same amount of minerals given to them. A good example would be corn. Corn needs lots and lots of nitrogen to grow properly. This means that if you want to grow corn, you have to know this and you have to be prepared to feed the corn nitrogen in your fertilizer. Other plants, such as legumes like the soybean, need no nitrogen given to them at all, since they get their nitrogen from the air.

In this section we learned about photosynthesis in more detail. One important thing to try to do is to link this knowledge with knowledge you have gained before in other units. For example, it is very important to understand that a plant is not just a photosynthesis machine! Remember back to the previous plant unit, and try to remember something else you learned about plants! Do they have any defense mechanisms? How are plants classified?

Another link you could try to make could be with the energy, force, and motion unit! Where did you see a transfer of energy in the photosynthesis system? Is there one specific type of energy that is transferred to another type of energy?

Photosynthesis: Activities and Experiments

1. Investigating the effect of sunlight deprivation

What you need:

- 2 inexpensive fast growing plants
- Water
- Light proof cupboard
- Ruler
- Pencil and lab book

What you do:

- Evaluate both plants in terms of color, height, and sturdiness. Does the plant look healthy?
- Record your observations.
- Place one plant on the windowsill and one plant in the cupboard.
- Over the period of 1 week, water the plants the same amount and at the same time, and make sure not to expose the plant in the dark to the light for too long.
- After 1 week, perform the same observations you did in the beginning.
- Record your results.

What you should learn:

- Sunlight is an integral part of a plant's growth and survival requirements. When you deprive them of it they cannot photosynthesize. This experiment shows you the drastic effect this can have on a plant's overall wellbeing.

Questions:

- What did the plant in the dark look like?
- How long did it take for these changes to occur?

2. Isolating chlorophyll

What you need:

- Handful of green plant leaves
- Cup
- Scissors
- Paper towel
- Oven
- Water
- Foil
- Test tubes with lids
- Mortar and pestle
- Acetone

What you do:

- Put the leaves in a cup.
- Pour boiling water over them, leave for 1 minute, then take out and dry them.

- Remove all veins from the leaves and throw them away, then cut the leaves up into small pieces.
- Put them on foil and put them in the oven for 20 min, at 40 degrees centigrade.
- Put the now dry leaves into a completely dry mortal and pestle and crush them.
- Put the crushed mixture into the test tube, and add 5-10 ml of acetone.
- Close the lid and shake, then wait 10 more minutes.
- Without shaking the it, return and look at the contents of the test tube.
- Observe and record any colors, layers of separation, and other characteristics of the mixture.

What you should learn:

- When you observe this mixture, you will see several things. The first think you may notice is that there seems to be a layer of greenish solution, under which there will be sediment of dark green powder. The chlorophyll, which is the green pigment responsible for absorbing the light, is now diluted in the acetone. The big pieces that you see are cellular debris, and smaller pieces may cause the solution to be foggy. If you would filter out the pieces, you should have an acetone solution with chlorophyll in it. In science, it is very common to have to separate different components of your samples with techniques similar to this.

Question:

- What would plants look like if there was no chlorophyll left in them?

3. Investigating oxygen release

What you need:

- Elodea- water plant
- Scissors
- Test tubes
- Water
- Baking soda
- Lamp
- Tape
- Clock or stopwatch
- Ruler
- Test tube rack or stand
- Pencil and lab book

What you do:

- Grab 1 sprig of your elodea plant.
- Tear off any leaves around the cut stem, and cut a small section of the stem again at an angle.
- Gently crush the cut end, and place the sprig cut-end-up in a test tube filled with water.
- Push it to the bottom.
- Place the lamp 5 cm from the test tube. Wait 1 minute
- Start your stopwatch and start counting bubbles. The bubbles will rise from the sprig, and your job is to count them for the next 5 minutes. If no bubbles appear, recut and recrush the end of the stem.
- Record your results.
- Add a small amount of baking soda to the solution and repeat the process.
- After 1 minute, count and record the number of bubbles again.

What you should learn:

- This experiment can be a bit tricky, but if you managed to achieve it properly, you should have been able to count the number of bubbles that this plant released in a five-minute period. During the process of photosynthesis, oxygen is generated. The more oxygen is released, the more photosynthesis is occurring.

When you add the baking soda, you are introducing more carbon dioxide to the plant, allowing faster photosynthesis rates.

Question:

- How many bubbles did the sprig release in a 5-minute period?
- Did the baking soda have the expected effect?

4. Making moss graffiti

What you need:

- A few handfuls of moss
- Non flavored yoghurt or buttermilk
- Beer
- Sugar
- Blender
- Paintbrush
- Container for moss paint
- Corn syrup

What you do:

- Wash the moss to remove as much dirt as possible.
- Add the moss, 2 cups of yoghurt or buttermilk, 2 cups of beer, and 1 teaspoon of sugar to the blender.
- Blend the mixture until smooth
- If it is very runny, add some cornstarch to make it more viscous.
- Transfer it to the moss paint container.
- Find a wall where you can apply the moss paint. The wall should have some sunlight reaching it, but should not be in the direct path of the sun all day long. A moister environment is best.
- Apply the paint with the brush on the wall, painting whatever design you like.
- Once you have painted your moss art, refrigerate the remaining mixture.
- Return every 2 days to spray it with a water bottle, and add more paint every other day as well. This is to encourage growth and thriving of the moss painting. It may grow very quickly, or it may grow a bit slower, depending on the environment.
- To remove the moss graffiti, it must be sprayed with limejuice.

What you should learn:

- Moss is also a photosynthesizing plant! This fun activity demonstrates the amazing ability for plants to grow under all kinds of conditions, and allows students to craft a fun and beautiful living mural.

Questions:

- Did your moss mural grow?
- If not, why do you think this was?
- What kind of environment does moss like? Was there too much or not enough light? Was it too dry?

5. Plant a seed of your choice and grow a plant for your desk at home

What you need:

- A pot

- Potting soil
- A seed of your choice
- Fertilizer of your choice
- Water

What you do:

- This experiment is simple. Plant and grow your seed.
- Do research to find out exactly how much water your plant needs, or what the best kind of fertilizer to use is.

What you should learn:

- This activity is one of reflection and giving back. Plants are the basis for all life here on earth. They allow us to live, and so it is nice to give something back, and to help one grow. After all the amazing things we learned about plants, don't you want one anyway?! You should cultivate this plant, take care of it, and enjoy having another living thing to share your space with.

Questions:

- What did you learn about plants and photosynthesis that was most fascinating for you?
- What kind of plant did you choose to grow?

Photosynthesis: Quiz

1. What 3 things are absolutely needed for photosynthesis to occur?

_____

2. What else do plants need to grow apart from these 3 things?

_____

_____

3. How do plants take up water?

_____

4. How do plants take up carbon dioxide?

_____

5-7. How do plants absorb sunlight? What cellular structure is important for this process, and what molecule inside this structure is responsible?

_____

_____

_____

8. What do plants produce as waste as a byproduct of the photosynthesis process?

_____

9. What is the main form of food that the plants get from photosynthesis?

_____

10. What do the plants then form from this food?

_____

True or false:

11. Plants need nitrogen to survive. _____

12. Plants do not only photosynthesize, but also undergo respiration. _____

13. Photosynthesis is 50% efficient in terms of light utilization. _____

14. Some algae can perform photosynthesis. _____

15. Leaves turn brown in the winter because they are rotten. _____

16. Photosynthesis is only important for the survival of plants. _____

17. Plants do not only produce oxygen as waste, but also utilize it. _____

18. Plants do not have any way of transpiring, or sweating. _____

19. Plants use photosynthesis to alter solar energy into chemical energy. _____

20. Waste from animals can be used as a natural fertilizer. _____

Chapter 10: Weather

The weather on earth is a constantly evolving force of nature. From rainstorms to dry deserts, from humid to dry; the world has it all. In this unit we will try to learn more about the different ways in which weather patterns form, and about weather in general.

The most important component of the earth's weather is probably the **water cycle.**

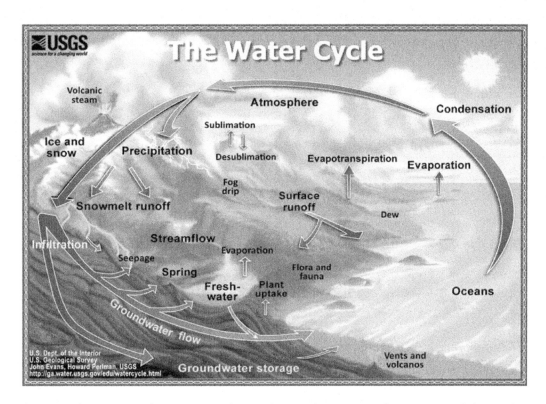

As illustrated above, the water cycle represents the continuous movement of water around the earth.

Water is always moving between the atmosphere, the surface of earth, and underground regions. Every step of the water cycle has different conditions that must be met for that particular type of change to take place:

Precipitation:

After condensation of water, or the forming of clouds, water droplets fall in various forms– these forms are called precipitation, and they include rain, snow, hail, and sleet, among others.

Temperature variation in cloud formations, as well as temperature variations in the area in general, is very instrumental in controlling what kind of precipitation will occur.

Evaporation:

Water enters the atmosphere as steam. This can be due to temperature changes, as well as to plants that release water vapor.

Condensation:

Condensation happens when water vapor transfers back to the form of water droplets. This causes the formation of clouds, eventually leading to precipitation again.

Run-off:

If precipitation falls onto the earth, the pattern of flow generally directs the precipitation back to ocean level, either in the form of surface water flow, or rather in the form of groundwater.

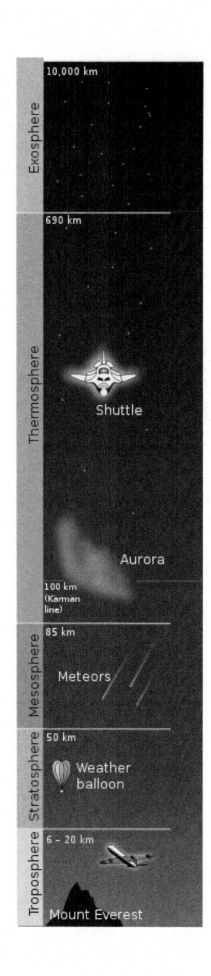

The earth's atmosphere

The earth has many layers surrounding it. These layers are made of gas and they are called **atmosphere**. In the order from closest to the earth's surface, to the farthest from the earth's surface, here are its layers.

- *Troposphere-* this is where all animals and plants live and breath air; it is also where all the weather forms, and where the temperature decreases as you go higher
- *Stratosphere-* The ozone later exists in the stratosphere, and prevents harmful levels of sunlight from reaching the earth; humans cannot breath at this altitude.
- *Mesoshpere-* At this level the temperature still decreases with altitude. This is where we see meteors burning up on their way to earth
- *Thermoshpere-* The air is thin here, and at this level the solar activity is what determines the temperature; it is usually very hot
- *Exosphere-* The air is extremely thin here- many molecules escape into space, and their density is so low that they no longer behave like gas.

The ozone layer

The ozone later is a pale blue gas that surrounds the earth. It resides mostly in the stratosphere, but there is also a little but of ozone in the troposphere. Funnily enough, ozone also has a strong smell! Good thing we are on the ground!

The ozone layer is extremely important for the earth, since it is the only gas that is absorbing all the ultraviolet radiation from the sun, protecting people from the UV's damaging effects.

Solar energy

The sun projects light at the earth, but on the way a lot of the light is reflected or absorbed by clouds and gasses in the atmosphere. The light that gets through to the earth is also subject to something called the **greenhouse effect.** The greenhouse effect tells us that light that is absorbed by the land and the water is transferred to heat, and that this heat is absorbed by the gas in the atmosphere. This is how the earth stays warm.

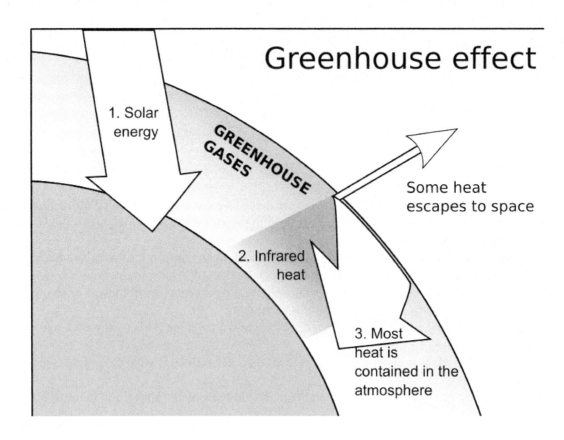

Clouds

Beneath the ozone layer, in the troposphere, is where the weather forms. There are many different types of clouds, and here you will learn how to identify them. They are classified by their shape, elevation, and the weather patterns that are associated with them. The 3 main types of clouds are:

- **Cumulus-** these clouds are formed at medium to low elevation. They are big puffy clouds that have flat bottoms. When these clouds get dark you know then that you should expect some kind of storm.

- **Stratus-** a type of cloud that spreads out to create a big thick later of cloud. When you see this type of cloud growing, you can expect some precipitation in the area

- **Cirrus-** a cloud that has a wispy appearance; they usually signal fair weather, or the approach of a warm front

Storms

When huge pressure differences cause airflow to move at a very high speed, this can be called a storm. This causes the weather gets rough, and encourages extreme conditions. Here we will focus on 3 types of storm:

- **Thunderstorm**- a storm with heavy rain, lightning, and thunder. They often also have strong winds

- **Hurricane**- a tropical storm that forms over warm water, a hurricane develops until it has a spinning circular pattern, with a so-called eye in the center. When the air pressure in the center is lower, the faster the hurricane's winds will blow.

- **Tornado**- a tunnel shaped, rapidly spinning cloud, the tornado comes down from a storm cloud, and can often cause massive damage

Measuring the weather

There are many ways to assess and try to predict the weather. An example of a factor that one can assess is humidity. It is one of the factors that a **meteorologist** might assess, since it tells you the state of the weather in terms of how much water is in the air. Humidity is relative, and when you are told what the humidity is you are given a percentage. At 100%, the air would be fully saturated. Humidity is measured with a **hygrometer**.

A Meteorologist is a person who studies the weather. They do not only measure the humidity levels! They can also measure many other factors:

- Wind speed with an **anemometer**
- Rain volume with a **rain gauge**
- Air pressure with a **barometer**

Meteorologists also want to predict the weather as accurately as possible. This has led to the use of **station**

models. A station model is an illustration that depicts many variables about the current weather situation at a single given reporting station. This means lots of information is known about this particular point, including factors like cloudiness, temperature, wind speed, precipitation, and others as well. Many station models from many different reporting stations can then be looked at all together, to give the meteorologists a good idea about trends in the weather.

Air Masses and fronts

An air mass is a large body of air that has a similar temperature, pressure, and humidity levels. Air masses get their properties because of their environments. For example, if an air mass spends a long time over the ocean, it will get more humid due to evaporation. If the air mass would spend more time over a desert, it would be come extremely dry.

There are 4 distinct types of air mass:

1. **Polar**
2. **Maritime**
3. **Continental**
4. **Tropical**

Polar air masses form at the pole regions of the earth, and normally characterized by cold temperatures.

Maritime air masses form over water, and are therefore extremely humid.

Continental air masses form over land and are relatively dry.

Tropical air masses form over tropical regions and are characterized by high temperatures.

When 2 air masses meet each other, they form a **front** at their border.

Cold fronts move very quickly, and are known for producing thunderstorms. While they pass through they may provoke thunderstorms, and after they have passed they will leave a cooler temperature behind them.

Warm fronts move very slowly, and they bring with them a lot of humidity. While they pass through it will often rain, and once they have passed temperatures will often be warmer. There are also **stationary fronts,** where two air masses meet, but the front does not move. This results in long periods of consistent unchanging weather.

High and low pressure systems

High pressure usually causes fairer weather, often resulting in winds circulating around the system in a clockwise manner. Low pressure, on the other hand, is prone to causing the formation of droplets, as well as an inward and counterclockwise wind circulation. This pattern of wind is often associated with rainy and stormy weather.

Convection

Another important concept in weather is **convection**. Convection happens when hot air rises up and then becomes cool. This creates tunnels of wind flow. This happens because of uneven heating from solar energy. Certain areas of the earth receive more light and are heated faster. This results in a temperature imbalance between areas. Then, the air above that area will become warmer, and therefore the air will become less dense, causing it to rise.

Challenge: Describe the weather you are experiencing right now using information you have learned in this unit! Why do you think you are having that weather at the moment?

Weather: Activities and Experiments

1. Investigating evaporation and condensation

What you need:

- Large plastic bowl
- A pitcher
- Ceramic coffee cup
- Large rubber band, or long piece of string
- Water
- Sheet of clear plastic wrap
- Pencil and lab book
- Small rock

What you do:

- Pour water into the bowl until it is about a quarter full.
- Place the coffee cup in the center of the bowl, and make sure there is no water inside.
- Cover the top of the bowl tightly with plastic wrap.
- Secure the wrap in place using the large plastic band or the long string.
- Place the small rock on the plastic wrap in the center, above the cup.
- Make sure the rock is large enough to cause a droop in the plastic wrap, but not large enough to drag it down completely.
- Place the bowl in a sunny warm place.
- Observe and record.

What you should learn:

- The water will evaporate due to the heat, and it will become mist. This mist will condense on the top of the plastic, and drip down into the mug. This is a simulation of the water cycle! Imagine that the water contained in the bowl is like the ocean, the condensation on plastic is like the clouds, and the dripping is like the rain.

Questions:

- What if the water was dirty?
- Would the water that drips in the mug after condensation also be dirty?
- Why or why not? If you are not sure, just give it a try!

2. Creating a tornado in a bottle

What you need:

- 2 1 liter plastic bottles
- Water
- Bowl
- Strong, duct tape
- Metal washer that fits on top of the mouth of a bottle

What you do:

- Remove the labels from the bottles and clean them.
- Fill 1 bottle to the top, and put the metal washer on the opening.
- Place the second, empty water bottle on top of the first one, so that the washer sits between them.
- Use the duct tape to secure the two bottles together. Make this connection very strong by tightly applying several layers of tape. No movement should occur.
- Turn the device over and swirl the water as it drains. The water will form a tornado as it drains into the second bottle!

What you should learn:

- This fun simulation of a tornado shows us how the vortex shape forms. The vortex is the shape that occurs in liquids and gasses that causes them to spin in spirals around a central point, as it does in a tornado.

Question:

- In what kind of conditions do tornados arise?
- Which parts of the world (and of your country, if applicable) are the most susceptible to tornados? You may need to research this question.

3. Simulating the greenhouse effect

What you need:

- 2 thermometers
- 2 small glass jars
- 2 liter soda bottle
- Scissors
- Pencil and lab book

What you do:

- Place the 2 thermometers in the small glass jars, and place the 2 glass jars in a sunny place.
- Using the scissors, remove the label and cut the top half of the bottle off.
- Keeping the cap on, use the top half of the bottle to cover one of the jars with its thermometer.
- Wait 1 hour.
- Observe and record the temperature from both thermometers.

What you should learn:

- The thermometer inside of the bottle should display a higher temperature. This is due to the greenhouse effect. The solar energy that passes into the contained area of the bottle half is turned into heat energy, which is trapped inside the bottle. The earth also has its own kind of 'bottle'. This bottle is the atmosphere. This is how our earth retains heat.

Question:

- Why is it important for us, as humans, to not alter the makeup of our atmosphere too much? This is a very broad question, and requires some research to answer. Do some research on greenhouse gasses and global warming to find out the answer!

4. Heat convection in liquid

What you need:

- Clear jar

- Water
- Freezer
- Spoon
- Liquid dropper
- Coffee cup
- Food coloring

What you do:

- Fill the jar three quarters with cold water, and put it in the freezer to cool even further. The water should become cold, but not freeze.
- Full the coffee mug half way with hot water.
- Add food-coloring drops until water is a strong shade of blue.
- Remove jar with cold water and put it on the bench.
- Fill the dropper with hot blue water, and lower the dropper to the bottom of the jar. Release a few drops of blue water and observe what happens.
- Record your results.
- Add more blue water, and observe what happens.
- Once you have added some blue water with dropper, wait 5 more minutes and observe what happens.
- Record your results.

What you should learn:

- When you squeeze the hot water drops out, they rise to the top. Because they are hotter and contain more kinetic energy, the molecules are moving around more and more, making the hot water less dense than the cold water. This causes it to rise. Over time, the temperatures equalize, and the blue liquid diffuses throughout the entire jar.

Question:

- What parallels can you draw between this experiment and what we learned in the unit?

5. Creating a weather chart an compare to predictions

What you need:

- Your pencil and lab book
- A computer with internet
- A thermometer
- A camera and printer (optional)

What you do:

- Go online and search for the weather for the next week in your city or place of residence.
- Draw a chart in your lab book, labeling the upcoming 7 days, and the expected weather forecast for those days.
- Each day go outside and assess the weather. Leave a thermometer somewhere outside and look at it once in the morning, once in the afternoon, and once in the evening.
- Use these measurements to give an average temperature for the day.
- Take photos of any clouds, and print them and include them in your lab book.
- Identify which cloud type they may be, and label them.
- Compare the weather forecast with the actual weather, and assess whether the forecast was accurate or not.

What you should learn:

- Forecasting the weather is not an easy job! Sometimes the forecast is correct, and sometimes it is flawed. Because of the great complexity of the task, and the great many number of variables involved, we are not yet perfect predictors of the weather, but still manage to do a pretty good job.

Questions:

- Was the weather forecast accurate or not?
- How do meteorologists forecast the weather in the first place?

Weather: Quiz

Link the instruments on the left with the variables they measure on the right.

1. Hygrometer   Rain volume

2. Anemometer   Air pressure

3. Rain gauge   Wind speed

4. Barometer   Humidity

We learned about 3 types of clouds. Below are the three different types. Please label them.

5.

_____

6.

_____

135

7.

8. Give a brief description of the greenhouse effect.

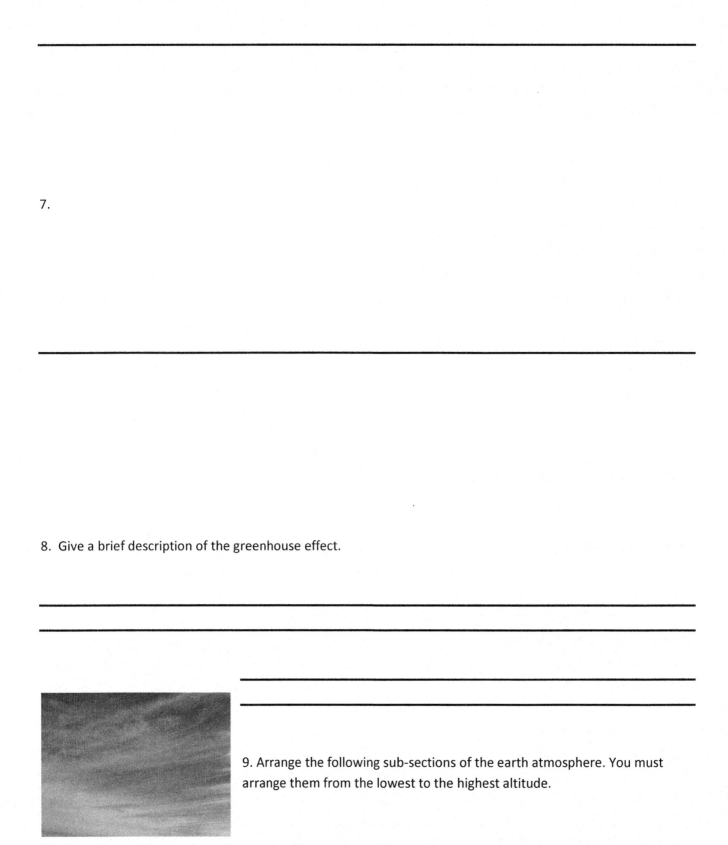

9. Arrange the following sub-sections of the earth atmosphere. You must arrange them from the lowest to the highest altitude.

Thermoshpere- Troposphere- Exosphere- Mesoshpere – Stratosphere

10-12. What is the ozone layer? In which layer of the atmosphere does the ozone reside? What does it protect us from?

_____
_____
_____
_____
_____
_____

13-15. Explain the differences between a **tornado**, a **hurricane**, and a **thunderstorm**.

_____
_____
_____
_____
_____
_____

True or false:

16. Meteorologists use station models to help predict the weather. _____

17. Convection happens when cool air rises up. _____

18. When 2 air masses meet each other they form a front at their border. _____

19. Condensation is when water droplets become water vapor. _____

20. High pressure often causes good weather, while low pressure often causes bad weather. _____

Answer Key

Chapter 1

1. Planning, conducting, processing, evaluating

2-11. F, T, T, F, T, T, T, F, F, T

12. Control variables are important and need to be taken care of to ensure that there are no confounding factors in the experiment; that is to say that you must be sure that the only thing altering the outcome of your experiment is the independent variable, and that no other variables can affect it.

13. The list of materials used in the experiment

14. The numbered step-by-step process that must be carried out when doing the experiment

15. Because it allows you to put all information about the experiments in one place. It is helpful to refer to it when you get confused, and it means that your data is not scattered around everywhere (students may give equally good but different answers.)

16. Dependent… — variable
17. Materials and… — methods
18. Title and… — aim
19. Planning phase — hypothesis
20. Conducting phase — recording data

Chapter 2

1. Chemistry

2-10. P, P, P, C, C, P, C, P, P

11-18. F, T, T, F, F, T, F, T

19. Liquid, Solid, Gas, Plasma. Examples may vary but can include: water, ice, steam, and lightning, respectively

20. Answers may vary

Chapter 3

1. Brain / Central nervous system

2. Heart

3. Lungs

4 – 11. F, T, T, F, F, F, T, T

12. There are multiple correct answers. E.g. eyes, ears, stomach, lungs, brain, skin

13. There are multiple correct answers. E.g. seeing, hearing, digesting, thinking

14. There are multiple correct answers. E.g. stomach and intestines for digesting, eyes and brain for seeing, etc..

15. Releasing hormones

16. Pumping blood around the body.

17. Fighting off pathogens.

18. Allowing pregnancy and childbirth.

19. To collect urine.

20. Sight, smell, hearing, touch, taste.

Chapter 4

1. Comet

2. Asteroid

3. Meteoroid

4. Meteor

5. Meteorite

6. Satellite

7. The moon and sun are responsible for another common phenomenon on earth: the tide. The tide is created because of the gravitational pull that the earth, sun, and moon exert on each other. Because the oceans are liquid, they are easier for gravity to manipulate.

BONUS: Some have theorized that evolution owes a lot of thanks to the tide, and that we would not be here today if it was not for this interaction of huge bodies that pull on each other with gravity. The idea is that because of the tide, there were areas of the earth that were exposed to both wet and dry conditions. This interface and switching between wet and dry allowed some organisms to experience both on land and off land conditions, helping them make the transition from one state of being to the other.

9-20. F, T, T, F, F, F, T, F, T, F, F, T

Chapter 5

1. Kingdom→Phylum→Class→Order→Family→Genus→Species

2. Plantae

3. **Autotrophs:** Autotrophs provide their own food, via a biological mechanism known as **photosynthesis**. You will learn more about that in a later unit, but all you need to know now is that autotrophs use photosynthesis to make their own energy. A plant is autotrophic.

Heterotrophs: Heterotrophs need to provide their own food, as they cannot produce their own. This requires hunting, grazing, scavenging, or any other form of food procurement that gets the food from an external source, like animals do.

4-10. F, T, F, T, F, T, T

11-13. **Leaves:** Leaves function as a site for many processes. Photosynthesis is carried out in leaves, as well as respiration (the exchange of oxygen and carbon dioxide).

Stems: Function as a storage site, or a structure to keep the plant ridged. They also serve as a structure to push the leaves up to the light.

Roots: Roots are the primary method for water absorption in plants. They also perform the mechanical function of anchoring the plant in place. They absorb nutrients as well. There are two types of roots: **fibrous roots**, and **taproots**.

- Fibrous roots have long branching segments that break off and branch out in all directions.
- Taproots are singular, long, thick roots, with very few smaller roots branching off.

14. Yes. Some plants, for example, have thorns that act as a deterrent against animals that may want to eat them otherwise. Some plants have poisonous fruits or leaves that prevent animals from eating them as well.

15. Growing towards water

16. Growing against gravity

17. Growing towards light

Chapter 6

1. Energy is defined as the ability to cause change

2-10. T, T, T, F, T, F, F, F, T

11-14.

- **Sliding friction** → force that comes into play when 2 surfaces slide along each other. An example of sliding friction would be when you scrub things with a sponge.
- **Rolling friction** → a force that slows down the movement of a rolling object. A good example of rolling friction can be seen in cars, skateboards, roller skates, and anything else that moves with wheels!
- **Fluid friction** → When an object moves through fluid or air it encounters a resistance force that slows it down. This is fluid friction. An example of fluid friction is swimming in water, or using a rowboat.
- **Static friction** → when the friction prevents the movement from starting. An example of static friction would be if you tried to push a very big rock, but it didn't move.

15. Potential energy and kinetic energy

16. The ball would keep going in the same direction at the same speed.

17. The car that is heavier will accelerate slower than the first car.

18. The third law of motion: *When one object exerts force on another object, the second object will have the equal, yet opposite reaction on the first object.* Examples given by students may vary e.g. a bird flapping its wings.

19-20. Answers may vary; there are many correct ones. The important aspect that should be addressed by the student is the relationship between the components of energy, force, and motion.

Chapter 7

1. Protons, neutrons, and electrons

143

2. Protons and neutrons in the nucleus, electrons in orbit

3. An electrical conductor is a material that is very good at taking up electrons, making the transfer of electricity possible. Examples may vary.

4. An electrical insulator is a material that is not good at taking up electrons, making the transfer of electricity more difficult. Examples may vary.

5-13. F, T, T, F, T, F, T, T, T

14. That electric current can produce a magnetic field.

15. Lines that represent force exerted on 2 objects by the other object, as caused by the electric field.

16.

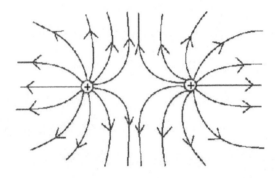

17. It can travel longer distances.

18. It is thought that the earth's magnetic field originates from moving charges, since the core of the earth is composed of metals that flow as the earth rotates, which creates electrical currents. These electrical currents then induce a magnetic field.

19. Answers may vary, but include all electrical devices.

20. Answers may vary, but the one likely known to the student is a compass.

Chapter 8

1. Dmitri Mendeleev

2. Most of these elements can be found under natural conditions, but there are also many on this list that could only have been observed under laboratory conditions. Elements 99 – 118 are elements that have only been synthesized in the lab. Some of the elements on the table were found in nature, but only sometime after they had already been synthesized in a lab, due to their rarity.

3. If you refer to the periodic table, you will notice that above every single element there is a number. This number is called the atomic number. It represents the total number of protons in the atom's nucleus. The atomic number is also equal to the number of electrons, assuming that the atom is in an uncharged state. Every chemical element is uniquely identified by its atomic number.

4-14. T, F, T, F, T, T, F, T, F, T, F

15-17. Answers may vary.

18-20. In atoms, the electrons are arranged around the nucleus. When there are many electrons, they arrange themselves in regions of orbit called **electron shells**. These shells are also called **energy levels**. Imagine these shells as kind of orbit paths around the atoms' nuclei. Each energy level has a different number of possible electrons positions. It is not necessary for each shell to be completely filled up before electrons occupy the outer shells. The outermost shell is called be **valence shell,** and the electrons that occupy this shell are called **valence electrons**.

Chapter 9

1. Water, CO_2, and light

2. Plants need various minerals to survive, such as potassium, nitrogen, phosphorus, and others. These help the plant in ways that photosynthesis cannot.

3. Through the roots.

4. On the bottom of plants' leaves, there are small holes called **stomata.** These stomata are then used for gas exchange, including absorption of carbon dioxide.

5-7. This absorption happens in the green leaves of the plant. Plants have special cellular structures, called **chloroplasts**. These chloroplasts contain **chlorophyll**, which is what gives them their green color, as well their ability to absorb light.

8. Oxygen

9. Sugar/glucose

10. Starch, fats, and oils.

11-20. T, T, F, T, F, F, T, F, T, T

Chapter 10

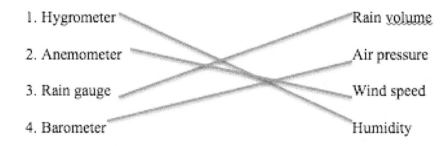

5. Cumulus

6. Stratus

7. Cirrus

8. The light that gets through to the earth is also subject to something called the **greenhouse effect.** The greenhouse effect tells us that light that is absorbed by the land and the water is transferred to heat, and that this heat is absorbed by the gas in the atmosphere. This is how the earth stays warm.

9. Troposphere → Stratosphere → Mesosphere → Thermosphere → Exosphere

10-12. The ozone later is a pale blue gas that surrounds the earth. It resides mostly in the stratosphere, but there is also a little but of ozone in the troposphere. The ozone layer is extremely important for the earth, since it is the only gas that is absorbing all the ultraviolet radiation from the sun, protecting people from the UV's damaging effects.

13-15. **Thunderstorm-** a storm with heavy rain, lightning, and thunder. They often also have strong winds

Hurricane- a tropical storm that forms over warm water, a hurricane develops until it has a spinning circular pattern, with a so-called eye in the center. When the air pressure in the center is lower, the faster the hurricane's winds will blow.

Tornado- a tunnel shaped, rapidly spinning cloud, the tornado comes down from a storm cloud, and can often cause massive damage

16-20. T, F, T, F, T

Sixth Grade Math
For Home School or Extra Practice

By Greg Sherman

Whole Numbers

Whole numbers are the base numbers for all the mathematics learned beginning essentially when a child first starts counting things. Whole numbers do not include fractions, decimals, or negative numbers. However, whole numbers are used throughout our society daily.

When we go shopping at the grocery store, we purchase whole portions of items such as loaves of bread, bags of chips, bottles of soda pop, boxes of crackers and cereal, fruits and vegetables, and a variety of other goods. The same concept can be applied to our purchases of several other goods like clothing, cars, houses, furniture, etc. Whole numbers are the core of how we function using math.

Addition

Addition is the first type of mathematical equation students learn in school. First, adding single whole numbers is taught followed by adding double-digit numbers and single numbers, then double-digit numbers to each other. Finally, adding triple-digit numbers to single numbers, to double-digit numbers, and to triple-digit numbers is taught. The concept of carrying the one and adding multiple numbers are also covered in sixth grade math.

The final answer calculated after adding whole numbers together is referred to as the Sum. The Sum is always larger than any of the numbers being added together (addends) unless the equation includes the Sum being added to zero.

Adding single-digit numbers involves applying mental math by sixth grade. By learning fact families, students will be better able to remember the sums of single-digit addends and perform better on timed math tests. After studying fact families, some patterns begin to emerge that both students and parents can use to their advantage.

One such pattern involves the equations including nine. Learning the sums of equations with ten is easy because students just replace the zero in the ten with the number being added. If students can remember than nine is just one less than ten, then the sum will be one less than the sum with ten. So, if the student knows $10 + 4 = 14$, then $9 + 4 = 13$, just one less than the equation with the ten.

Another pattern involves the addition of the number to itself. If the student can remember 5 + 5 = 10, then adding one less to five would have the sum of 9, and adding one more to five would have the sum of 11.

Subtraction

Subtracting whole numbers is defined as finding the Difference between numbers. When finding the difference, the smaller number is subtracted from the larger number. Finding the difference between whole numbers is a mathematical operation that most of us perform several times daily.

For example, whenever we calculate someone's age, we are finding the difference between the person's birth year and the current year. For example, if someone was born in 1968 and it is now 2013, their current age is 2013 – 1968 = 45, so the person is 45-years-old.

Subtraction is also used for calculating a variety of comparisons. Some common comparisons are finding the distance between points, figuring out which locations are closer or farther from each other, and calculating whether a specific point is closer to one location of another.

For example, when calculating the distance traveled during a car trip, the difference between the starting odometer value and ending odometer value is calculated. If, the odometer reading at the start of the trip is 13,478 miles and the odometer reading at the end of the trip is 13,623 miles, the distance traveled is 13,623 miles – 13,478 miles = 145 miles.

After another car trip, the odometer reads 13,789 miles, so the distance traveled is the difference between 13,789 miles and 13,623 miles. In equation form, the difference is expressed as 13,789 – 13,623 = 166 miles.

From these two calculations, it can be determined that the distance of the second car trip was longer than the first, the second location was farther from the first than the first was from the original start point, and the original start point was closer to the first location than the second location was to the first. This information can be important when planning a trip for the purposes of time management, cost of gas, and determining how far the destinations are from the start point and from each other.

In sixth grade, students will use the difference between numbers to interpret their location on a number line relative to each other and relative to other specific values and points. Differences between numbers will also be taught in story problems.

A story problem using the difference between two numbers is presented below:

The students of a sixth grade class held a bake sale. The girls baked cupcakes and the boys made cookies. 127 cupcakes were sold and 213 cookies were sold during the sale. How many more cookies were sold than cupcakes?

To find the answer, the difference between what the boys sold and what the girls sold needs to be calculated. The difference between 213 and 127 is 86. So, the boys sold 86 more cookies than the girls sold cupcakes.

Multiplication

The answer to a multiplication problem is defined as the Product. Whether we realize it or not, multiplication is used constantly throughout out daily routines. One example is how we are cooking a meal or baking desserts, we multiply how many servings we need to prepare to be sure everyone gets a proper portion.

For example, 18 people are attending a dinner party. How many desserts does the chef need to prepare if each guest is going to get three? The multiplication equation would be 18 x 3 = 54. The chef will need to prepare 54 desserts for the dinner party.

A school-related example involves the distribution of books. If the entire sixth grade class needs new math and science books and there are 64 students in the sixth grade, how many books total need to be ordered? The factors are 2 and 64 and the product is the multiplication of 2 and 64. The equation is 64 x 2 = 128. A total of 128 books will be ordered for the sixth grade.

Division

Division is also used on a daily basis by most of our society. The answer to a division problem is called the Quotient. To take a quantity and break it up into equal evenly distributed parts requires division. Dealing cards during a card game, distributing money earned during a fundraising event, splitting up birthday favors to be sure each child gets the same amount of each prize, etc. are all examples of using division.

Another example involves a school bake sale. If the students want to earn at least 400 dollars and they have 200 cookies to sell, how much should they charge for each cookie? The equation is 400 ÷ 200 = 2, so the students should charge 2 dollars per cookie to earn 400 dollars for their bake sale.

Factor Families

By sixth grade, students are expected to be proficient at mental math for multiplication and division using their factor families. Factors are the numbers that divide completely into another number.

Examples of Factors include the following:

Factors of 12 = 1, 12, 2, 6, 3, and 4

Factors of 24 = 1, 24, 2, 12, 3, 8, 4, and 6

Factors of 15 = 1, 15, 3, and 5

Factors of 18 = 1, 18, 2, 9, 3, and 6

Common factors are those that are found in each factor group for different numbers. For the above numbers, three share common factors: 12, 24 and 18 all share the factors 4 and 6. The Least Common Factor is 4 and the Greatest Common Factor is 6.

When learning the factor families, some patterns become noticeable and can be helpful for students and parents when memorizing and using these factor families. One pattern observed from the multiplication tables is that all the products calculated when 5 is one of the multipliers end with 5 or 0. Another pattern is found when multiplying with 10. All the products are the number being multiplies by 10 with a 0 added to the right. For example, 1 x 10 = 10, 2 x 10 = 20, 24 x 10 = 240, and 506 x 10 = 5,060. So, when multiplying by ten, just take the other multiplier and add a zero to get the answer. A division pattern observed is that products ending in 0 are divisible by 2, 5, and 10.

Whole Numbers – Practice Sheet

1. True or False: Whole Numbers include all numbers along a number line.

2. True or False: Mental math involves memorizing single-digit addition, subtraction, multiplication and division.

3. True or False: After studying the fact family table, certain patterns regarding adding and subtracting become visible.

4. True or False: The answer to an addition problem is called the Sum.

5. True or False: The answer to a subtraction problem is called the Divisor.

6. True or False: ⅚ is a whole number.

7. True or False: Adding together non-whole numbers like fractions or decimals can produce an answer that is a whole number.

8. True or False: A whole number subtracted from another whole number can produce an answer that is NOT a whole number.

9. Which of the following is NOT a whole number: 1, 5, ½, 12, -4, 18, 25, 1.2, 7, -8

10. Which of the following is a whole number: 1.52, -8, 3, 12½, 6, -14, 9, 1¼

11. What is the Sum of 5 and 4?

12. What is the Sum of 15 and 5?

13. What are the factors of 12 and 18? What is the Least Common Factor and what is the Greatest Common Factor between 12 and 18?

14. What is the Difference between 19 and 7?

16. What is the Difference between 25 and 5?

17. What is the Difference between 18 and 3?

18. What is the Product of 4 and 7?

19. What is the Product of 20 and 13?

20. What is the Quotient of 25 and 5?

Whole Numbers – Quiz

1. True or False: Negative numbers are whole numbers.

2. True or False: Whole numbers are the numbers zero and greater including fractions and decimals.

3. What is the Sum of 14 and 15?

4. What is the Sum of 18 and 5?

5. What is the Difference between 19 and 6?

6. Which number is closer to 100, 85 or 123?

7. What is the product of 5 and 25?

8. What is the Product of 8 and 4?

9. What is the Quotient of 12 and 3?

10. What are the factors of 30 and 48? What is the Least Common Factor between 30 and 48?

Operations with Whole Numbers

Operations with whole numbers include addition, subtraction, multiplication, and division.

Students are encouraged to become more proficient using mental math with the single-digit numbers. Memorizing these addition and subtraction equations allows the student to calculate the answers more quickly, especially during timed math tests. Below is the fact family table for whole numbers one through nine:

Zero	One	Two	Three	Four	Five	Six	Seven	Eight	Nine
0 + 1 = 1	1 + 1 = 2	2 + 1 = 3	3 + 1 = 4	4 + 1 = 5	5 + 1 = 6	6 + 1 = 7	7 + 1 = 8	8 + 1 = 9	9 + 1 = 10
1 + 0 = 1	2 − 1 = 1	1 + 2 = 3	1 + 3 = 4	1 + 4 = 5	1 + 5 = 6	1 + 6 = 7	1 + 7 = 8	1 + 8 = 9	1 + 9 = 10
1 − 0 = 1		3 − 2 = 1	4 − 3 = 1	5 − 4 = 1	6 − 5 = 1	7 − 6 = 1	8 − 7 = 1	9 − 8 = 1	10 − 9 = 1
		3 − 1 = 2	4 − 1 = 3	5 − 1 = 4	6 − 1 = 5	7 − 1 = 6	8 − 1 = 7	9 − 1 = 8	10 − 1 = 9
0 + 2 = 2	1 + 2 = 3	2 + 2 = 4	3 + 2 = 5	4 + 2 = 6	5 + 2 = 7	6 + 2 = 8	7 + 2 = 9	8 + 2 = 10	9 + 2 = 11
2 + 0 = 2	2 + 1 = 3	4 − 2 = 2	2 + 3 = 5	2 + 4 = 6	2 + 5 = 7	2 + 6 = 8	2 + 7 = 9	2 + 8 = 10	2 + 9 = 11
2 − 0 = 2	3 − 2 = 1		5 − 3 = 2	6 − 4 = 2	7 − 2 = 5	8 − 6 = 2	9 − 7 = 2	10 − 8 = 2	11 − 9 = 2
	3 − 1 = 2		5 − 2 = 3	6 − 2 = 4	7 − 5 = 2	8 − 2 = 6	9 − 2 = 7	10 − 2 = 8	11 − 2 = 9
0 + 3 = 3	1 + 3 = 4	2 + 3 = 5	3 + 3 = 6	4 + 3 = 7	5 + 3 = 8	6 + 3 = 9	7 + 3 = 10	8 + 3 = 11	9 + 3 = 12
3 + 0 = 3	3 + 1 = 4	3 + 2 = 5	6 − 3 = 3	3 + 4 = 7	3 + 5 = 8	3 + 6 = 9	3 + 7 = 10	3 + 8 = 11	3 + 9 = 12
3 − 0 = 3	4 − 1 = 3	5 − 2 = 3		7 − 4 = 3	8 − 5 = 3	9 − 6 = 3	10 − 7 = 3	11 − 8 = 3	12 − 9 = 3
	4 − 3 = 1	5 − 3 = 2		7 − 3 = 4	8 − 3 = 5	9 − 3 = 6	10 − 3 = 7	11 − 3 = 8	12 − 3 = 9
0 + 4 = 4	1 + 4 = 5	2 + 4 = 6	3 + 4 = 7	4 + 4 = 8	5 + 4 = 9	6 + 4 = 10	7 + 4 = 11	8 + 4 = 12	9 + 4 = 13
4 + 0 = 4	4 + 1 = 5	4 + 2 = 6	4 + 3 = 7	8 − 4 = 4	4 + 5 = 9	4 + 6 = 10	4 + 7 = 11	4 + 8 = 12	4 + 9 = 13
4 − 0 = 4	5 − 1 = 4	6 − 2 = 4	7 − 3 = 4		9 − 5 = 4	10 − 6 = 4	11 − 7 = 4	12 − 8 = 4	13 − 9 = 4
	5 − 4 = 1	6 − 4 = 2	7 − 4 = 3		9 − 4 = 5	10 − 4 = 6	11 − 4 = 7	12 − 4 = 8	13 − 4 = 9
0 + 5 = 5	1 + 5 = 6	2 + 5 = 7	3 + 5 = 8	4 + 5 = 9	5 + 5 = 10	6 + 5 = 11	7 + 5 = 12	8 + 5 = 13	9 + 5 = 14
5 + 0 = 5	5 + 1 = 6	5 + 2 = 7	5 + 3 = 8	5 + 4 = 9	10 − 5 = 5	5 + 6 = 11	5 + 7 = 12	5 + 8 = 13	5 + 9 = 14
5 − 0 = 5	6 − 1 = 5	7 − 2 = 5	8 − 3 = 5	9 − 4 = 5		11 − 6 = 5	12 − 7 = 5	13 − 8 = 5	14 − 9 = 5
	6 − 5 = 1	7 − 5 = 2	8 − 5 = 3	9 − 5 = 4		11 − 5 = 6	12 − 5 = 7	13 − 5 = 8	14 − 5 = 9
0 + 6 = 6	1 + 6 = 7	2 + 6 = 8	3 + 6 = 9	4 + 6 = 10	5 + 6 = 11	6 + 6 = 12	7 + 6 = 13	8 + 6 = 14	9 + 6 = 15
6 + 0 = 6	6 + 1 = 7	6 + 2 = 8	6 + 3 = 9	6 + 4 = 10	6 + 5 = 11	12 − 6 = 6	6 + 7 = 13	6 + 8 = 14	6 + 9 = 15
6 − 0 = 6	7 − 1 = 6	8 − 2 = 6	9 − 3 = 6	10 − 4 = 6	11 − 5 = 6		13 − 7 = 6	14 − 8 = 6	15 − 9 = 6
	7 − 6 = 1	8 − 6 = 2	9 − 6 = 3	10 − 6 = 4	11 − 6 = 5		13 − 6 = 7	14 − 6 = 8	15 − 6 = 9
0 + 7 = 7	1 + 7 = 8	2 + 7 = 9	3 + 7 = 10	4 + 7 = 11	5 + 7 = 12	6 + 7 = 13	7 + 7 = 14	8 + 7 = 15	9 + 7 = 16
7 + 0 = 7	7 + 1 = 8	7 + 2 = 9	7 + 3 = 10	7 + 4 = 11	7 + 5 = 12	7 + 6 = 13	14 − 7 = 7	7 + 8 = 15	7 + 9 = 16
7 − 0 = 7	8 − 1 = 7	9 − 2 = 7	10 − 3 = 7	11 − 4 = 7	12 − 5 = 7	13 − 6 = 7		15 − 8 = 7	16 − 9 = 7
	8 − 7 = 1	9 − 7 = 2	10 − 7 = 3	11 − 7 = 4	12 − 7 = 5	13 − 7 = 6		15 − 7 = 8	16 − 7 = 9
0 + 8 = 8	1 + 8 = 9	2 + 8 = 10	3 + 8 = 11	4 + 8 = 12	5 + 8 = 13	6 + 8 = 14	7 + 8 = 15	8 + 8 = 16	9 + 8 = 17
8 + 0 = 8	8 + 1 = 9	8 + 2 = 10	8 + 3 = 11	8 + 4 = 12	8 + 5 = 13	8 + 6 = 14	8 + 7 = 15	16 − 8 = 8	8 + 9 = 17
8 − 0 = 8	9 − 1 = 8	10 − 2 = 8	11 − 3 = 8	12 − 4 = 8	13 − 5 = 8	14 − 6 = 8	15 − 7 = 8		17 − 9 = 8
	9 − 8 = 1	10 − 8 = 2	11 − 8 = 3	12 − 8 = 4	13 − 8 = 5	14 − 8 = 6	15 − 8 = 7		17 − 8 = 9
0 + 9 = 9	1 + 9 = 10	2 + 9 = 11	3 + 9 = 12	4 + 9 = 13	5 + 9 = 14	6 + 9 = 15	7 + 9 = 16	8 + 9 = 17	9 + 9 = 18
9 + 0 = 9	9 + 1 = 10	9 + 2 = 11	9 + 3 = 12	9 + 4 = 13	9 + 5 = 14	9 + 6 = 15	9 + 7 = 16	9 + 8 = 17	18 − 9 = 9
9 − 0 = 9	10 − 1 = 9	11 − 2 = 9	12 − 3 = 9	13 − 4 = 9	14 − 5 = 9	15 − 6 = 9	16 − 7 = 9	17 − 8 = 9	
	10 − 9 = 1	11 − 9 = 2	12 − 9 = 3	13 − 9 = 4	14 − 9 = 5	15 − 9 = 6	16 − 9 = 7	17 − 9 = 8	

* Part of the zero fact family is not included because zero minus a whole number creates a negative number and negative numbers are NOT whole numbers.

During sixth grade students will be learning how to add and subtract multi-digit numbers and include the concepts of "carrying" in addition and "borrowing" in subtraction. Some examples are presented below:

Addition

100	37	123	247	89	892	623	96	375
+ 20	+17	+123	+ 85	+ 52	+ 146	+104	+ 23	+ 34
120	54	246	332	141	1,038	727	119	409

Subtraction

100	37	123	247	89	892	623	96	375
- 20	- 17	- 123	- 85	- 52	- 146	- 104	- 23	- 34
80	20	0	162	37	846	519	73	341

Similar to using the addition and subtraction fact families, students are expected to be familiar proficient using mental math to calculate single-digit multiplication and division equations. The following table represents the factor families that should be memorized:

Three	Four	Six	Seven	Eight	Nine	Eleven	Twelve
1 x 3 = 3	1 x 4 = 4	6 x 1 = 6	7 x 1 = 7	8 x 1 = 8	9 x 1 = 9	11 x 1 = 11	12 x 1 = 12
3 x 1 = 3	4 x 1 = 4	1 x 6 = 6	1 x 7 = 7	1 x 8 = 8	1 x 9 = 9	1 x 11 = 11	1 x 12 = 12
3 ÷ 1 = 3	4 ÷ 1 = 4	6 ÷ 1 = 6	7 ÷ 1 = 7	8 ÷ 1 = 8	9 ÷ 1 = 9	11 ÷ 1 = 11	12 ÷ 1 = 12
3 ÷ 3 = 1	4 ÷ 4 = 1	6 ÷ 6 = 1	7 ÷ 7 = 1	8 ÷ 8 = 1	9 ÷ 9 = 1	11 ÷ 11 = 1	12 ÷ 12 = 1
2 x 3 = 6	4 x 2 = 8	6 x 2 = 12	7 x 2 = 14	8 x 2 = 16	9 x 2 = 18	11 x 2 = 22	12 x 2 = 24
3 x 2 = 6	2 x 4 = 8	2 x 6 = 12	2 x 7 = 14	2 x 8 = 16	2 x 9 = 18	2 x 11 = 22	2 x 12 = 24
6 ÷ 2 = 3	8 ÷ 4 = 2	12 ÷ 6 = 2	14 ÷ 7 = 2	16 ÷ 8 = 2	18 ÷ 9 = 2	22 ÷ 11 = 22	24 ÷ 12 = 2
6 ÷ 3 = 2	8 ÷ 2 = 4	12 ÷ 2 = 6	14 ÷ 2 = 7	16 ÷ 2 = 8	18 ÷ 2 = 9	22 ÷ 2 = 11	24 ÷ 2 = 12
3 x 3 = 9	4 x 3 = 12	6 x 3 = 18	7 x 3 = 21	8 x 3 = 24	9 x 3 = 27	11 x 3 = 33	12 x 3 = 36
9 ÷ 3 = 3	3 x 4 = 12	3 x 6 = 18	3 x 7 = 21	3 x 8 = 24	3 x 9 = 27	3 x 11 = 33	3 x 12 = 36
	12 ÷ 4 = 3	18 ÷ 6 = 3	21 ÷ 7 = 3	24 ÷ 8 = 3	27 ÷ 9 = 3	33 ÷ 11 = 3	36 ÷ 12 = 3
	12 ÷ 3 = 4	18 ÷ 3 = 6	21 ÷ 3 = 7	24 ÷ 3 = 8	27 ÷ 3 = 9	33 ÷ 3 = 11	36 ÷ 3 = 12
3 x 4 = 12	4 x 4 = 16	6 x 4 = 24	7 x 4 = 28	8 x 4 = 32	9 x 4 = 36	11 x 4 = 44	12 x 4 = 48
4 x 3 = 12	16 ÷ 4 = 4	4 x 6 = 24	4 x 7 = 28	4 x 8 = 32	4 x 9 = 36	4 x 11 = 44	4 x 12 = 48
12 ÷ 3 = 4		24 ÷ 6 = 4	28 ÷ 7 = 4	32 ÷ 8 = 4	36 ÷ 9 = 4	44 ÷ 11 = 4	48 ÷ 12 = 4
12 ÷ 4 = 3		24 ÷ 4 = 6	28 ÷ 4 = 7	32 ÷ 4 = 8	36 ÷ 4 = 9	44 ÷ 4 = 11	48 ÷ 4 = 12
3 x 5 = 15	4 x 5 = 20	6 x 5 = 30	7 x 5 = 35	8 x 5 = 40	9 x 5 = 45	11 x 5 = 55	12 x 5 = 60
5 x 3 = 15	5 x 4 = 20	5 x 6 = 30	5 x 7 = 35	5 x 8 = 40	5 x 4 = 45	5 x 11 = 55	5 x 12 = 60
15 ÷ 5 = 3	20 ÷ 4 = 5	30 ÷ 6 = 5	35 ÷ 7 = 5	40 ÷ 8 = 5	45 ÷ 9 = 5	55 ÷ 11 = 5	60 ÷ 12 = 5
15 ÷ 3 = 5	20 ÷ 5 = 4	30 ÷ 5 = 6	35 ÷ 5 = 7	40 ÷ 5 = 8	45 ÷ 5 = 9	55 ÷ 5 = 11	60 ÷ 5 = 12
3 x 6 = 18	4 x 6 = 24	6 x 6 = 36	7 x 6 = 42	8 x 6 = 48	9 x 6 = 54	11 x 6 = 66	12 x 6 = 72
8 x 3 = 18	6 x 4 = 24	36 ÷ 6 = 6	6 x 7 = 42	6 x 8 = 48	6 x 9 = 54	6 x 11 = 66	6 x 12 = 72
18 ÷ 3 = 6	24 ÷ 4 = 6		42 ÷ 7 = 6	48 ÷ 8 = 6	54 ÷ 9 = 6	66 ÷ 11 = 6	72 ÷ 12 = 6
18 ÷ 6 = 3	24 ÷ 6 = 4		42 ÷ 6 = 7	48 ÷ 6 = 8	54 ÷ 6 = 9	66 ÷ 6 = 11	72 ÷ 6 = 12
3 x 7 = 21	4 x 7 = 28	6 x 7 = 42	7 x 7 = 49	8 x 7 = 56	9 x 7 = 63	11 x 7 = 77	12 x 7 = 84
7 x 3 = 21	7 x 4 = 28	7 x 6 = 42	49 ÷ 7 = 7	7 x 8 = 56	7 x 9 = 63	7 x 11 = 77	7 x 12 = 84
21 ÷ 3 = 7	28 ÷ 4 = 7	42 ÷ 6 = 7		56 ÷ 8 = 7	63 ÷ 9 = 7	77 ÷ 11 = 7	84 ÷ 12 = 7
21 ÷ 7 = 3	28 ÷ 7 = 4	42 ÷ 7 = 6		56 ÷ 7 = 8	63 ÷ 7 = 9	77 ÷ 7 = 11	84 ÷ 7 = 12
3 x 8 = 24	4 x 8 = 32	6 x 8 = 48	7 x 8 = 56	8 x 8 = 64	9 x 8 = 72	11 x 8 = 88	12 x 8 = 96
8 x 3 = 24	8 x 4 = 32	8 x 6 = 48	8 x 7 = 56	64 ÷ 8 = 8	8 x 9 = 72	8 x 11 = 88	8 x 12 = 96
24 ÷ 3 = 8	32 ÷ 4 = 8	48 ÷ 6 = 8	56 ÷ 7 = 8		72 ÷ 9 = 8	88 ÷ 11 = 8	96 ÷ 12 = 8
24 ÷ 8 = 3	32 ÷ 8 = 4	48 ÷ 8 = 6	56 ÷ 8 = 7		72 ÷ 8 = 9	88 ÷ 8 = 11	96 ÷ 8 = 12
3 x 9 = 27	4 x 9 = 36	6 x 9 = 54	7 x 9 = 63	8 x 9 = 72	9 x 9 = 81	11 x 9 = 99	12 x 9 = 108
9 x 3 = 27	9 x 4 = 36	9 x 6 = 54	9 x 7 = 63	9 x 8 = 72	81 ÷ 9 = 9	9 x 11 = 99	9 x 12 = 108
27 ÷ 3 = 9	36 ÷ 4 = 9	54 ÷ 6 = 9	63 ÷ 7 = 9	72 ÷ 8 = 9		99 ÷ 11 = 9	108 ÷ 12 = 9
27 ÷ 9 = 3	36 ÷ 9 = 4	54 ÷ 9 = 6	63 ÷ 9 = 7	72 ÷ 9 = 8		11 ÷ 9 = 11	108 ÷ 9 = 12
3 x 10 = 30	4 x 10 = 40	6 x 10 = 60	7 x 10 = 70	8 x 10 = 80	9 x 10 = 90	11 x 10 = 110	12 x 10 = 120
10 x 3 = 30	10 x 4 = 40	10 x 6 = 60	10 x 7 = 70	10 x 8 = 80	10 x 9 = 90	10 x 11 = 110	10 x 12 = 120
30 ÷ 10 = 3	40 ÷ 4 = 10	60 ÷ 6 = 10	70 ÷ 7 = 10	80 ÷ 8 = 10	90 ÷ 9 = 10	110 ÷ 11 = 10	120 ÷ 12 = 10
30 ÷ 3 = 10	40 ÷ 10 = 4	60 ÷ 10 = 6	70 ÷ 10 = 7	80 ÷ 10 = 8	90 ÷ 10 = 9	110 ÷ 10 = 11	120 ÷ 10 = 12
3 x 11 = 33	4 x 11 = 44	6 x 11 = 66	7 x 11 = 77	8 x 11 = 88	9 x 11 = 99	11 x 11 = 121	12 x 11 = 132
11 x 3 = 33	11 x 4 = 44	66 x 6 = 11	11 x 7 = 77	11 x 8 = 88	11 x 9 = 99	121 ÷ 11 = 11	11 x 12 = 132
33 ÷ 3 = 11	44 ÷ 4 = 11	66 ÷ 6 = 11	77 ÷ 7 = 11	88 ÷ 8 = 11	99 ÷ 9 = 11		132 ÷ 12 = 11
33 ÷ 11 = 3	44 ÷ 11 = 4	66 ÷ 11 = 6	77 ÷ 11 = 7	88 ÷ 11 = 8	99 ÷ 11 = 9		132 ÷ 11 = 12
3 x 12 = 36	4 x 12 = 48	6 x 12 = 72	7 x 12 = 84	8 x 12 = 96	9 x 12 = 108	11 x 12 = 132	12 x 12 = 144
12 x 3 = 36	12 x 4 = 48	12 x 6 = 72	12 x 7 = 84	12 x 8 = 96	12 x 9 = 108	12 x 11 = 132	144 ÷ 12 = 12
36 ÷ 3 = 12	48 ÷ 4 = 12	72 ÷ 6 = 12	84 ÷ 7 = 12	96 ÷ 8 = 12	108 ÷ 9 = 12	132 ÷ 11 = 12	
36 ÷ 12 = 3	48 ÷ 12 = 4	72 ÷ 12 = 6	84 ÷ 12 = 7	96 ÷ 12 = 8	108 ÷ 12 = 9	132 ÷ 12 = 11	

* Zero, One, and Two tables were omitted because they have been covered extensively in previous grades. The fives and tens tables wee omitted because they are also extensively covered in previous grades.

The following multiplication and division problems are similar to those that the sixth grade students will be studying this year. Concepts including "carrying over" in multiplication and remainders in division will also be covered during sixth grade.

Multiplication

```
   100        37       123       247        89       892       623       96       375
x   20     x  17    x  123    x   85     x  52    x  146    x  104    x  23    x   34
   000       259       369      1235       178      5352      2492      288      1500
 +200       + 37     + 246      1976      +445     + 3568      0000      192      1125
  2000       629     +123      20995      4628       892        623     2208     12750
                    15129                          130232      64792
```

* Commas for proper number notation were not used in these equations so the numbers would line up in their appropriate columns.

Exponents

A specific multiplication operation involves exponents. The exponent is the small number to the upper right of a whole number that tells you how many times the number is multiplies by itself. An example using the number 2 is presented below:

$2^2 = 2 \times 2 = 4$

$2^3 = 2 \times 2 \times 2 = 4 \times 2 = 8$

$2^4 = 2 \times 2 \times 2 \times 2 = 4 \times 4 = 16$

Using exponents is like using a short hand for multiplication. Rather than write $2 \times 2 \times 2 \times 2 \times 2 = 32$, it is easier to use the exponent $2^5 = 32$

Division

$2,000 \div 100 = 20$ $629 \div 37 = 17$ $15,129 \div 123 = 123$ $20,995 \div 247 = 85$

2,000 ÷ 20 = 100   629 ÷ 17 = 37   20,995 ÷ 85 = 247

4,628 ÷ 89 = 52   130,232 ÷ 892 = 146   64,792 ÷ 623 = 104   2,208 ÷ 96 = 23
4,628 ÷ 52 = 89   130,232 ÷ 146 = 892   64,792 ÷ 104 = 623   2,208 ÷ 23 = 96

12,750 ÷ 375 = 34
12,750 ÷ 34 = 375

Order of Operations

When equations are composed of more than one kind of mathematical operation, they need to be solved in a specific order to obtain the correct answer. The following is the order of operations for adding, subtracting, multiplying and dividing:

Parentheses, Exponents, Multiply and Divide from left to right, then Add and Subtract from left to right. Examples of the Order of Operations are presented below:

1. $5 + 2 - 3 =$ first add, then subtract $= 7 - 3 = 4$

2. $18 + 4 - (3 + 5) \times 2 =$ simplify parentheses first

    $18 + 4 - 5 \times 2 =$ then multiply

    $18 + 4 - 10 =$ add then subtract

    $22 - 10 = 12$

3. $2^3 + (8 - 3) - 3 \times 3 \div 3 = 2^3 + (8 - 3) - 3 \times 3 \div 3 = 8 + 5 - 3 \times 3 \div 3 = 8 + 5 - 9 \div 3 = 8 + 5 - 3 = 13 - 3 = 10$

Operations with Whole Numbers – Practice Sheet

1. What are the four main whole number operations learned and practiced in sixth grade?

2. Fill in the blank

Students use _____ families to help them memorize single-digit addition and subtraction operations.

Fill in the blanks for the following fact families:

1. ___ + 2 = 5, 5 - _____ = 2, 2 + _____ = 5, 5 – 2 = _____

2. 8 + _____ = 15, _____ + 8 = 15, 15 - 8 = _____, 15 - _____ = 8

3. _____ + 5 = 20, 5 + _____ = 20, 20 - _____ = 5, 20 – 5 = _____

Fill in the blanks for the following factor families:

1. 2 x _____ = 12, _____ x 2 = 12, 12 ÷ 2 = _____, 12 ÷ _____ = 2

2. 3 x _____ = 12, _____ x 3 = 12, 12 ÷ _____ = 3, 12 ÷ 3 = _____

3. 7 x _____ = 35, _____ x 7 = 35, 35 ÷ _____ = 7, 35 ÷ 7 = _____

Complete the following mathematical operations:

1. 23 + 8 = _____   5. 34 x 5 = _____

1. Write the Product for the following exponents: 2^3, 4^2, 5^4, 10^6

2. $18 + 17 =$ _____	6. $23 \times 8 =$ _____
3. $31 - 12 =$ _____	7. $25 \div 5 =$ _____
4. $57 - 19 =$ _____	8. $63 \div 7 =$ _____

2. Explain the order of operations to correctly solve the following problem:

$(10 + 20) - 3^2 + 1 - 4 \times 2 \div 8 = 21$

Operations with Whole Numbers – Quiz

1. Name one mathematical operation that uses whole numbers.

2. Write all the single-digit equations for calculating a Sum of 8.

3. What are the factors for 27?

4. Which factors can you multiply to calculate 90?

Solve the following problems:

1. $184 + 2,376 =$

2. $1,007 - 38 =$

3. $832 \times 23 =$

4. $255 \div 5 =$

Write the answers for:

1. $5^2 =$ _____, $3^4 =$ _____, $10^2 =$ _____

2. Properly solve the following equation using the correct order of operations:

    $15 + 5 - (2 + 7) \times 2 \div 3 =$ _____

Decimals

Decimals are numbers that have values on both sides of the decimal point. Whole numbers are represented to the left of the decimal point in values of ones, tens, hundreds, thousands, etc. and decimal place numbers are represented to the right of the decimal point in values of tenths, hundredths, thousandths, etc.

Examples of decimal numbers include

1.315	2.67	8.31	12.256	117.212
20.67	18.756	2.6	3.4	5.895

Decimals can be written with zeros as placeholders to the right of the last whole value to make it visually easier to perform operations like addition, subtraction, multiplication and division. If these operations are not being used as part of a decimal problem, the decimal numbers can be simplified.

For example, the following examples present decimal numbers with extra zeros and their simplified versions:

3.03030 =	0.00400 =	5.67000 =	413.4500 =	2.560600 =	1.23000 =
3.0303	0.004	5.67	413.45	2.5606	1.23

Sometimes zeros are added or decimals are simplified for the purpose of comparing decimal numbers and learning concepts like "greater than," "less than," and "equal to."

The above examples are "equal to" types of comparisons using decimal numbers. The following are examples of "greater than" and "less than" comparisons:

Greater Than and Less Than

1. Is 0.101 greater than or less than 0.1?

First, to make the problem visually easier, zeros are added to 0.1 to give it the same number of decimal places as 0.101.

Is 0.101 greater than or less than 0.100?

By adding the zeros, it becomes clearer than 0.101 is greater than 0.100.

The answer, written as an equation, looks like this: 0.101 > 0.1

2. Is 0.03050 greater than or less than 0.305?

First, to make the problem visually easier, one zero is added to 0.305 and one zero is taken away from 0.03050 to give them both equal decimal places.

Is 0.0305 greater than or less than 0.3050?

By using the zeros as placeholders, it becomes clearer that 0.0305 is less than 0.3050.

The answer written as an equation, looks like this: 0.0305 < 0.3050

More examples:

Indicate the relationship between the following decimals - less than (<), equal to (=), or greater than (>):

0.23 _____ 0.145   2.51 _____ 0.2   0.01250 _____ 0.0125

1.25 _____ 1.250   4.510 _____ 4.53   0.2 _____ 0.153

Answers to the above are >, >, = and =, <, >

Adding or subtracting zeros can also make it easier to determine the proper order of numbers regarding their values.

For example, a student is asked to put the following decimal numbers in increasing order:

0.205   0.5   0.35   0.221   0.14   0.22   0.371   0.17

If we add zeros to convert each number to three decimal places they look like this:

0.205   0.500   0.350   0,221   0.140   0.220   0.371   0.170

The student can now put them in the correct increasing order and eliminate the place holding zeros.

0.14   0.17   0.205   0.22   0.221   0.35   0.371   0.5

Adding and Subtracting Decimals

Place-holding zeros are an essential conversion for adding and subtracting decimal numbers. The mistake most often made by students when adding and subtracting decimal numbers is forgetting where to line up the decimal point. If the decimal point is not in the correct place when adding and subtracting decimal numbers, the place values will be incorrect and the student will calculate the wrong answer.

The following are examples of not lining up the decimal points:

0.125	1.23	100	1.786	0.256
+ 4.1	+ 0.3	+ 0.1	+ 0.23	+ 0.44
0.166	1.26	10.1	1.809	300

The above equations have been calculated to produce the wrong answers because the decimal points are not lined up. When the decimal points are lined up correctly, the proper columns and aligned and the correct answers can be solved.

0.125	1.23	100.0	1.786	0.256
+ 4.100	+ 0.30	+ 0.1	+ 0.230	+ 0.440
4.225	1.53	100.1	2.016	0.696

Multiplying and Dividing Decimals

When multiplying and dividing decimal numbers, the numbers are lined up instead of the decimal points. After the product or quotient is calculated, then the decimal point is placed in the correct place in the new number.

For example, if 1.25 is multiplied by 0.5, the answer is 0.625. The reason for the placement of the decimal point before the six is because the total number of decimal places between the two factors is three.

After the original multiplication operation, the value of the answer is 625, but to be correct as the product for this calculation the decimal point needs to be moved from the end of the number, three places to the left to get 0.625

$$
\begin{array}{r} 1.25 \\ \times\ 0.5 \\ \hline 625 \end{array}
\quad \longrightarrow \quad
\begin{array}{r} 1.25 \\ \times\ 0.5 \\ \hline \mathbf{0.625} \end{array}
$$

Additional multiplication examples:

3.5 x 2 = 7.0 = 7 (simplified)

2.56 x 0.3 = 0.768 (moved the decimal 3 places to the left after calculating the product)

7.25 x 0.2 = 1.45 (moved the decimal 3 places to the left after calculating the product)

0.25 x 0.25 = 0.0625 (moved the decimal point 4 places)

Division problems are a bit different. Movement of the decimal point still occurs, but before and after the division calculation.

For example, if 1.25 is going to be divided by 0.5, the decimal points of the dividend (number being divided) and divisor (number doing the dividing) need to be moved to the right until the divisor is represented as a whole number, the dividing calculation can be completed:

- Take 0.5 and move the decimal point one space to the right to create the whole number 5.
- Take 1.25 and move the decimal point one place to the right to create the decimal 12.5. The (answer) will have one decimal place like the dividend.
- Now divide 5 into 12.5 to get 2.5

The equation looks like this: 1.25 ÷ 0.5 = 12.5 ÷ 5 = 2.5

Additional Examples:

1. 2.32 ÷ 0.2 = 23.2 ÷ 2 = 11.6
2. 6.36 ÷ 0.3 = 63.6 ÷ 3 = 21.2
3. 5.45 ÷ 0.5 = 54.5 ÷ 5 = 10.9

Decimals – Practice Sheet

Write the following as decimal numbers:

1. One and Seventeen Hundredths

2. Five and One Hundredths

3. Two and One Hundred Twelve Thousandths

4. Five and Sixteen Thousandths

5. Four Hundred Eighteen Thousandths

6. Fifty-Six Hundredths

Add zeros as placeholders to extend each of the following decimals to the Ten Thousandths place:

1. 2.56_____

2. 0.546___

3. 8.2_____

4. 13.44____

5. 9.573____

6. 1.502____

Compare – Greater Than, Less Than, Equal to

1   0.142 _____ 0.024   2. 0.573 _____ 0.0889   3. 0.0350 _____ 0.035

Complete the following problems:

1. 0.25 x 0.2 =

2. 4.5 ÷ 0.09 =

3. 18.759 + 2.65 =

4. 15.67 − 1.875 =

5. 1.25 x 8.36 =

Decimals – Quiz

Write the Name or Number for the following:

1. 1.351

2. Twelve and Forty-Two Thousandths

Greater Than, Less Than, Equal to

1. 0.135 _____ 1.35

2. 1.237 _____ 1.27

3. 0.0852 _____ 0.895

Complete the following Problems:

1. 0.75 x 0.2 =

2. 5.4 ÷ 0.9 =

3. 13.8 + 2.65 =

4. 7.9 – 1.875 =

5. 2.77 x 10 =

Integers

Integers include all the whole numbers, zero, and all the negative equivalents of the whole numbers. Fractions and decimal numbers are not considered to be integers.

$$-10 \; -9 \; -8 \; -7 \; -6 \; -5 \; -4 \; -3 \; -2 \; -1 \; 0 \; 1 \; 2 \; 3 \; 4 \; 5 \; 6 \; 7 \; 8 \; 9 \; 10$$

The number line above ranges from -10 to +10. As you move to the right from zero, the numbers are positive and to the left from zero the numbers are negative. Using the number line as a reference tool for adding and subtracting integers is helpful until the student becomes more familiar with the process.

A basic addition or subtraction problem begins at the zero point and moves either left or right depending on the "sign" of the first number. A number's sign is designated as either positive (+) or negative (-) and determines its place on the number line. Try finding the following numbers on the above number line: +5, -5, +8, -8, +2, -2, zero, +6, and -6.

To visualize an addition problem using this number line, put your finger on the zero as a starting point. Now move your finger to +5. This represents the first number in an addition problem. Next, move your finger to the right 3 points to +8. This movement represents adding a +3 to the +5. The +8 is the Sum of the equation +5 + (+3).

The parentheses around the +3 are used in the equation to prevent confusion with the addition sign and the positive sign of the +3. Another way positive integers are written is as a plain number with no sign. It is implied that all numbers without a designating positive sign or negative sign are positive. This rule also helps minimize confusion with the addition sign. Parentheses are also used for negative numbers being subtracted to avoid confusion with the minus sign. Subtracting a negative number is discussed in the Subtraction section below.

Another math problem using the above number line involves a positive integer and a negative integer. If you start with your finger again on the zero and move it to -6, you have selected moved to the left of the zero in the negative direction and selected -6 as the first integer in the equation. If you move your finger from the -6 to the -1 you have moved in the positive direction 5 points. The equation for this movement looks like -6 + (+5) = -1

Once the student is comfortable with the concept of moving along the number line in a positive and/or negative direction, the operations of adding, subtracting, multiplying and dividing integers become easier and the need for a number line diminishes.

Integers can be added, subtracted, multiplied and divided just like whole numbers, but having the negative numbers included means being aware of some differences and rules involved.

Addition

Adding integers from the same side of the number line is treated the same as adding whole numbers. A negative number added to another negative number equals a larger negative number and a positive number added to another positive number equals a larger positive number.

Examples

1. -2 + -3 = -5
2. -8 + - 2 = -10
3. 2 + 3 = 5
4. 8 + 2 = 10

```
-10 -9 -8 -7 -6 -5 -4 -3 -2 -1  0  1  2  3  4  5  6  7  8  9  10
←───────────────────────────────────────────────────────────────→
```

By using the number line above, it can be seen that as positive numbers are added together, their value increases to the right, and as negative numbers are added together, their values increase to the left.

However, when adding a negative number and a positive number together, subtraction is the operation that occurs. The number values go to the right or left along the number line depending on whether a positive is being added to a negative or a negative is being added to a positive.

Examples

1. 10 + -2 = 8: the value of 10 is moves to the left (negative direction) 2 places to get a positive 8

2. 5 + -2 = 3: the value of 5 is moved to the left 2 places to get a positive 3

3. -10 + 3 = -7: the value of -10 is moved to the right (positive direction) 3 places to get a -7

4. -10 + 7 = -3: the value of -10 is moved to the right 7 places to get -3

Subtraction

When subtracting mixed integers, it becomes an addition operation. Subtracting a negative integer makes it a positive integer.

For example: - (-9) = 9, - (-5) = 5, and - (-45) – 4

When placed into an equation the operation looks like the following:

1. 15 – (-1) = 16: add the 1

2. 20 – (-2) = 22: add the 2

3.   -4 – (-2) = -2: add the 2 (move in the positive direction on the number line 2 spaces)

4.   -12 – (-5) = -7: add the 7 (move in the positive direction on the number line 5 spaces)

A method for remembering to add when subtracting a negative is to turn the minus sign to a plus sign and the negative sign to a positive sign. Then complete the operation as an addition problem.

For example: -(-2) = + 2, - (-7) = + 7, - (-31) = + 31

Multiplication and Division

There are two basic rules for multiplying and dividing integers:

- ⇒ If both numbers are positive or negative, the answer is always positive.
- ⇒ If the problem includes both positive and negative numbers, the answer is always negative.

OR   Examples:

(+) x (+) AND (-) x (-) = (+)	3 x 4 = 12 AND -3 x -4 = 12
(+) ÷ (+) AND (-) ÷ (-) = (+)	12 ÷ 4 = 3 AND -12 ÷ -4 = 3
(+) x (-) AND (-) x (+) = (-)	3 x -4 = -12 AND -3 x 4 = -12
(+) ÷ (-) AND (-) ÷ (+) = (-)	12 ÷ -3 = -4 AND -12 ÷ 3 = -4

Integers – Practice Sheet

1. What is the largest (+) number on this time line?

2. What is the largest (-) number on this time line?

```
-10 -9 -8 -7 -6 -5 -4 -3 -2 -1 0 1 2 3 4 5 6 7 8 9 10
```

3. If you start at zero and move three points to the left, what is the integer?

4. What integer will you be at if you move 6 points to the right from -4?

5. If the beginning integer in a problem is 4 and -7 is added, what integer will you end up on?

Calculate the Answer

1. 5 + 7 =

    10. -100 – (-10) =

2. 14 + 11 =

    11. -12 x -12 =

3. 12 – 5 =

    12. 5 x -25 =

4. 27 – 9 =

    13. 8 x 14 =

5. -12 + -13 =

6. 18 + (-7) =

7. 39 − (-5) =

8. 53 − (-7) =

9. -34 − (-4) =

14. -8 ÷ -2 =

15. 18 ÷ -9 =

Integers – Quiz

```
-10 -9 -8 -7 -6 -5 -4 -3 -2 -1 0 1 2 3 4 5 6 7 8 9 10
```

1. What is the range of integers represented on the above time line?

2. True or False

Positive integers are to the left of the zero and negative integers are to the right of the zero.

3. If you start at zero, move three points to the left and then six points to the right, what integer will you end at?

4. If you start at +9 and move 13 points to the left and then 5 points to the right, what integer will you end on?

Calculate the Answer

1. -5 + -27 =

2. -33 + 21 =

3. -83 – (-5) =

4. 97 – (-3) =

5. 12 x -12 =

6. -38 ÷ 2 =

Graphing

Graphs are the visual representation of a set or several sets of numbers. Their purpose is to allow the student to look at a picture version of specific numbers and make comparisons, interpretations and decisions regarding the data shown in the graph. There are several types of graphs: coordinate graphs, bar graphs, pie charts, line graphs, etc.

Bar Graphs are good for comparing different totals or groups, Pie Charts are good for displaying totals represented as percentages or fractions of a pie, and Line Graphs are usually created to track the changes in a measurement or changing value.

Interpreting Graphed Data

	Cookies	Cupcakes	Brownies
6th Grade	100	153	95
7th Grade	112	127	113
8th Grade	97	134	185
All	309	414	393

The following graphs represent the data in the above table:

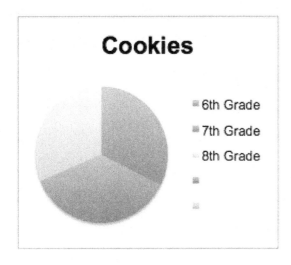 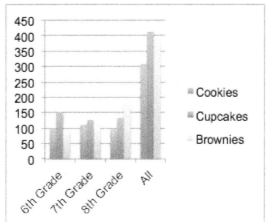

The Pie Chart shows the comparison between the number of cookies each grade sold. Based on the function of the Pie Chart, it can only show one set of data spread between two or more data groups. To look at the number of cupcakes and number of brownies per grade using Pie Charts, each set of data would have its own chart. So, Pie Charts are better for comparing one set of data between several data groups.

The Bar Graph is a better representation of the total data gathered and provides a comparison between the data and the groups from which the data was gathered. Based on the table of data gathered, the Bar Graph provides the best visual representation of the data and is easier to visually interpret.

The Line Graph below, it not a good representation of the data gathered and presented in the table. Line Graphs are better representations of single point data like measurements and changes in the data gathered. The line graph presented below is a bit confusing with regard to the bake sale data.

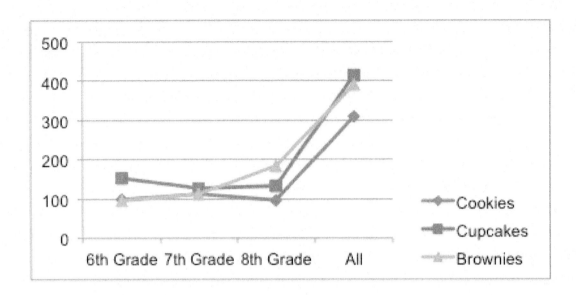

So, to properly present the data gathered for the student bake sale and interpret that data, the table and bar graph are presented below:

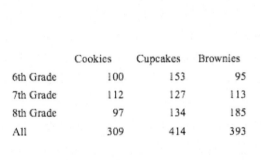
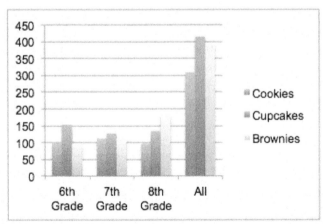

Just using the Bar Graph as a source of data, it is easy to see that more cupcakes were sold than brownies or cookies. It is also easy to interpret the data in general: the 8th Grade sold the most brownies, 6th Grade sold the most cupcakes, and the 7th grade class sales of all three bake sale items was mostly evenly distributed.

General totals can be determined from the Bar Graph. For example, just slightly more than 400 cupcakes were sold, the 8th Grade sold almost 200 brownies, the 6th grade sold just about 150 cupcakes, and the 7th grade sold around 100-120 of each item.

The table containing the hard (actual) data, provides more specific data, but requires more time to interpret the numbers, class data, and data regarding each item sold.

Interpretation of Data (continued)

	Cookies	Cupcakes	Brownies
6th Grade	100	153	95
7th Grade	112	127	113
8th Grade	97	134	185
All	309	414	393

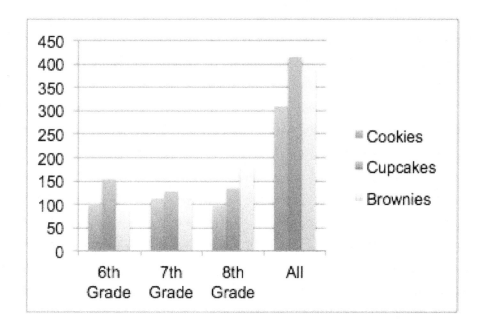

From interpreting the data presented in the table, the students can conclude the following:

1. The 6th Grade sold significantly more cupcakes than brownies or cookies. Specifically, they sold 53 more cupcakes than cookies and 58 more cupcakes than brownies.

2. By calculating the difference between the number of brownies sold by the 6th Grade and the 8th Grade and then the difference between the 7th Grade and the *the 8th Grade, it becomes evident that the 8th Grade class sold many more brownies than any other class: 185 − 95 = 90 and 185 − 113 = 72. So, 90 more brownies were sold by the 8th Grade than the 6th Grade and 72 more brownies were sold by the 8th Grade than the 7th Grade.

3. The greatest number of items sold by the classes was 414 total cupcakes. The second greatest item sold was the brownies with a total of 393, and the item that sold the least was cookies at 309 total.

Creating Graphs

To create a graph, first data must be gathered and organized. Sometimes the data can be directly plotted on to a graph and sometimes the data needs to be organized into a table and then plotted on to a graph. The graph below shows how data can be visually organized directly to the graph:

A student asked his fellow classmates whether they liked chocolate or did NOT like chocolate. He collected the answers in chart form.

Days	Temp °F
1	10
2	12
3	13
4	10
5	5
6	-2
7	-5
8	0
9	-1
10	5

The previous chart can be interpreted visually and it is easily noticeable that just about an equal number of girls and boys like chocolate and that more boys than girls do not like chocolate. Since the data is represented directly in the chart, the student can also present numerical data: 8 girls like chocolate, 3 girls do not like chocolate, 7 boys like chocolate, and 5 boys do not like chocolate.

Liked Chocolate		Do Not Like Chocolate	
X X X			
X X X X			X
X X X X		X	X X
X X X X		X X	X X
Girls	Boys	Girls	Boys

Students can also collect measured data and plot the changes over time on a line graph.

Students in Mr. Smith's class measured the temperature outside their classroom for ten days. They took each day's temperature reading and plotted the result on a graph. After the ten days, they connected the points and the graph below presents their results.

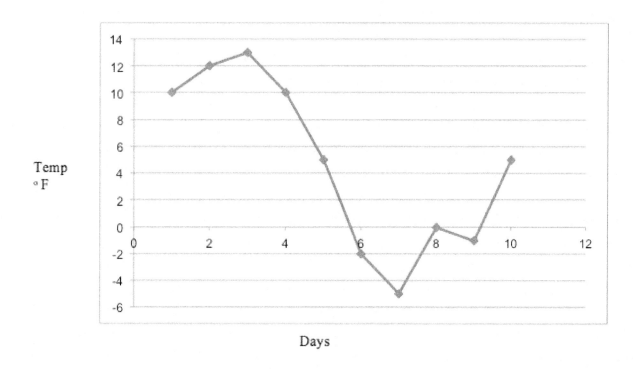

The students found that when they connected the points that they could make some conclusions about the data they collected:

1. The high temperature during the 10 days was 13 °F and the low temperature was -5 °F.

2. The temperature dropped significantly between Day 3 and Day 7 and began to rise again by Day 9.

Graphing – Practice Sheet

1. Label the following graphs : Bar Graph, Pie Chart, or Line Graph:

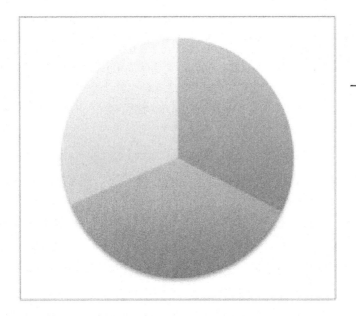   _____

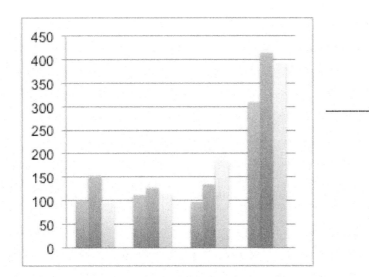   _____

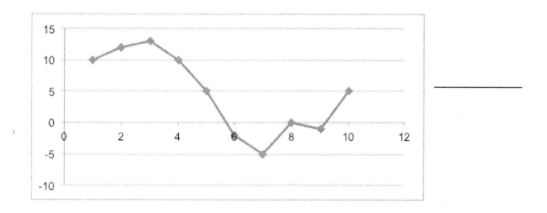

2. Which graph shows data with negative values?

Without any data other to use, interpret the information presented in the Pie Chart below:

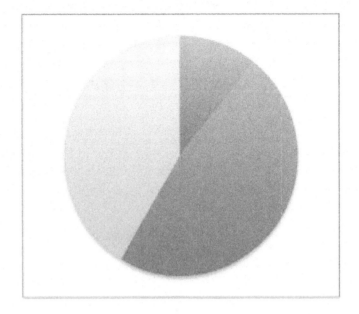

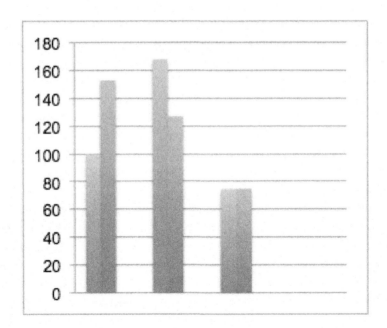

1. Which color covers the greatest area of the Pie Chart?

2. Which color covers the smallest area of the Pie Chart?

3. Which two colors are closest in area?

4. Which two colors, if you add them together will be almost equal to the third?

Without any data other to use, interpret the information presented in the Bar Graph below:

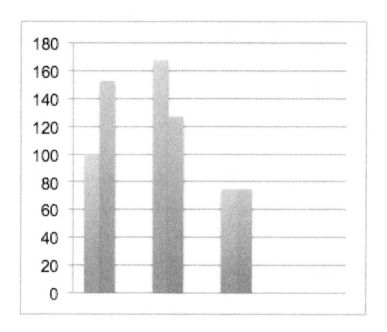

1. Which group shows an even amount of data in both colors?

2. Which color has the greatest data value?

3. Which color's greatest value was approximately 150?

4. Which color, between the first and second groups of data, is the smallest?

5. When totaled, which color has a greater value, Red or Blue?

Graphing – Practice Sheet

Girls – Juice or Soda at Lunch
Girls – Water at Lunch
Boys – Juice or Soda at Lunch
Boys – Water at Lunch

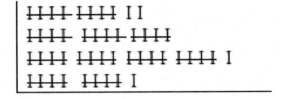

The above data/graph represents the types of drinks the 6th grade class typically has at lunch.

1. How many girls drink juice or soda at lunch?

2. How many boys drink juice or soda at lunch?

3. How many more boys than girls drink juice or soda at lunch?

4. Do more boys drink juice or soda at lunch or water at lunch?

5. How many more girls drink water at lunch than juice or soda?

Number of Weeks Measured

	Height Day 1	Height Day 2	Height Day 3	Height Day 4	Height Day 5	Height Day 6	Height Day 7
Sunflower Growth	1 inch	2 inches	2 inches	3 inches	4 inches	4 inches	5 inches

1. Plot the data points on the graph provided.

2. Connect the points to form a line graph.

3. How long did it take for the sunflower to reach 4 inches?

4. If the current growth pattern continues, when will the sunflower reach 10 inches?

Graphing - Quiz

1. Which of the two graphs below is better for interpreting changing data points?

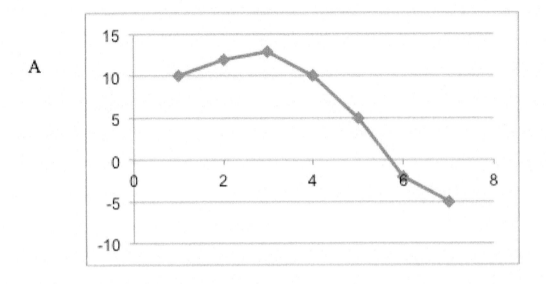

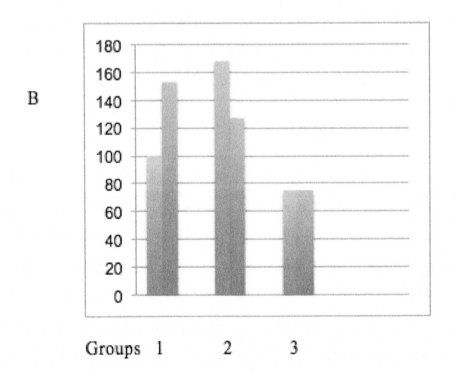

2. Which of the two graphs better represents a comparison of groups of data?

3. Does Graph A show an increase in the measured data or a decrease?

4. What is the smallest measurement plotted on Graph A?

5. Create a table with the following data and plot the points on Graph A: x-axis = 0 through 8 days, plot one value per day, 0, 3, 6, 2, 7, 8, 9, 12

6. Which group has the greatest Blue value in Chart B?

7. Which group for Chart B has the smallest Blue data value?

8. Which group for Chart B has equal values for both the Red and Blue data?

9. In Chart B, which group shows the Red Data greater than the Blue Data?

10. What is the approximate value of the largest data group?

Fractions

Basic fractions are shown with the Numerator on top and Denominator on the bottom and represent a portion of a whole number, whole object or whole idea. Fractions are very prevalent throughout our daily activities. When serving birthday cake to the class or family, it is divided into equal parts. If the cake is divided into 10 equal slices, the portion that each person gets can be represented as the fraction 1/10. When money is discussed, it is common to refer to 25 cents as a quarter, 1/4, because it is one quarter of a whole dollar.

Examples of simple fractions include the following:

1/2, 1/3, 1/4, 1/5, 1/6, 1/7, 2/3, 3/4, 5/6, 5/7, 1/16

Adding and subtracting fractions requires that they have a Common Denominator. Which means the denominator of the fractions being added or subtracted need to be equal. The denominators remain the same and the numerators are added or subtracted.

Examples

1. 1/4 + 1/4 = 2/4
2. 3/8 + 2/8 = 5/8
3. 1/5 + 1/5 = 2/5
4. 3/5 − 1/5 = 2/5
5. 6/7 − 2/7 = 4/7
6. 5/16 − 1/16 = 4/16
7. 9/10 − 3/10 = 4/10
8. 11/12 − 4/12 = 7/12

If the fractions already share a **common denominator**, like those above, then there is no need to convert any of the fractions in the equation. However, if the denominators are not the same, one or more of the fractions in the equation will need to be converted to create a common denominator.

To create a **Common Denominator**, the fraction in question is multiplied by a special fraction with a numerator and denominator that are equal. This type of fraction does not change the actual value of the fraction to be converted because it is equal to one. For example, 2/2 = 1, 3/3 = 1, 4/4 = 1, 5/5 = 1, 23/23 = 1 etc. When multiplying the fraction to be changed by the special value "1" fraction, both the numerator and denominator are multiplied.

Examples

1/2 + 1/4 = ?   Since 2 is a factor of 4, the common denominator of 4 can be used. To convert 1/2 to fourths, it is multiplies by 2/2 which converts it to 2/4. Now, 2/4 + 1/4 = 3/4.

1/2 + 1/3 = ?   Since neither denominator is a factor of the other, the next common factor needs to be calculated. The smallest common denominator for both 2 and 3 is 6. So, 1/2 is multiplied by 3/3 and 1/3 is multiplied by 2/2 to get the following equation: 3/6 + 2/6 = 5/6.

The proper term for the smallest common denominator is **Lowest Common Denominator**. The Lowest Common Denominator is usually calculated to minimize the need to reduce the fraction. Reduction will be discussed later in this section.

The problems below provide examples of finding the Lowest Common Denominator for the purpose of adding and subtracting fractions with different denominators:

1. 1/4 + 1/8 = (2/2 x 1/4) + 1/8 = 2/8 + 1/8 = 3/8
2. 2/3 + 1/6 = (2/2 x 2/3) + 1/6 = 4/6 + 1/6 = 5/6
3. 3/4 + 1/8 = (2/2 x 3/4) + 1/8 = 6/8 + 1/8 = 7/8
4. 1/3 + 1/4 = (4/4 x 1/3) + (3/3 x 1/4) = 4/12 + 3/12 = 7/12
5. 1/3 + 2/5 = (5/5 x 1/3) + (3/3 x 2/5) = 5/15 + 6/15 = 11/15

Multiplying Fractions

Common denominators are not needed to multiply fractions. Since the numerators are multiplied together and the denominators are multiplied together, an entirely new fraction is calculated. Examples of multiplying fractions are shown below:

1.   1/2 x 1/2 = 1/4
2.   1/2 x 1/3 = 1/6
3.   1/2 x 1/4 = 1/8
4.   1/2 x 1/5 = 1/10
5.   1/3 x 1/4 = 1/12
6.   2/3 x 2/3 = 4/9
7.   1/3 x 2/3 = 2/9
8.   3/5 x 1/2 = 3/10

Since the above products of multiplying fractions are already simplified to their lowest form, they do not need to be "reduced" any smaller. Reducing a fraction to its lowest form means that neither the numerator nor denominator can be divided to a smaller amount using common factors. For example, 1/3, 2/3, 1/5, 1/4, 2/5, 3/4, etc. cannot be reduced because their numerators and denominators do not share any common factors.

The process of reducing fractions is presented below:

1.   2/4, 2/8, and 2/6

A common factor of 2, 4, 6, and 8 is 2, so the numerator and denominator are both divided by 2 to get the **reduced fractions** of 1/2, 1/4, and 1/3.

2.   3/6, 3/9, and 3/12

A common factor of 3, 6, 9, and 12 is 3, so the numerator and denominator are both divide by 3 to get the **reduced fractions** of 1/2, 1/3, and 1/4.

Dividing Fractions

When dividing whole numbers, the question essentially is how many divisors will fit into the dividend? For example, when dividing 18 by 9 the question of how many 9's are in 18? It is the same with fractions. When dividing 1/2 by 1/4, the question of how many 1/4's are in 1/2?

Dividing fraction is usually a two-step process: First, calculate how many divisors are in 1. Essentially we divide 1 by a divisor like 1/4. This changes 1/4 to it's reciprocal 4/1. A **reciprocal** of a fraction is the fraction with the numerator and denominator places switched. For example, the **reciprocal** of 2/3 = 3/2, the **reciprocal** of 3/5 is 5/3, and the **reciprocal** of 2/5 is 5/2.

So, dividing 1/2 by 1/4 first involves changing 1/4 into it's reciprocal, 4/1 and then completing the Second Step of finding 1/2 of 4/1 by multiplying to get the answer 4/2. Reducing 4/2 involves dividing the numerator and denominator by a common factor, in this case 2, to get the final answer of 2.

So, 1/2 ÷ 1/4 = 1/2 x 4/1 = 4/2 = 2

Another Example of Dividing Fractions:

3/4 ÷ 1/3 = 3/4 x 3/1 = 9/4

Now, in this case, the numerator is larger than the denominator and there are no common factors between 9 and 4 to be able to reduce this answer to a whole number. The number 9/4 will be reduced to what is called a **mixed number**. To calculate this **Mixed Number**, the denominator is divided into the numerator as completely as possible. The remaining numerator becomes a fraction and is represented as part of the whole number calculated.

So, 9/4 is actually 9 ÷ 4 = 2 with 1/9 left over. The mixed number is represented as 2 1/9 and is named as Two and One-Ninth.

Finally, the entire problem of 3/4 ÷ 1/3 can be solved: 3/4 ÷ 1/3 = 3/4 x 3/1 = 9/4 = 2 1/9.

More Division Examples

1. 2/3 ÷ 1/4 = 2/3 x 4/1 (reciprocal of 1/4) = 8/3 = 8 ÷ 3 = 2 with 2 left over = 2 2/3 = Two and Two-Thirds.

2. 3/4 ÷ 1/2 = 3/4 x 2/1 = 6/4 = 3/2 (reduced) = 1 1/2 = One and One-Half.

3. 3/5 ÷ 2/3 = 3/5 x 3/2 = 9/10 = Nine-Tenths

Fractions – Practice Sheet

1. True or False: If the numerator and denominator are equal the fraction equals 1.

2. True or False: To add and subtract fractions, the denominators need to be the same.

3. True or False: A common denominator is created by multiplying the fractions.

4. True or False: When multiplying fractions, the numerators and denominators are multiplied to get the final product.

4. True or False: To divide fractions, the divisor fraction is converted to its reciprocal and multiplied with the dividend.

5. True or False: A mixed number is a whole number with a fraction represented.

Solve and Reduce the Following Problems

1. 2/3 + 2/3 =

2. 1/5 + 1/5 =

3. 2/3 + 1/4 =

4. 5/6 + 1/2 =

5. 1/2 + 1/2 =

9. 3/4 x 1/2 =

10. 2/3 x 3/5 =

11. 1/2 x 2/3 =

12 1/2 ÷ 1/3 =

13. 3/4 ÷ 1/3 =

6. 2/3 − 1/3 =

7. 3/5 − 1/2 =

8. 7/8 − 1/4 =

14. 2/3 ÷ 1/3 =

15. 5/6 ÷ 2/3 =

Fractions – Quiz

1. True or False: The number 2 1/3 is considered a Mixed Number.

2. True or False: The reciprocal of 2/3 is 3/2.

Solve and Reduce the following Problems

1. 2/3 + 1/6 =

2. 3/4 + 1/8 =

3. 1/3 + 1/6 + 1/2 =

4. 3/16 – 1/8 =

5. 2/3 – 1/9 =

6. 1/8 x 1/2 =

7. 3/4 x 3/5 =

8. 2/3 x 1/3 x 1/9 =

9. 3/5 ÷ 1/3 =

10. 4/5 ÷ 1/2 =

Ratios / Proportions / Percents

Ratios, Proportions, and Percents are all mathematical descriptions of relationships between numbers.

Ratios

A Ratio is the expression of a relationship between two ideas, objects, or numbers. For example, if there are 5 oranges and 3 apples, what is the ratio of oranges to apples? The answer is 5 to 3, or expressed mathematically as 5:3 or 5/3.

Write the following examples as ratios:

1. If there are 5 red apples and 7 green apples, what is the ratio? 5:7 or 5/7

2. If there are 9 horses and 4 cows in the pasture, what is the ratio of horses to cows? 9:4 or 9/4 (NOTE: ratios do not get reduced to mixed numbers)

3. If a classroom has 22 desks and 25 students, what is the ratio of desks to students? 22:25 or 22/25

Ratios can also be expressed in a table to show a pattern:

1	3
2	6
3	9
4	12
5	18

4	5
8	10
12	15
16	20
20	25

10000	400
2000	200
400	100
80	50
16	25

1	1
3	4
5	7
7	10
9	13

The first table expressed a ratio of counting by ones to counting by threes, the second table represents a ratio of multiples of 4 multiples to multiples of 5, the third table shows a ratio of dividing by 5 to dividing by 2, and the fourth table shows a ratio of adding 2 to adding 3.

Comparing Ratios

Ratios can be compared as being greater than one or the other, less than one or the other, or equivalent. To determine the relationship between the ratios, the cross numbers are multiplied.

Example: To compare 2:3 = 4:6, the ratios are re-written as fractions. So, 2:3 = 2/3 and 4:6 = 4/6. Then, cross-multiply the numbers of the fractions. The denominator of 2/3, which is 3, multiplies the numerator of 4/6, which is 4, for a product of 12 and the denominator of 4/6, which is 6, multiplies the numerator of 2/3, which is 2, for a product of 12. So, these ratios are equivalent.

More Examples:

1. There are 12 ducks to 18 ducklings and 4 geese to 6 goslings. Are the ratios ducks to ducklings and geese to goslings equivalent?

Convert the ratios to fractions. Now, are 12/18 and 4/6 equivalent? Multiply 18 and 4 for a product of 72, and multiply 6 and 12 for a product of 72. So, the ratios are equivalent.

2. Are 2/3 and 6/7 equivalent? Multiply 3 and 6 for 18, and 2 and 7 for 14. So these ratios are not equivalent.

Proportions

Proportions are two ratios that are equivalent. If the ratios are not equivalent, they are not proportional. Ratios that are proportional are described like A is to B as C is to D. For example, the written proportion is stated one is to three as two is to six. To write the proportion numerically, the numbers need to be written in the order they are stated. So, one is to three = 1/3 and two is to six = 2/6. To show they are equivalent and thus proportional, the ratios are written as 1/3 = 2/6.

Examples:

1 Which ratio pairs are proportional?

a) 3/4 = 9/12   b) 1/3 = 3/6   c) 2/3 = 8/12   d) 4/5 = 8/10

To get the answer, cross-multiply the ratios.

Answers:

a) does 4 x 9 = 3 x 12? 36 = 36, yes, the ratios are proportional

b) does 3 x 3 = 6 x 1? 9 ≠ 6, no, the ratios are not proportional

c) does 3 x 8 = 12 x 2? 24 = 24, yes, they are proportional

d) does 10 x 4 = 5 x 8, 40 = 40, yes, they are proportional

Completing / Solving Proportions

Solving proportions involves cross-multiplying and then solving for an unknown portion of one of the ratios. Many times, story problems are solved using proportions.

Basic Example: 3/7 = x/21 Cross-multiply 7x = 63 and solve for x, x = 63/7 = 9, x = 9

1/3 = x/9 Cross-multiply 3x = 9 and solve for x, x = 9/3 = 3, x = 3

Story Problem with Proportions

The ratio of cardinals to blue jays in Karen's backyard is 2 to 7. If 28 blue jays were spotted one day, how many cardinals were there?

So, the ratios are 2 cardinals to 7 blue jays are equivalent to C cardinals to 28 blue jays. Numerically written the proportion is 2/7 = C/28. To solve for the number of cardinals (C), the ratios are cross-multiplied. So, 7C = 2 x 28 = 56 and solve for C, 7C = 56, C = 8. So, there were 8 cardinals in Karen's yard the same day 28 blue jays were spotted.

Percents

A percent is a fraction with 100 in the denominator written using the % symbol. So, 20/100 = 20%, 33/100 = 33%, and 47/100 = 47%.

Fractions can also be expressed as percents when converted to a denominator equal to 100. For example, what is 3/5 expressed as a percent? Since 5 x 20 = 100, the percent is expressed as a numerator of 3 x 20 = 60, over the denominator of 5 x 20 = 100 or 60/100, which is 60%.

Finding percents using proportions:

1. If 34/68 = x/100, solve for x by cross-multiplying. So, 3,400 = 68x, x = 3,400/68, x = 50. So, 34/68 = 50/100 = 50%

2. If 24/96 = x/100, what percent is 24 out of 96? Cross-multiply to get 2,400 = 96x, solve for x, x = 2,400/96 = 25, x = 25. So, 24/96 = 25/100 = 25%

Solving percents as story problems

If Twenty percent of the 6th grade participated in a fundraising event and 10 students earned over $100 each, how many students participated in the event?

First a Ratio Table is made:

Students Participating	Ratio	Actual
Earned over $100	20	10
Earned Less than $100	80	X
Total	100	Y

If 20/100 = 10/y, y = 50

If 80/100 = 10/x, x = 40

So total number of students participating in the event was 40 + 10 = 50

How many students are in the 6th Grade? $20/100 = 50/z$, $20z = 5{,}000$, $z = 5{,}000/20 = 250$. So, 50 out of 250 students participated and 10 earned more than $100.

Ratios / Proportions / Percent's - Practice Sheet

Fill in the Blanks

1. A _____ is an expression of the relationship between two numbers.

2. A _____ is the representation of two _____ that are equivalent.

3. _____ are fractions that have 100 in the denominator and are designated by using the _____ symbol.

Express the following as Ratios

1. A shopper buys 6 pears and 5 apples. What is the ratio of pears to apples? What is the ratio of apples to pears?

2. Seven ducks and 3 geese are spotted on a neighborhood lake. What is the ratio of ducks to geese and then geese to ducks?

Write the Proportions as Ratios and Fractions

1. Two is to four as three is to six

2. Three is to nine as four is to twelve

3. Seven is to fourteen as eight is to sixteen

True or False

1. To determine whether a pair of ratios are equivalent or not, the fraction representation of the ratios are cross-multiplied.

2. Ratios are proportional if they are NOT equivalent.

3. Percents can be determined by cross-multiplying the ratios.

4. Ratios, when expressed as fractions, are always reduced.

5. The order of the numbers in ratios is not a factor when solving for equivalency or calculating a proportionate value.

6. Sixty percent can be written as 60/100 and 60%

Solve the Problems

1. Are the ratios 2:3 and 6:9 equivalent?

2. Are the ratios 3:4 and 5:6 equivalent?

3.

4	5
8	?
12	15
16	20
20	25

4. What percent of 64 is 16? (hint: the problem set up looks like this 16/64 = x/100)

5. The ratio of fox to deer in the nature center is 3 to 12. If 24 deer were counted on Tuesday, how many fox were present as well?

6. If 30 percent of the total number of student drivers of 90 passed their driving exam, how many students total passed? How many did not pass?

Ratios / Proportions / Percent's - Quiz

Are the following ratio pairs proportional?

1. 3/4 = 9/12
2. 1/3 = 3/6
3. 2/3 = 8/12
4. 4/5 = 8/10

Solve for x (percent)

1. What percentage of 52 is 13?

2. What is 25 percent of 180?

3.

1	1
3	4
5	x
7	10
9	13

5. If the ratio of blue pencils to red pencils in a classroom is 6 to 3, and one box of colored pencils contains 24 blue pencils, how many red pencils are in the box?

6. If 20 percent of the graduating class of 600 seniors are already accepted to a college, what number of students have not yet been accepted?

Measurements

We use a mixture of measurements throughout our society. Both standard and metric units of measurement are used throughout our daily routines. Standard units include feet, yards, pounds, cups, gallons, Fahrenheit, etc. Metric units include meters, grams, kilograms, liters, Celsius, etc.

During sixth grade students learn how to convert and compare both types of measurements.

Standard Units of Measurement (U.S. Standard Units)

The most common units of standard measurement are:

Length: inches, feet and yards (in, ft, yd)

Weight: ounces and pounds (oz, lb)

Volume: cups, pints, quarts, and gallons (C, pt, qt, gal)

These Standard Units of Measurement can also be expressed as equivalent values:

12 inches = 1 foot

3 feet = 1 yard

5,280 feet = 1 mile

1,760 yards = 1 mile

16 ounces = 1 pound

2 cups = 1 pint

2 pints = 1 quart

4 quarts = 1 gallon

By using the standard units of measurement, students can calculate a variety of lengths, widths, depths, areas, weights, and volumes. Practice in the classroom using these units of measure prepares the students for measuring items, objects, and containers in their daily life outside school. We use these standard measurements to decorate our homes, bake cookies, prepare emergency kits, plan car trips, track our weight gain or loss, etc.

For example, if a decorator wants to hang a specific picture in the living room, the picture and wall need to be measured to determine if the picture will fit on the wall and to calculate the best spot on the wall to hang the picture. The proper units of measure for this activity are inches to measure the picture and feet to measure the wall.

Solve the following measurement problems using standard units:

1. If a dresser measures 24 inches in width and 6 feet in length, will it fin into a room 10 feet long and 15 feet wide? Yes, because the length of the dresser is only 6 feet and both the length and width of the room are long enough to accommodate the dresser easily.

2. A cart can handle carrying a total weight of 500 lbs. If three items weighing 100 lbs each and 5 items weighing 16 oz each are loaded on to this cart, will it be able to handle the total weight?

3. The water level in a 1,200 gal pool is down to 900 gal. If 200 gal, 20 qts, and 16 pints are added, will the pool overflow?

Converting Standard Units

In order to change from one unit of measure to another, a unit multiplier needs to be used. The unit multiplier is a fraction that equals one and is composed of the two units being compared and changed.

To convert from inches and feet, the unit multiplier is 1 foot/12 inches and 12 inches/1 foot depending on which unit is being converted. To convert inches to feet, inches needs to be the unit in the denominator of the unit multiplier and to convert feet to inches, the unit multiplier needs to have feet in the denominator.

For example, to convert 24 inches to feet, the following equation is used: 24 inches x 1 foot/12 inches. Since inches/inches = 1, the units are canceled out. The equation becomes 24 x 1 foot/12 = 24 feet/12 = 2 feet.

To convert cups to pints the unit multiplier is 1pint/2 cups. So, converting 6 cups to pints involves the following equation: 6 cups x 1 pint/2 cups = 6 x 1 pint/2 = 3 pints.

Converting pounds to oz uses the multiplier 16 oz/1 lb. So, 18 lbs x 16oz/1 lb = 18 x 16 oz/1 = 288 oz.

Metric Units of Measurement

Metric Units are based on powers of ten and units are converted from one size to another by moving the decimal point to reflect the unit value. The most popular Metric Units of Measurement are the following:

Length: Kilometer, meter, centimeter, millimeter (km, m, cm, mm)

Mass: Kilograms, grams, milligrams (kg, g, mg)

Volume: Liter and milliliter (l and ml)

Converting metric units is relatively easy and involves moving the decimal point to reflect the appropriate place value. Equivalent metric units are presented below:

1 m = 100 cm

1 m = 1,000 mm

1 cm = 10 mm

1 km = 1,000 m

1 kg = 1,000 g

1 g = 1,000 mg

1 l = 1,000 ml

Examples of Using and Converting Metric Units

1. If a race is measured to be 5 km, how many meters will be run? Since 1 km = 1,000 m, then 5 km = 5,000 meters. The decimal point for 5.000 is moved three spaces to the right to represent thousands. So, 5 becomes 5,000.

A unit multiplier can also be used like that used in standard unit conversions. For this problem, the unit multiplier is 1,000 m/1 km and the equation is 5 km x 1,000 m/1 km = 5 x 1,000 m/1 = 5,000 m.

2. An object weighs 210 kg. How much does the object weigh in grams? Since there are 1,000 g in each kg, the decimal point is moved 3 places to the right to get the answer 210,000 g or the unit multiplier 1,000 g/1 kg is used to convert the units. The equation using the unit multiplier is 210 kg x 1,000 g/1 kg = 210,000.

3. A scientist has a total volume of 2.5 liters of a liquid that needs to be tested using milliliter volumes. To convert from l to ml by moving the decimal to the right three places gives an answer of 2,500 ml. A unit multiplier can also be used to find the answer. The unit multiplier for this problem is 1,000 ml/1 l, so, the equation is 2.5 l x 1,000 ml/1 l = 2,500 ml. Therefore, the scientist needs 2,500 ml tubes of the liquid to conduct the tests.

Converting between Popular Standard Units and Most Common Metric Units

1 inch = 2.54 cm   1 cm = 0.39 in

1 mile = 1.6 km   1 km = 0.62 mi

1 gal = 3.79 l

1 kg = 2.2 lbs   1 lb = 0.45 kg

To convert Celsius to Fahrenheit, multiply the temperature value by 9/5 then add 32.

To convert Fahrenheit to Celsius, subtract 32 from the temperature value then multiply by 5/9.

To convert between metric units and standard units of measurement, one or more unit multipliers are needed.

To convert from inches to centimeters, the following unit multiplier is used:

2 inches x 2.54 cm/1 inch = 2 x 2.54 cm/1 = 4.9 cm

Remember that the unit being converted needs to be in the denominator of the unit multiplier.

To convert from miles to kilometers the following unit multiplier is used:

5 miles x 1.6 km/1 mile = 5 x 1.6 km/1 = 8 km

To convert gallons to liters, the following unit multiplier is used:

3 gallons x 3.79 liters/1 gallon = 3 x 3.79 l/1 = 11.37 l

To convert pounds to kilograms, the following unit multiplier is used:

150 lbs x 0.45 kg/1 lb = 150 x 0.45 kg/1 = 67.5 kg

To convert Fahrenheit to Celsius use the following formula: temperature x 9/5 + 32

85 degrees Fahrenheit becomes 85 x 9/5 = 153 degrees Celsius

Measurements – Practice Sheet

Standard Conversions	Metric Conversions	Standard to Metric Conversions	
12 inches = 1 foot	1 m = 100 cm	1 inch = 2.54 cm	1 cm = 0.39 in
3 feet = 1 yard	1 m = 1,000 mm	1 mile = 1.6 km	1 km = 0.62 mi
5,280 feet = 1 mile	1 cm = 10 mm	1 gal = 3.79 l	
1,760 yards = 1 mile	1 km = 1,000 m	1 kg = 2.2 lbs	1 lb = 0.45 kg
16 ounces = 1 pound	1 kg = 1,000 g	Celsius to Fahrenheit = Temp x 9/5 + 32	
	1 g = 1,000 mg		
2 cups = 1 pint		Fahrenheit to Celsius = Temp - 32 x 5/9	
2 pints = 1 quart	1 l = 1,000 ml		
4 quarts = 1 gallon			

1. Which units, standard and metric, are the best for measuring the top of a small table?

2. Which units, standard and metric, are best for measuring a person's weight?

3. Which units, standard and metric, are best for measuring the amount of water in a bathtub?

Solve the following problems:

1. How many inches are in 37 feet?

2. How many feet are in 18 yards?

3. How many inches are in 2 yards?

4. How many pounds equal 64 oz?

5. How many yards in 3 miles?

6. How many gallons equal 84 quarts?

7. How many pints in 3 gallons?

8. How many mm in 25 cm?

9. How many meters equal 827 cm?

10. How many kg equal 340 g?

11. A race is 12 km long. How many meters is the racing course?

12. If a tree is 18 meters tall, how many cm tall is the tree?

13. A package weighs 3 kg, what is its weight in grams?

14. A laboratory assistant needs to prepare 320 ml containers with a special solution. How many Liters are needed to fill all the ml containers?

15. A car mechanic is working on a car that needs some hosing replaced. The hosing is sold by the foot, but the car's parts use metric units. How many feet are needed to replace a 81cm hose?

16. How many miles are in 23 km?

17. A teacher needs to fill a 24-liter tub using 1-gallon containers of punch. How many gallons will she need to fill the tub?

18. A rock climber scales a 300 ft rock face. How many meters has he covered?

19. The temperature outside today is 34 degrees Fahrenheit. What is the same temperature in degrees Celsius?

20. In Hawaii today, it is a balmy 25 degrees Celsius. What is the temperature in Fahrenheit?

Measurements – Quiz

True or False

1. Length can be measured using kilometers and yards.

2. Kilograms and pounds are unit measurements for weight.

3. Liters and pints are about equal in measurement.

4. Miles and meters are equivalent lengths of measurement.

Standard Conversions	Metric Conversions	Standard to Metric Conversions	
12 inches = 1 foot	1 m = 100 cm	1 inch = 2.54 cm	1 cm = 0.39 in
3 feet = 1 yard	1 m = 1,000 mm	1 mile = 1.6 km	1 km = 0.62 mi
5,280 feet = 1 mile	1 cm = 10 mm	1 gal = 3.79 l	
1,760 yards = 1 mile	1 km = 1,000 m	1 kg = 2.2 lbs	1 lb = 0.45 kg
16 ounces = 1 pound	1 kg = 1,000 g	Celsius to Fahrenheit = Temp x 9/5 + 32	
	1 g = 1,000 mg		
2 cups = 1 pint		Fahrenheit to Celsius = Temp - 32 x 5/9	
2 pints = 1 quart	1 l = 1,000 ml		
4 quarts = 1 gallon			

Solve the following problems:

1. A football field is 100 yards long. How many feet long is the same football field?

2. A fish tank at a famous celebrity's house holds 2,000 gallons. How many liters does it contain?

3. How many football fields equal 10 miles? (remember 1 football field is 100 yards)

4. If it is 10 degrees Fahrenheit on January 1, 2014 in Montana, what is the same temperature in Celsius?

5. If a professional basketball player is 6 feet 7 inches tall, what is his total height in inches?

6. How many cm tall is the basketball player from Question 5?

Functions and Probability

Functions

A function is the pairing of one unknown number with exactly one other unknown, and different, number. To use a function to solve mathematical problems, the formula for the function must have three components: input value, the output value and the relationship that unites them in a formula.

The notation for a function is usually written as f(x), where x equals the input value. The whole formula for a function is usually written as f(x) = the relationship between x and the output.

Some examples of functions are:

1. $f(x) = x^2$ This function takes the value (x) [input] squares it [relationship], and generates an answer [output].

    The above function is described as follows: f of x equals x squared.

2. $f(x) = (x) \times 2$ This function takes the value (x) and multiplies it by two to generate an answer.

    The above function is described as follows: f of x equals (x) times 2

Functions are used to process several elements of a specific group to generate another specific group of values. These specific elements or groups are referred to as sets. Another definition for Function is that a specific function relates each element (values) of a set to exactly one other element (value) of another set.

Examples

1. Using the function f(x) = x + 2, what is the output if x = 5. The function would be written as f(5) = 5 + 2 = 7, so f(5) = 7.

What would the output be for an input set of 2, 5, 8, 13, and 21? By understanding that the function is x + 2, each number will have 2 added to get the output answers. So, the outputs are 4, 7, 10, 15, and 23.

2. Using the function $f(x) = x^3$, determine the output for x = 3. So, $f(3) = 3^3 = 3 \times 3 \times 3 = 27$ and $f(3) = 27$. Using an input set of 1, 2, 3, 4, and 5, the output data will be 1, 8, 27, 64, and 125.

When using sets, the input, relationship, and output have specific qualities and names. The names of these sets are Domain, Codomain, and Range.

The Domain is the set of specific input numbers for a function.

The Codomain is the set of all numbers possible by using the function.

The Range is the set of numbers that are actually generated by the function.

(NOTE: The Range is actually a subset of the Codomain)

However, the Codomain can determine whether a formula or calculation is a function or not. So, when specifying a Codomain from which the Range is taken from, be sure it meets the definition of a function when paired with a function formula and Domain.

The basic process for using Domain (input) and Range (output) is:

Domain ---> Function ----> Range

For the purpose of ease, the Domain and Codomain will be taken from whole numbers and fractions separately.

Examples

1. $f(x) = x^2 - 1$ and the Domain is {even numbers 2 through 12}, what is the Range?

Range = {3, 15, 35, 63, 99, and 143}

2. f(x) = (x + 3) x 2 and the Domain is {1 through 10, whole numbers}, What is the Range?

Range = {8, 10, 12, 14, 16, 18, 20, 22, 24, and 26}

In summary, functions allow numbers to be processed in a specific manner to get a specific answer to a specific question.

Probability

Probability is the likelihood that a specific event or outcome will occur based on a specific set of circumstances.

The general equation for calculating Probability=

$$\frac{\text{Number of Desired Outcomes}}{\text{Total Possible Outcomes}} \quad \text{OR} \quad \frac{\text{Desired Outcomes}}{\text{Total Possible}}$$

OR

Because Probability is expressed as a fraction, its value will always be between 0 and 1. A number line shows this concept more clearly:

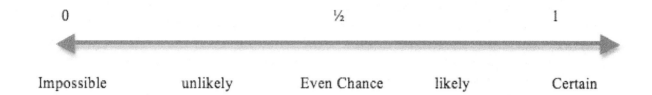

Examples of Calculating Probability:

1. Flipping a coin has a historical record for deciding many outcomes and decisions for various situations. Since a coin has 2 sides, that is the value for the Total Possible Outcomes and because only 1 side at a time is chosen each time the coin is flipped, the desired outcome is 1. Therefore, if Desired Outcome/Total Possible Outcomes equals the Probability of the specific result, the Probability of flipping heads or tails is ½. According to the number line above, that means there is an even chance each time the coin is flipped to get either heads or tails.

2. Another Probability example involves a deck of 52 playing cards. Each card is represented in the deck 4 times, so there are 4 desired cards regardless of which card is chosen. However, to be more specific, the question of what is the Probability of drawing a 5 from a deck of 52 cards will be calculated.

Since there are 4 desired cards out of 52 possible cards, the ratio of desired outcome to possible outcome is 4/52. Since ratios are normally reduces, the Probability of drawing a 5 from 52 playing cards is 1/13.

3. Sometimes Probability is referred to as a Chance expressed as a percent. The meteorologists are always reporting future weather as an x% chance of rain, snow, sleet, sun, etc. Since percents are also ratios, a Probability can be calculated regarding the weather. If the meteorologist reports that there is a 30% chance (probability) of snow on Sunday, what is the chance it will not snow?

Since 100% means it will definitely snow, and 0% means it will definitely not snow, and the ratio has to use whole positive numbers, the Probability that it will snow is 30/100 or 3/10. The number 100 is the value for the total possible outcomes because percents need to total 100. Since we were given the value for the probability of snow, the difference between 100 and 30 = 70, which gives the value for the desired outcome. So, 70 (desired outcome)/100 Total Possible Outcome = 70/100 or 70%. So, the answer is there is a 70% chance that it will not snow.

The above examples calculated the probability of a single event, but could still be defined as experiments or trials with just one event. However, if the coin is repeatedly flipped and heads or tails predicted and several cards were drawn successively from the deck of 52 cards trying to find a 5, they would be considered to be a series of events.

The basic formula for finding the Probability of a Series of Events is by multiplying the individual event probabilities with each other. In the case of the coin flipping experiment, each time the coin was flipped, the probability that either heads or tails would show was calculated to be ½.

If, we flip the coin two times in a row, what is the probability that it will show heads both times. To calculate the probability of both flips, each individual probability is multiplied together: ½ x ½ = ¼. So the probability that two heads will show in a row is ¼.

Functions and Probability – Practice Sheet

Functions

True or False

1. The formula for the function must have three components: input value, the output value and the relationship that unites them in a formula.

2. The formula $f(x) = x^3$ by using this formula, all values of x will be cubed.

3. Domain is the set of numbers calculated from the function (output).

4. Range is the set of numbers calculated from the function (output).

Solve

1. $f(x) = x + 5$, when $x = 4$, what is the output?

2. $f(x) = x - 2$, when $x = 7$, what is the output?

3. $f(x) = x^2$, when $x = 3$, what is the output?

4. $f(x) = x/2$, when $x = 12$, what is the output?

5. $f(x) = x^2 + 3$, when $x = 6$, what is the output?

6. $f(x) = x - 3$, where x = {even numbers from 4 to 12}, what is the Range?

7. f(x) = 3x + 1, where x = {1, 2, 3, 4, 5, and 6}, what is the Range?

8. f(x) = 5x, where x = {odd numbers 3 through 13}, what is the Range?

Probability

True or False

1. The Probability of an occurrence or event can also be referred to as a Chance the occurrence or event will happen.

2. To calculate Probability, a ratio of Desired Outcome to Total Possible Outcomes is created and solved.

3. It is not possible to calculate the Probability of a series of events occurring.

Solve

1. What is the Probability of showing heads when you flip a coin?

2. What is the Probability of rolling a 6 when you roll a single die?

3. What is the Probability of drawing the 5 of Hearts from a deck of 52 cards?

4. What is the probability of showing heads twice in a row when flipping a coin?

5. What is the Probability of a Sunny Day if the meteorologist predicts a 30% chance of rain showers on Sunday?

Functions and Probability – Quiz

True or False

1. Domain and Range are used as input and output values for functions.

2. Probability is the likelihood that an event will occur during a specific set of circumstances.

3. The percent chance that an event will occur is an aspect of Probability.

Solve

1. $f(x) = 2x + 3$, when $x = 4$, what is the output?

2. $f(x) = x^3 - 5$, when $x = 3$, what is the output?

3. $f(x) = 4x - 2$, where the Domain is {1,2,3,4,5,and 6}, what is the Range?

4. What is the Probability that out of a set of 3 red pencils, 4 blue pencils, and 4 yellow pencils, a student will choose a red pencil?

5. If there is an 80% chance that a student will get above 90% on a math test, what is the Probability that the student will not get 90%?

Geometry

Geometry is all about shapes: drawing shapes, naming shapes, calculating both Perimeter and Area for shapes, and understanding the angles that hold them together.

The following are the shapes that will be discussed in this section and their Names:

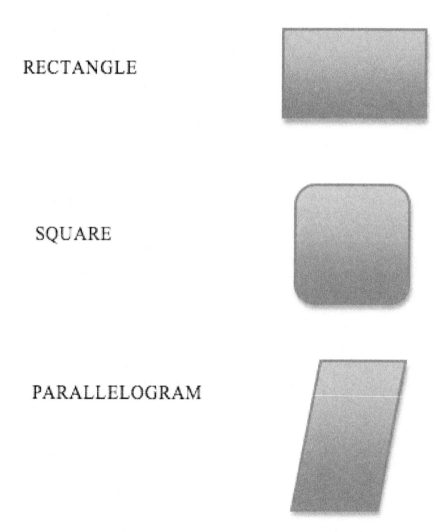

RECTANGLE

SQUARE

PARALLELOGRAM

RIGHT TRIANGLE

ACUTE TRIANGLE

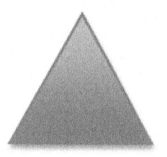

The above shapes are defined by their mathematical qualities and specific dimensions with regard to their angles. All shapes are called polygons. A polygon is any straight-sided closed shape

Rectangles, squares, and parallelograms are called quadrilaterals and are composed of four sides and four angles. Triangles have three sides and three angles. Polygons are generally named for their number of sides and angles. For example, an octagon has eight angles and eight sides, a hexagon has six angles and sides, and a pentagon has five angles and sides.

Triangles are a special polygon. They are the smallest form of polygon, since only two sides cannot be enclosed and instead form an angle. Triangles are classified according to the length of their sides and their types of angles.

The triangles classified by their sides are equilateral (all sides are equal), isosceles (at least two sides are equal), and scalene (all sides are different lengths). The triangles classified by their angles are acute triangle (all three angles are less than 90 degrees), right triangle (one angle is a right angle or 90 degrees), and an obtuse triangle (one angle is obtuse or greater than 90 degrees).

There are also a few special quadrilaterals. The parallelogram is characterized by having two pairs of parallel sides, the rectangle is a parallelogram with right angles, and a square is a rectangle with four equal sides.

Perimeter

One of the calculations regarding quadrilaterals and triangles that Sixth Grade students will need to learn is Perimeter. The Perimeter of a polygon is the line surrounding the shape. It is calculated by adding the lengths of each side to get a total length around the entire shape. **Regular polygons** are those where all their sides are equal. For example, a regular octagon, like a stop sign, has eight equal sides and eight equal angles.

Presented below are some formulas that will help the student calculate Perimeter for quadrilaterals and triangles:

Square = 4 x side (each side is equal, so multiplying one side by 4 will calculate the Perimeter.

Rectangle = 2 x length + 2 x width or 2 x (l + w) (since the widths are the same length and the lengths are the same lengths, multiplying each by 2 and adding their products will calculate the Perimeter.

Parallelogram = 2 x the base + 2 x a side, similar in calculation to the Perimeter of a rectangle.

Triangle = side 1 + side 2 + side 3

Example Problems

1. What is the Perimeter of an equilateral triangle where s = 4? Since the sides are all equal, one side can be multiplied 3 times to get the Perimeter. So, Perimeter = 3 x 4 = 12.

2. What is the Perimeter of a rectangle with a length of 8 and a width of 3? Perimeter equals 2l + 2w = 16 + 6 = 22

3. What is the Perimeter of a square with sides measuring 7 inches? Perimeter of a square = 4 x side = 4 x 7 = 28 inches.

4. What is the Perimeter of a parallelogram with a base of 12 and a side measurement of 3? Perimeter = 2b + 2s = 24 + 6 = 30.

Area

Another value calculated for polygons is Area. The Area of a polygon is the space surrounded and enclosed by the Perimeter. The following formulas apply to calculating Area for quadrilaterals and triangles:

Square = side x side or s^2

Rectangle = length x width or lw

Parallelogram = base x height or bh

Triangle = ½ bh

Example Problems

1. What is the area of a rectangle with a length of 12 and a width of 5? Since Area = lw, 12 x 5 = Area = 60

2. What is the area of a square if its sides each measure 8? Area = s^2 = 8^2 = 64

3. What is the Area of a parallelogram with a base of 13 and a height of 2? Area = bh, so, the Area = 13 x 2 = 26

4. What is the Area of a triangle with a base of 4 and a height of 7? Area = ½ bh, so, Area = ½ (4)(7) = ½ x 28 = 14

Angles of Polygons

The Sum of the inside angles of a polygon equals 360 degrees, with the exception of triangles which have an interior angle total of 180 degrees. The types of angles found within polygons are acute, right, and obtuse. As long as they add up to 360 degrees, the number of angles and types of angles are only constrained by the type of polygon.

Example Problems

1. A right triangle has two angles at 45 degrees. What is the measurement of the remaining angle? Since the total of all the angles equals 180 degrees, the remaining angle = 180 – 90 = 90 degrees.

2. What do each of the six angles in a regular hexagon measure? Answer: 360 ÷ 6 = 60 degrees.

3. An irregular polygon with four sides has three angles measuring 30 degrees, 40 degrees, and 100 degrees. What is the measurement of the fourth angle? Answer: 360 –170 = 190 degrees.

Mixed Problems

1. A rectangle has a length of 23 meters and a width of 10 meters. What are the Perimeter and Area of the rectangle? Answer: Perimeter = 2l + 2w = 46 + 20 = 66 meters. Area = lw = 23 x 10 = 230 square meters.

2. An equilateral triangle has sides measuring 7 feet and a height of 10 feet. What is the Perimeter and the Area and what is the measurement of each angle? Perimeter = 3 x 7 = 21 feet, Area = ½ 7 x 10 = 70/2 = 35 square feet. The measurement of each angle is 180 degrees ÷ 3 = 60 degrees.

3. An irregular polygon with five sides with each side measuring as follows: 3 inches, 5 inches, 7, inches, 5 inches, and 3 inches. What is the Perimeter of this polygon? Perimeter = Sum of the sides = 3 + 5 + 7 + 5 + 3 = 23 inches.

Geometry – Practice Sheet

1. Which type of polygon has three sides?

2. Which type of polygon has four equal sides and four interior angle measurements of 90 degrees each?

3. Which type of polygon has eight sides and eight equal interior angles?

4. Which type of triangle has three equal sides?

5. True or False: A rectangle is a parallelogram.

6. What is the Perimeter of a rectangle with a length of 30 inches and a width of 15 inches?

7. What is the Area of the rectangle in Problem 6?

8. What is the Perimeter of a square with each side measuring 8 feet?

9. What is the Area of the square in Problem 8?

10. Why is the area of a triangle ½ bh, while the area of a parallelogram is bh?

11. If a polygon with five sides has four angles measuring a total of 195 degrees. What is the value of the fifth angle?

12. What is the total area of a house's footprint if the footprint is composed of 5 squares, each with a side measurement of 15 feet?

13. What is the Perimeter of a parallelogram with a base of 14 and a side measurement of 6?

14. What are the angle measurements of a right triangle?

15. True or False: There are six triangle types. Three are classified by the lengths of their sides and three are classified according to their angle measurements.

16. What are the lengths of the sides of a square if the Area is 16?

17. What is the Perimeter of a regular Octagon if each side is 32 inches long?

18. True or False: A parallelogram is a regular polygon.

19. True or False: An obtuse triangle has at least one angle that is greater than 90 degrees.

20. True or False: an isosceles triangle has at least two equal sides.

Geometry – Quiz

1. Which type of polygon has four equal sides and four interior angles measuring 90 degrees each?

2. Which triangle has at least one angle greater than 90 degrees?

3. What is the definition of a parallelogram?

4. What is the total inside angle measurement of a triangle?

5. What is the definition of a Regular Polygon?

6. What is the Perimeter of a rectangle with a length of 25 feet and a width of 10 feet?

7. What is the Area of a square with sides each measuring 6 feet?

8. What is the value of the fourth angle of a quadrilateral, if the total of the other three is 220 degrees?

9. What is the Area of a triangle with a height of 10 feet and a base of 10 feet?

10. The Perimeter of a rectangular pool is 60 feet. If the width is 10 feet, what is the Area the pool covers?

Answer Key

Whole Numbers – Practice Sheet

1. True or **False**: Whole Numbers include all numbers along a number line.

2. **True** or False: Mental math involves memorizing single-digit addition, subtraction, multiplication and division.

3. **True** or False: After studying the fact family table, certain patterns regarding adding and subtracting become visible.

4. **True** or False: The answer to an addition problem is called the Sum.

5. True or **False**: The answer to a subtraction problem is called the Divisor.

6. True or **False**: ⅚ is a whole number.

7. **True** or False: Adding together non-whole numbers like fractions or decimals can produce an answer that is a whole number.

8. **True** or False: A whole number subtracted from another whole number can produce an answer that is NOT a whole number.

9. Which of the following is NOT a whole number: 1, 5, ½, 12, -4, 18, 25, 1.2, 7, -8   ANSWER: ½, -4, 1.2, -8

10. Which of the following is a whole number: 1.52, -8, 3, 12½, 6, -14, 9, 1¼

    ANSWER: 3, 6, 9

11. What is the Sum of 5 and 4? 9

12. What is the Sum of 15 and 5?   20

13.   What are the factors of 12 and 18?   1

   2: 1, 12, 3, 4, 2, 6   18: 1, 18, 2, 9, 3, 6   What is the Least Common Factor (not including 1) and what is the Greatest Common Factor between 12 and 18?

   Least = 2, Greatest = 6

14. What is the Difference between 19 and 7?   12

16. What is the Difference between 25 and 5?   20

17. What is the Difference between 18 and 3?   15

18. What is the Product of 4 and 7?   28

19. What is the Product of 20 and 13? 260

20. What is the Quotient of 25 and 5?   5

Whole Numbers – Quiz

1. True or **False**: Negative numbers are whole numbers.

2. True or **False**: Whole numbers are the numbers zero and greater including fractions and decimals.

3. What is the Sum of 14 and 15?   29

4. What is the Sum of 18 and 5?   23

5. What is the Difference between 19 and 6?   13

6. Which number is closer to 100, 85 or 123?   123

7. What is the product of 5 and 25?   125

8. What is the Product of 8 and 4?   32

9. What is the Quotient of 12 and 3?   4

10. What are the factors of 30 and 48? What is the Least Common Factor between 30 and 48?

    30 = 1, 30, 2, 15, 3, 10, 5, 6

    48 = 1, 48, 2, 24, 3, 16, 4, 12

    Least Common Factor (not including 1) = 2

    Greatest Common Factor = 3

Operations with Whole Numbers – Practice Sheet

1. What are the four main whole number operations learned and practiced in sixth grade? Addition, Subtraction, Multiplication, Division

2. Fill in the blank

Students use _____ families to help them memorize single-digit addition and subtraction operations.
 FACT

Fill in the blanks for the following fact families:

1. _3_ + 2 = 5, 5 - _3_ = 2, 2 + _3_ = 5, 5 – 2 = _3_

2. 8 + _7_ = 15, _7_ + 8 = 15, _15_ - 8 = 7, 15 – _7_ = 8

3. _15_ + 5 = 20, 5 + _15_ = 20, 20 - _15_ = 5, 20 – 5 = _15_

Fill in the blanks for the following factor families:

1. 2 x _6_ = 12, _6_ x 2 = 12, 12 ÷ 2 = _6_, 12 ÷ _6_ = 2

2. 3 x _4_ = 12, _4_ x 3 = 12, 12 ÷ _4_ = 3, 12 ÷ 3 = _4_

3. 7 x _5_ = 35, _5_ x 7 = 35, 35 ÷ _5_ = 7, 35 ÷ 7 = _5_

Complete the following mathematical operations:

1. 23 + 8 = _31_   5. 34 x 5 = _170_

1. Write the Product for the following exponents: $2^3, 4^2, 5^4, 10^6$

2. $18 + 17 = \_\_\_35\_\_\_$

3. $31 - 12 = \_\_\_19\_\_\_$

4. $57 - 19 = \_\_\_36\_\_\_$

6. $23 \times 8 = \_\_\_\_184\_\_\_\_$

7. $25 \div 5 = \_\_\_\_5\_$

8. $63 \div 7 = \_\_\_9\_\_\_$

ANSWER: 8, 16, 625, 1,000,000

2. Explain the order of operations to correctly solve the following problem:

$(10 + 20) - 3^2 + 1 - 4 \times 2 \div 8 = 21$

Solve Parentheses first, then exponents, then multiplication, division, adding and subtracting from left to right.

Operations with Whole Numbers – Quiz

1. Name one mathematical operation that uses whole numbers. Addition

2. Write all the single-digit equations for calculating a Sum of 8.

ANSWER $1 + 7 = 8, 2 + 6 = 8, 3 + 5 = 8, 4 + 4 = 8$

3. What are the factors for 27? 1, 27, 3, 9

4. Which factors can you multiply to calculate 90?

ANSWER: 1 and 90, 2 and 45, 3 and 30, 5 and 18, 10 and 9

Solve the following problems:

1. 184 + 2,376 = 2,560

2. 1,007 – 38 = 969

3. 832 x 23 = 19,136

4. 255 ÷ 5 = 51

Write the answers for:

1. 5^2 = ___25___, 3^4 = __81_____, 10^2 = ___100___

2. Properly solve the following equation using the correct order of operations:

   15 + 5 –(2 +7) x 2 ÷ 3 = ___14_____

Decimals – Practice Sheet

Write the following as decimal numbers:

1. One and Seventeen Hundredths 1.17

2. Five and One Hundredths 5.01

3. Two and One Hundred Twelve Thousandths
   2.112

4. Five and Sixteen Thousandths
   5.016

5. Four Hundred Eighteen Thousandths
   0.418

6. Fifty-Six Hundredths
   0.56

Add zeros as placeholders to extend each of the following decimals to the Ten Thousandths place:

1. 2.5600

2. 0.5460

3. 8.2000

4. 13.440

5. 9.5730

6. 1.5020

Compare – Greater Than, Less Than, Equal to

1   0.142 ____>____ 0.024   2. 0.573 _____>____ 0.0889   3. 0.0350 _____=___ 0.035

Complete the following problems:

1. 0.25 x 0.2 = 0.05

2. 4.5 ÷ 0.09 = 4.59

3. 18.759 + 2.65 = 21.409

4. 15.67 − 1.875 = 13.795

5. 1.25 x 8.36 = 10.45

Decimals – Quiz

Write the Name or Number for the following:

1. 1.351   One and Three Hundred Fifty-One Thousandths

2. Twelve and Forty-Two Thousandths   12.042

Greater Than, Less Than, Equal to

1. 0.135 ___<___ 1.35

2. 1.237 ___<___ 1.27

3. 0.0852 ___<___ 0.895

Complete the following Problems:

1. 0.75 x 0.2 = 0.15

2. 5.4 ÷ 0.9 = 6

3. 13.8 + 2.65 = 16.45

4. 7.9 – 1.875 = 6.025

5. 2.77 x 10 = 27.7

Integers – Practice Sheet

1. What is the largest (+) number on this time line?   10

2. What is the largest (-) number on this time line? -10

3. If you start at zero and move three points to the left, what is the integer? -3

4. What integer will you be at if you move 6 points to the right from -4? 2

5. If the beginning integer in a problem is 4 and -7 is added, what integer will you end up on?   -3

Calculate the Answer

1. 5 + 7 = 11

2. 14 + 11 = 25

3. 12 – 5 = 7

4. 27 – 9 = 18

5. -12 + -13 = -25

6. 18 + (-7) = 11

7. 39 – (-5) = 44

10 -100 – (-10) = -90

11. -12 x -12 = 144

12. 5 x -25 = -125

13. 8 x 14 = 112

14. -8 ÷ -2 = 4

15. 18 ÷ -9 = -2

8. 53 − (-7) = 60

9. -34 − (-4) = -30

Integers – Quiz

1. What is the range of integers represented on the above time line?

-10 to 10

2. True or False   FALSE

Positive integers are to the left of the zero and negative integers are to the right of the zero.

3. If you start at zero, move three points to the left and then six points to the right, what integer will you end at?
3

4. If you start at +9 and move 13 points to the left and then 5 points to the right, what integer will you end on?
1

Calculate the Answer

1. -5 + -27 = -32

2. -33 + 21 = -12

3. -83 – (-5) = -78

4. 97 – (-3) = 100

5. 12 x -12 = -144

6. -38 ÷ 2 = -19

Graphing – Practice Sheet

1. Label the following graphs : Bar Graph, Pie Chart, or Line Graph:

   _____Pie Chart_____

   _____Bar Graph_____

   Line Graph

2. Which graph shows data with negative values? Line graph Without any data other to use, interpret the information presented in the Pie Chart below:

1. Which color covers the greatest area of the Pie Chart? RED

2. Which color covers the smallest area of the Pie Chart?   BLUE

3. Which two colors are closest in area? GREEN AND RED

4. Which two colors, if you add them together will be almost equal to the third? BLUE AND GREEN

Without any data other to use, interpret the information presented in the Bar Graph below:

1. Which group shows an even amount of data in both colors? 3

2. Which color has the greatest data value? BLUE

3. Which color's greatest value was approximately 150? RED

4. Which color, between the first and second groups of data, is the smallest? BLUE

5. When totaled, which color has a greater value, Red or Blue? RED

Interpret the following Data/Graph

The above data/graph represents the types of drinks the 6th grade class typically has at lunch.

1. How many girls drink juice or soda at lunch? 12
2. How many boys drink juice or soda at lunch? 21
3. How many more boys than girls drink juice or soda at lunch? 9
4. Do more boys drink juice or soda at lunch or water at lunch? JUICE OR SODA
5. How many more girls drink water at lunch than juice or soda? 2

Number of Weeks Measured

	Height Day 1	Height Day 2	Height Day 3	Height Day 4	Height Day 5	Height Day 6	Height Day 7
Sunflower Growth	1 inch	2 inches	2 inches	3 inches	4 inches	4 inches	5 inches

1. Plot the data points on the graph provided.
2. Connect the points to form a line graph.
3. How long did it take for the sunflower to reach 4 inches? 5 days
4. If the current growth pattern continues, when will the sunflower reach 10 inches? Day 14

Graphing - Quiz

1. Which of the two graphs below is better for interpreting changing data points? A

2. Which of the two graphs better represents a comparison of groups of data? B

3. Does Graph A show an increase in the measured data or a decrease? DECREASE

4. What is the smallest measurement plotted on Graph A? (1, 10)

5. Create a table with the following data and plot the points on Graph A: x-axis = 0 through 8 days, plot one value per day, 0, 3, 6, 2, 7, 8, 9, 12

6. Which group has the greatest Blue value in Chart B? 2

7. Which group for Chart B has the smallest Blue data value? 3

8. Which group for Chart B has equal values for both the Red and Blue data? 3

9. In Chart B, which group shows the Red Data greater than the Blue Data? 1

10. What is the approximate value of the largest data group? 160

Fractions – Practice Sheet

1. True or False: If the numerator and denominator are equal the fraction equals 1.   TRUE

2. True or False: To add and subtract fractions, the denominators need to be the same. TRUE

3. True or False: A common denominator is created by multiplying the fractions.   FALSE

4. True or False: When multiplying fractions, the numerators and denominators are multiplied to get the final product.   TRUE

4. True or False: To divide fractions, the divisor fraction is converted to it's reciprocal and multiplied with the dividend.   TRUE

5. True or False: A mixed number is a whole number with a fraction represented.   TRUE

Solve and Reduce the Following Problems

1. 2/3 + 2/3 = 4/3 = 1 1/3

2. 1/5 + 1/5 = 2/5

3. 2/3 + 1/4 = 11/12

4. 5/6 + 1/2 = 8/6 = 1 1/3

9. 3/4 x 1/2 = 3/8

10. 2/3 x 3/5 = 6/15 = 2/5

11. 1/2 x 2/3 = 2/6 = 1/3

12. 1/2 ÷ 1/3 = 3/2 = 1 1/2

5. 1/2 + 1/2 = 1

6. 2/3 − 1/3 = 1/3

7. 3/5 − 1/2 = 1/10

8. 7/8 − 1/4 = 5/8

13. 3/4 ÷ 1/3 = 9/4 = 2 1/4

14. 2/3 ÷ 1/3 = 6/3 = 2

15. 5/6 ÷ 2/3 = 15/12 = 1 1/4

Fractions – Quiz

1. True or False: The number 2 1/3 is considered a Mixed Number.

    TRUE

2. True or False: The reciprocal of 2/3 is 3/2.

    TRUE

Solve and Reduce the following Problems

1. 2/3 + 1/6 = 5/6

2. 3/4 + 1/8 = 7/8

3. 1/3 + 1/6 + 1/2 = 6/6 = 1

4. 3/16 – 1/8 = 1/16

5. 2/3 – 1/9 = 5/9

6. 1/8 x 1/2 = 1/16

7. 3/4 x 3/5 = 9/20

8. 2/3 x 1/3 x 1/9 = 2/81

9. 3/5 ÷ 1/3 = 9/5 = 1 4/5

10. 4/5 ÷ 1/2 = 8/5 = 1 3/5

Ratios / Proportions / Percent's – Practice Sheet

Fill in the Blanks

1. A __RATIO_ is an expression of the relationship between two numbers.

2. A __PROPORTION is the representation of two ___RATIOS___ that are equivalent.

3. ____PERCENTS_ are fractions that have 100 in the denominator and are designated by using the ___%____ symbol.

Express the following as Ratios

1. A shopper buys 6 pears and 5 apples. What is the ratio of pears to apples? What is the ratio of apples to pears? 6:5 AND 5:6

2. Seven ducks and 3 geese are spotted on a neighborhood lake. What is the ratio of ducks to geese and then geese to ducks? 7:3 AND 3:7

Write the Proportions as Ratios and Fractions

1. Two is to four as three is to six 2:4 = 3:6 AND 2/4 = 3/6

2. Three is to nine as four is to twelve 3:9 = 4:12 AND 3/9 = 4/12

3. Seven is to fourteen as eight is to sixteen 7:14 = 8:16 AND 7/14 = 8/16

True or False

1. To determine whether a pair of ratios are equivalent or not, the fraction representation of the ratios are cross-multiplied. TRUE

2. Ratios are proportional if they are NOT equivalent. FALSE

3. Percents can be determined by cross-multiplying the ratios. TRUE

4. Ratios, when expressed as fractions, are always reduced. FALSE

5. The order of the numbers in ratios is not a factor when solving for equivalency or calculating a proportionate value. FALSE

6. Sixty percent can be written as 60/100 and 60% TRUE

Solve the Problems

1. Are the ratios 2:3 and 6:9 equivalent? YES

2. Are the ratios 3:4 and 5:6 equivalent? NO

3. = 10

4. What percent of 64 is16? (hint: the problem set up looks like this 16/64 = x/100)   25%

5. The ratio of fox to deer in the nature center is 3 to 12. If 24 deer were counted on Tuesday, how many fox were present as well? 6

6. If 30 percent of the total number of student drivers of 90 passed their driving exam, how many students total passed? How many did not pass?

27 AND 63

Ratios / Proportions / Percent's – Quiz

Are the following ratio pairs proportional?

1. 3/4 = 9/12   YES

2. 1/3 = 3/6 NO

3. 2/3 = 8/12   YES

4. 4/5 = 8/10   YES

Solve for x (percent)

1. What percentage of 52 is 13?   25%

2. What is 25 percent of 180?   45%

3. X = 7

5. If the ratio of blue pencils to red pencils in a classroom is 6 to 3, and one box of colored pencils contains 24 blue pencils, how many red pencils are in the box?   12

6. If 20 percent of the graduating class of 600 seniors are already accepted to a college, what number of students have not yet been accepted?

   120 ACCEPTED, 480 NOT YET ACCEPTED

Measurements – Practice Sheet

Standard Conversions	Metric Conversions	Standard to Metric Conversions
12 inches = 1 foot	1 m = 100 cm	1 inch = 2.54 cm 1 cm = 0.39 in
3 feet = 1 yard	1 m = 1,000 mm	1 mile = 1.6 km 1 km = 0.62 mi
5,280 feet = 1 mile	1 cm = 10 mm	1 gal = 3.79 l
1,760 yards = 1 mile	1 km = 1,000 m	1 kg = 2.2 lbs 1 lb = 0.45 kg
16 ounces = 1 pound	1 kg = 1,000 g	Celsius to Fahrenheit = Temp x 9/5 + 32
	1 g = 1,000 mg	
2 cups = 1 pint		Fahrenheit to Celsius = Temp - 32 x 5/9
2 pints = 1 quart	1 l = 1,000 ml	
4 quarts = 1 gallon		

1. Which units, standard and metric, are the best for measuring the top of a small table? INCHES AND CM

2. Which units, standard and metric, are best for measuring a person's weight?   LBS AND KG

3. Which units, standard and metric, are best for measuring the amount of water in a bathtub?   GAL AND L

Solve the following problems:

1. How many inches are in 37 feet? 444

2. How many feet are in 18 yards?   54

3. How many inches are in 2 yards? 72

4. How many pounds equal 64 oz? 4

5. How many yards in 3 miles? 5,280

6. How many gallons equal 84 quarts? 21

7. How many pints in 3 gallons? 24

8. How many mm in 25 cm? 2,500

9. How many meters equal 827 cm? 8.27

10. How many kg equal 340 g? 0.34

11. A race is 12 km long. How many meters is the racing course? 12,000

12. If a tree is 18 meters tall, how many cm tall is the tree? 1,800

13. A package weighs 3 kg, what is its weight in grams? 3,000

14. A laboratory assistant needs to prepare 320 ml containers with a special solution. How many Liters are needed to fill all the ml containers? 0.00032

15. A car mechanic is working on a car that needs some hosing replaced. The hosing is sold by the foot, but the car's parts use metric units. How many feet are needed to replace a 81cm hose? 2.6

16. How many miles are in 23 km?   14.26

17.   A teacher needs to fill a 24 liter tub using 1 gallon containers of punch. How many gallons will she need to fill the tub?   6.3

18.   A rock climber scales a 300 ft rock face. How many meters has he covered?   91.44

19.   The temperature outside today is 34 degrees Fahrenheit. What is the same temperature in degrees Celsius?   16.2

20.   In Hawaii today, it is a balmy 25 degrees Celsius. What is the temperature in Fahrenheit? 77

Measurements – Quiz

True or False

1. Length can be measured using kilometers and yards. TRUE

2. Kilograms and pounds are unit measurements for weight. TRUE

3. Liters and pints are about equal in measurement. FALSE

4. Miles and meters are equivalent lengths of measurement. FALSE

Solve the following problems:

1. A football field is 100 yards long. How many feet long is the same football field?   300

2. A fish tank at a famous celebrity's house holds 2,000 gallons. How many liters does it contain?   7,580

3. How many football fields equal 10 miles? (remember 1 football field is 100 yards)   176

4. If it is 10 degrees Fahrenheit on January 1, 2014 in Montana, what is the same temperature in Celsius?   -7.8

5. If a professional basketball player is 6 feet 7 inches tall, what is his total height in inches? 79

6. How many cm tall is the basketball player from Question 5?   200.66

Functions and Probability – Practice Sheet

Functions

True or False

1. The formula for the function must have three components: input value, the output value and the relationship that unites them in a formula. TRUE

2. The formula $f(x) = x^3$ by using this formula, all values of x will be cubed.

   TRUE

3. Domain is the set of numbers calculated from the function (output).

   FALSE

4. Range is the set of numbers calculated from the function (output).

   TRUE

Solve

1. $f(x) = x + 5$, when $x = 4$, what is the output?   9

2. $f(x) = x - 2$, when $x = 7$, what is the output? 5

3. $f(x) = x^2$, when $x = 3$, what is the output?   9

4. $f(x) = x/2$, when $x = 12$, what is the output? 6

5. $f(x) = x^2 + 3$, when $x = 6$, what is the output?   39

6. $f(x) = x - 3$, where x = {even numbers from 4 to 12}, what is the Range?

   {1, 3, 5, 7, AND 9}

7. f(x) = 3x + 1, where x = {1, 2, 3, 4, 5, and 6}, what is the Range?

    {4, 7, 10, 13, AND 19}

8. f(x) = 5x, where x = {odd numbers 3 through 13}, what is the Range?

    {15, 25, 35, 45, 55, AND 65}

Probability

True or False

1. The Probability of an occurrence or event can also be referred to as a Chance the occurrence or event will happen. TRUE

2. To calculate Probability, a ratio of Desired Outcome to Total Possible Outcomes is created and solved. TRUE

3. It is not possible to calculate the Probability of a series of events occurring. FALSE

Solve

1. What is the Probability of showing heads when you flip a coin? 1/2

2. What is the Probability of rolling a 6 when you roll a single die? 1/6

3. What is the Probability of drawing the 5 of Hearts from a deck of 52 cards?

    1/52

4. What is the probability of showing heads twice in a row when flipping a coin?   1/4

5. What is the Probability of a Sunny Day if the meteorologist predicts a 30% chance of rain showers on

Sunday?   70/100 OR 70%

Functions and Probability – Quiz

True or False

1. Domain and Range are used as input and output values for functions.

    TRUE

2. Probability is the likelihood that an event will occur during a specific set of circumstances.   TRUE

3. The percent chance that an event will occur is an aspect of Probability.

    TRUE

Solve

1. $f(x) = 2x + 3$, when $x = 4$, what is the output?   11

2. $f(x) = x^3 - 5$, when $x = 3$, what is the output? 22

3. $f(x) = 4x - 2$, where the Domain is {1,2,3,4,5,and 6}, what is the Range?

    {2, 6, 10, 14, 18, AND 22}

4. What is the Probability that out of a set of 3 red pencils, 4 blue pencils, and 4 yellow pencils, a student will choose a red pencil? 3/11

5. If there is an 80% chance that a student will get above 90% on a math test, what is the Probability that the student will not get 90%? 20%

Geometry – Practice Sheet

1. Which type of polygon has three sides?   TRIANGLE

2. Which type of polygon has four equal sides and four interior angle measurements of 90 degrees each?
   SQUARE

3. Which type of polygon has eight sides and eight equal interior angles?

   OCTAGON

4. Which type of triangle has three equal sides?

   EQUILATERAL

5. True or False: A rectangle is a parallelogram.

   TRUE

6. What is the Perimeter of a rectangle with a length of 30 inches and a width of 15 inches?

   90

7. What is the Area of the rectangle in Problem 6?

   450

8. What is the Perimeter of a square with each side measuring 8 feet?

   32 FEET

9. What is the Area of the square in Problem 8?

   64 SQUARE FEET

10. Why is the area of a triangle ½ bh, while the area of a parallelogram is bh?

    BECAUSE A TRIANGLE IS ½ THE SIZE AND SHAPE OF A PARALLELOGRAM

11. If a polygon with five sides has four angles measuring a total of 195 degrees. What is the value of the fifth angle?   165

12. What is the total area of a house's footprint if the footprint is composed of 5 squares, each with a side measurement of 15 feet?   375 SQUARE FEET

13. What is the Perimeter of a parallelogram with a base of 14 and a side measurement of 6? 40

14. What are the angle measurements of a right triangle? 90, 45, 45

15. True or False: There are six triangle types. Three are classified by the lengths of their sides and three are classified according to their angle measurements. TRUE

16. What are the lengths of the sides of a square if the Area is 16?

    4

17. What is the Perimeter of a regular Octagon if each side is 32 inches long?

    256 SQUARE INCHES

18. True or False: A parallelogram is a regular polygon.

FALSE

19. True or False: An obtuse triangle has at least one angle that is greater than 90 degrees.   TRUE

20. True or False: an isosceles triangle has at least two equal sides. TRUE

Geometry – Quiz

1. Which type of polygon has four equal sides and four interior angles measuring 90 degrees each? SQUARE

2. Which triangle has at least one angle greater than 90 degrees? OBTUSE

3. What is the definition of a parallelogram? A QUADRILATERAL WITH 2 PAIRS OF PARALLEL SIDES

4. What is the total inside angle measurement of a triangle?

   180 DEGREES

5. What is the definition of a Regular Polygon?

   A SHAPE WITH SIDES ALL EQUAL

6. What is the Perimeter of a rectangle with a length of 25 feet and a width of 10 feet? 70 FEET

7. What is the Area of a square with sides each measuring 6 feet?

   36 SQUARE FEET

8. What is the value of the fourth angle of a quadrilateral, if the total of the other three is 220 degrees? 140 DEGREES

9. What is the Area of a triangle with a height of 10 feet and a base of 10 feet? 50 SQUARE FEET

10. The Perimeter of a rectangular pool is 60 feet. If the width is 10 feet, what is the Area the pool covers? 600 SQUARE FEET

Sixth Grade Social Science
For Home School or Extra Practice

By Terri Raymond

Chapter 1: Paleolithic-Agricultural Revolution

Humans have not been around forever. In fact, it has been one of the pressing questions of science and history to determine exactly where and when humans originated. Thanks to modern technology, we have a pretty good sense of our roots. We do know that human beings evolved from chimpanzees; eventually, we gained the ability to walk upright, to speak, and think at a much higher level. But the transition from chimpanzee to today's human being was not a quick one. It took thousands upon thousands of years.

Humans at first were extremely hairy, much hairier than we are today. Our language was not developed beyond a few distinct signals; we used spears and rocks to hunt animals; and it was not common sense to stay in a single place. Early humans were *nomadic* creatures, meaning that they moved from place to place. It made no sense to them to remain in a single area, when they could always be on the move, hunting animals freely. The decision to stay on a piece of land, grow plants, and keep animals would come much later, as would the process of burying dead ones.

Also, humans lived in Africa. They roamed the grasslands and the savannahs, hunting down animals. Eventually, humans found a path that led them out of Africa; from there, they traveled into Europe and Asia; from Asia, they traveled to North America and populated the Americas. This is only a theory, however, called the "Out of Africa" theory.

But how do we know all of this? How do we know that early humans used spears, or that they originated in Africa? How do we know that they sometimes carried the limbs of the dead, because they had not yet discovered the ritual of burying those who have died? We know all of this because of *anthropologists.* An *anthropologist* is someone who studies humans, both present and past. They try to find clues in bones or *fossils,* and piece together the past in order to get a better understanding of the present.

Anthropologists have traced the history of humans as far back as four and a half million years; throughout that time there have been various "types" of humans, each developing over a certain amount of time. Early humans are called *hominids;* they were not exactly humans yet, but they were on the right evolutionary track. *For* example, anthropologists often think that the first species of humans was about four feet tall; they ate fruit, nuts, leaves, and meat; they used sticks and rocks to fight; today, we call them the *Australopithecus.*

While, over the course of four million years, there were many different types of hominids, anthropologists have noted the landmark three. The first of them is called *Homo habilis. Homo habilis* means "person with abilities," and they lived 1.5 million years ago and is often called the "handy man," because he was the first hominid to invent tools. These tools were often made of stone; it is for this reason that this era is called the *Stone Age.*

The next type of hominid was the *Homo erectus,* which roamed the earth 150,000 years ago. *Homo erectus* means "person who walks upright"; the word "erect" means upright. We know that *Homo erectus* walked straight because anthropologists have found their bones and examined their spines. When they compare the spines of *Homo erectus* with *Homo habilis*, they can spot the differences and see that *Homo erectus* walked very differently.

The final type of hominid is one that you are probably familiar with; the *homo sapien*. *Homo sapien* means "person who can think," and they currently populate the earth! You are a *homo sapien*, and the current development in human evolution. You are a *homo sapien* because of the millions of years of hominid development that has come before you.

But the evolution of the human species was not an uneventful one. When the hominids moved out of Africa, they faced many dangers far and wide. After all, they were moving into undiscovered territory. But there was more than just land they had to face: they also had to confront weather different from anything they had seen before.

The Ice Age is something that you may have heard before, and it has happened more than once in the past. In fact, in the past two million years, Earth has experienced four Ice Ages. An Ice Age occurs when cold weather comes from the North and South Poles and cause massive storms and glaciers to form around the world. Despite this, however, the area around the equator manages to stay warm and maintain most of its former temperature. Everywhere else around the world, though, the temperature will drop drastically. Some water in the ocean freezes, and when water freezes, it compresses. This means that the level of the ocean drops, which also affected the humans. This is also a pressing issue in today's world, because many scientists claim that global warming is causing ocean levels to *rise*.

The Ice Age posed many challenges for early hominids. When they were pressed with cooler weather when they moved out of Africa, they had to learn to *adapt*. To *adapt* means to make a change in order to survive; for example, if the hominids entered cold weather, they could *adapt* by using animal fur to keep themselves warm. They also needed *fire* to keep themselves warm. If a group of hominids could not spark fire, they would likely die out. Hence, those that were smartest and strongest survived when the Ice Age came.

The development of hominids was also marked by how they used tools. The *Homo habilis*, or handy man, indicated the beginning of the Stone Age because they used stone tools. The Stone Age is also called the *Paleolithic Era*. With the use of tools, hominids were able to better fend for themselves against wild animals and other enemies.

Some historians say that *Homo habilis* was the first hominid to leave Africa, while others say that the later hominid, *Homo erectus*, was most definitely the first. The evidence tends to lean towards *homo erectus*, and anthropologists estimate that they found a route out of Africa about one a half million years ago. Their route would likely have been through what is today known as the Middle East; from there, the *homo erectus* spread into

Asia and Europe. Arriving on these other continents was not a quick process, however; it took generations and generations of hominids to accomplish this. It took *Homo erectus* approximately one million years to spread into Asia and Europe, at least according to fossil evidence.

The hominids that had remained in Africa eventually developed into a species known as the *Neanderthal*. The Neanderthals had brains even larger than today's humans, and they were, on average, larger than us too. They could stand anywhere from five to six feet high, and they had large bodies that supported tons of muscle.

Neanderthals were some of the first humans to bury their dead. Burial rituals are one of the signatures of modern humanity; few other animals recognize their dead with a ritual, nevermind putting them in the ground. It represents that you can come back and visit their burial place, which is an advanced level of thinking in animals. Sometimes, Neanderthals put pretty flowers above their dead, or even buried them with food. This is also when anthropologists think than humans developed the concept of an afterlife, or something that comes after die.

Along with burying humans, anthropologists believe that Neanderthals developed ways to heal themselves. Today, when an anthropologists looks at ancient bones, they can see if the bones had been broken at all. So, for example, an anthropologist looks at the femur of a Neanderthal, and sees that the Neanderthal had severely injured himself and broken the bone; the anthropologist can determine how exactly the bone healed, and many have determined that Neanderthals may have even developed forms of medicine to help their injured.

At this point in time, there were two different species of hominids on the planet: the *homo sapien* that had spread into Europe and Asia, and the *Neanderthal* in Africa that was just leaving the continent. The *Homo sapiens* and the Neanderthals eventually clashed; how the Neanderthals eventually disappeared, no one knows for sure. Some historians speculate that, through war, the *Homo sapiens* completely destroyed the Neanderthal species, while others believe that the Neanderthals and *Homo sapiens* bred together, and the two species merged.

Eventually, *Homo sapiens* evolved into a new form, commonly called *Homo sapiens sapiens*. The addition of another *sapien* indicates the next level in human evolution. The first form of *Homo sapiens sapiens* was called *Cro-Magnon*, and they were discovered in France in the middle of the 1800s. Anthropologists have found evidence of the Cro-Magnon species across three continents: Africa, Asia, and Europe. As evolution will have it, the Cro-Magnons were more advanced than the Neanderthal. They stood much higher, and they had a better sense of craftsmanship, as well as a more developed language system.

The Stone Age and the Paleolithic Era long behind them, the Cro-Magnons sought many other materials for making their tools than stones. They would still use rocks, of course, but they also used the bones of animals they killed; other popular items included ivory from elephant tusks and antlers from moose. A new variety of tools allowed the Cro-Magnons to accomplish new feats. The tools and artifacts that they left behind tell us that they knew how to fish; they used bows and arrows to hunt down their prey, as well as spears; and they had axes, most likely for taking down big trees. These trees could be used for firewood, or even for long canoes, a fashion often recognized as Native American.

It was during the Cro-Magnon era that anthropologists believe hominids began settling down in single areas, which required the materials and tools to build homes, communities, and villages. As people settled down, they looked for people to lead them: sometimes tribes would war against each other. Other times supplies were low and they needed leadership to find new ones. With rulers came rules, and with rules came people appointed to enforce these rules. And so we see the inklings of the rise of civilization.

Following the development of the Cro-Magnon and the evolution into higher species of humans, there arrived a momentous era known as the *Agricultural Revolution*. "Agricultural" refers to something involving food, vegetables, and farming, while a "revolution" is a drastic change, introducing something new to replace something in the past.

In the past, hominids had been reliant on the world around them to eat. If they were hungry, they would go into the wilderness and take food, by either hunting it or picking it. But now that groups of hominids were settling into permanent areas, hunting became a little more difficult. Some villages sent hunters to foray in the wilderness and bring back food, while others had a very different idea.

The idea was this: farming. Take plants and put them in one area; let them grow; pick the fruits and vegetables and plants, and let the seeds grow once again. While this may seem very common to us today, it was absolutely revolutionary at the time. The introduction of farming occurred approximately eight thousand years ago, and it has sparked the rise of the human race ever since.

But plants were not the only thing that could be "farmed." People took animals and ate them; their babies grew up, and the people waited for their babies to be born before eating them too. Animals, like plants, can be cultivated, and this a process that continues today.

Hominids did not like to waste, however; because supplies were spare, it was difficult to put anything to waste. Bones were used for tools; goats and cows were milked; fat and flesh were eaten; sometimes even the intestines were used for tools, and furs were used for blankets or clothes. With animals and plants being drawn into permanent settlements along with the humans, we now see the first real resemblance to today's modern civilizations. Thus marked the end of the Agricultural Revolution, which planted the seeds of dozens of civilizations to come.

Paleolithic-Agricultural Revolution Discussion Questions

(1) When you first think about it, what similarities might human beings share with chimpanzees? Do you see any differences? There is a lot of discussion about the theory of evolution; do you believe that humans evolved from other primates?

(2) Discuss the "Out of Africa" theory. While it is likely, it is still only a theory because there is no direct evidence. if you wanted to present evidence for the "Out of Africa" theory, what might you point to?

(3) What does the term "handy man" imply, and why was this given to *Homo habilis*?

(4) Why is the Paleolithic Era called the Stone Age? Do you think this reason is significant enough that it gives the era the nickname "Stone Age?"

(5) The Ice Age was a pressing situation for hominids across the globe. What are the disadvantages of facing an Ice Age? Can you think of any advantages? What connections can you make between the Ice Age and the adaptations of hominids?

(6) The development of burial rituals was one of the most significant moments in human history. Why is this so important? What do burial rituals show about humans?

(7) Hominids did not often waste any part of an animal. Why was this? Do you think we waste more today? If so, why do you think we waste more today?

(8) Why was the Agricultural Revolution called a "revolution?" What changed from the past to the present, and why was this change made?

(9) Describe the difference between farming and hunting. What are the advantages and disadvantages?

(10) Some historians say that the Agricultural Revolution is the reason that humanity rose to such greatness. Why might the Agricultural Revolution have put the human race at an advantage over other species?

Paleolithic-Agricultural Revolution Activities

(1) Evolution is the driving evidence behind the development of the human species. Visit the following link, learn about Charles Darwin and natural selection, and even play a fun game where you get to pick species and try to make them survive in certain environments. Compare your experiences in the game to your knowledge of human evolution. http://www.sciencechannel.com/games-and-interactives/charles-darwin-game.htm

(2) Create five columns on a piece of paper, and give them the following respective titles: *Australopithecus, Homo habilis, Homo erectus, homo sapien, Neanderthal*. Compare each of these species in the development of humans.

(3) Find a map of the world and label the following continents: Africa, Asia, Europe, and North America. Beginning in Africa, trace the route that hominids would have had to take to enter the other three continents.

(4) You may be wondering how hominids reached North America – after all, it's not connected to Europe or Asia! Research a strip of land known as the *Bering Strait* and draw it on your map. This is what humans used to reach North America from Asia.

(5) Read the following article about an *Australopithecus* named "Lucy." She helped modern anthropologists understand a lot about out ancient ancestors. After you've read the article, write three new things that you have learned. http://news.nationalgeographic.com/news/2006/09/060920-lucy.html

(6) Now that you have some background knowledge about Lucy, watch the following video, which compares the skeletons of chimpanzees, Lucy, and a modern human. After you've watched the video, go back and write down three differences you've noticed between the modern human and the other two skeletons. http://www.youtube.com/watch?v=xT8Np0gI1dI

(7) On a piece of paper, create a Venn diagram. One circle will be "hunting" and the other will be "farming." Write down how humans may have lived their lives while their daily activities were focused on hunting or farming. What similarities did they have?

(8) Imagine that *Homo erectus* had the ability to speak—and even more than that, to write! You are a member of a *Homo erectus* tribe, and you are keeping a journal as your tribe moves out of Africa and into unknown lands. What new dangers do you face? Write at least three journal entries about your daily activities.

(9) Look at the following map of the lands affected by the Ice Age. The map is from the position of the North Pole, looking at North America, Europe, Asia, and Northern Africa. On your map of the world, make a rough sketch in blue of the areas that were touched by the Ice Age. Was your hometown once covered in enormous glaciers of ice and snow?

(10) You are living in a village during the time of the Agricultural Revolution. While you have spent most of your life hunting animals, your tribe is now settling down and attempting to farm plants. Write down your process of cultivating plants and animals, and why this might be more advantageous than being a nomadic species.

Paleolithic-Agricultural: For Further Reading

Bailey, Linda. *Adventures in the Ice Age*. Kids Can Press, 2004.

DK Publishing. *Early Humans*. DK Children, 2005.

Facchini, Fiorenzo. *A Day with Homo Habilis: Life 2,000,000 Years Ago*. 21st Century, 2003.

Fleming, Fergus. *Stone Age Sentinel*. E.D.C. Publishing, 1998.

Gibbons, Gail. *Farming*. Holiday House, 1990.

Greenburg, Dan. *Zack Files 25: Trapped in the Museum of Unnatural History*. Grosset & Dublap, 2002.

Hynes, Margaret. *The Best Book of Early People*. Kingfisher, 2003.

Peters, Lisa Westberg. *Our Family Tree: An Evolution Story*. HMH Books for Young Readers, 2003.

Robertshaw, Peter. *The Early Human World*. Oxford University Press, 2005.

Rosen, Michael J. *Our Farm: Four Seasons with Five Kids on One Family's Farm*. Darby Creek Pub, 2008.

Rubino, Michael. *Bang!: How We Came to Be*. Prometheus Books, 2011.

Saucier, C. A. P. *The Lucy Man: The Scientist Who Found the Most Famous Fossil Ever*. Prometheus Books, 2011.

Scieszka, Jon. *Your Mother Was A Neanderthal: Time Warp Trio, Book 4*. Penguin Group, 2009.

Weaver, Anne H. *Children of Time: Evolution and the Human Story.* University of New Mexico Press, 2012.

Zihlman, Afrienne L. *The Human Evolution Coloring Book.* HarperCollins, 2001.

Paleolithic-Agricultural Revolution: Quiz

(1) What primate do anthropologists believe humans evolved from?
    (A) Bonobo
    (B) Chimpanzee
    (C) Gorilla
    (D) Orangutan

(2) Early humans liked to roam from place to place, which means that they were _____.
    (A) Nomadic
    (B) Self-serving
    (C) Farming creatures
    (D) Chimpanzees

(3) On what continent did humans originate?
    (A) North America
    (B) Africa
    (C) Asia
    (D) Europe

(4) What do you call someone who studies humans, past and present?
    (A) Biologist
    (B) Chimpologist
    (C) Homologist
    (D) Anthropologist

(5) What was the first type of hominid?

(A) *Homo sapien*
(B) *Homo erectus*
(C) *Homo habilis*
(D) *Australopithecus*

(6) What type of hominid was referred to as the "handy man?"
   (A) *Homo sapien*
   (B) *Homo erectus*
   (C) *Homo habilis*
   (D) *Australopithecus*

(7) The Stone Age is a nickname for what era?
   (A) The Jurassic Era
   (B) The Paleomythic Era
   (C) The Age of Heroes
   (D) The Paleolithic Era

(8) Which hominid's name means "person who walks upright?"
   (A) Neanderthal
   (B) *Homo sapien*
   (C) *Homo erectus*
   (D) *Homo Australopithecus*

(9) Which hominid's name means "person who can think?"
   (A) *Homo sapien*
   (B) *Homo habilis*
   (C) *Homo erectus*
   (D) *Homo Neanderthalis*

(10) What hominid do you classify as?
   (A) *Homo sapien*
   (B) *Homo habilis*
   (C) *Homo erectus*
   (D) *Homo Australopithecus*

(11) During the Agricultural Revolution, what did hominids begin to do?
   (A) Foray and hunt
   (B) Bury their dead
   (C) Settle and farm
   (D) Heal their wounded

(12) Anthropologists believe what hominid first started to introduce burial rites into their culture?
   (A) Cro-Magnon
   (B) Neanderthal
   (C) *Australopithecus*

(D) *Homo sapien*

(13) Anthropologists believe what hominid was the first to settle down and start farming?
(A) Cro-Magnon
(B) Neanderthal
(C) *Australopithecus*
(D) *Homo sapien*

(14) How did humans get to North America?
(A) They sailed by boat from Europe.
(B) They sailed by boat from Africa.
(C) They crossed by land from Asia.
(D) They crossed by land from Australia.

(15) Anthropologists believe what hominid developed ways to heal itself?
(A) Cro-Magnon
(B) *Homo habilis*
(C) Neanderthal
(D) *Homo erectus*

(16) The Ice Age's massive glaciers reached every continent on the globe.
(A) True
(B) False

(17) Both plants and animals were a major part of the Agricultural Revolution for humans.
(A) True
(B) False

(18) The Out of Africa theory has been proved undeniably true.
(A) True
(B) False

(19) The Paleolithic Era is often called the Iron Age.
(A) True
(B) False

(20) Early humans often wasted no part of any animal they killed.
(A) True
(B) False

Paleolithic-Agricultural Revolution: Quiz Answers

(1) **B.** Anthropologists believe humans evolved from chimpanzees.
(2) **A.** Early humans liked to roam from place to place, which means they were nomadic.
(3) **B.** Humans originated on Africa.
(4) **D.** An anthropologist studies humans, past and present.
(5) **D.** The first type of hominid was *Australopithecus.*
(6) **C.** *Homo habilis* was referred to as the "handy man."
(7) **D.** The Stone Age is a nickname for the Paleolithic Era.
(8) **C.** "Person who walks upright" is the meaning of *Homo erectus.*
(9) **A.** *Homo sapien* means "person who can think."
(10) **A.** You classify as a *homo sapien.*
(11) **C.** During the Agricultural Revolution, humans began to settle and farm.
(12) **B.** Anthropologists believe that Neanderthals were the first to introduce burial rites into their culture.
(13) **A.** Anthropologists believe that the Cro-Magnons were the first to settle down and farm.
(14) **C.** Humans reached Asia by crossing by land from Asia.
(15) **C.** Anthropologists believe that Neanderthals developed healing methods.

(16) **False.** The Ice Age's glaciers did not reach ever continent.
(17) **True.** Both plants and animals were a major part of the Agricultural Revolution.
(18) **False.** The Out of Africa theory has not been proved undeniably true; it is a theory, but a likely one.
(19) **False.** The Paleolithic Era is often called the Stone Age, not the Iron Age.
(20) **True.** Early humans often wasted no part of any animal they killed.

Paleolithic-Agricultural Revolution: Works Cited

http://news.nationalgeographic.com/news/2006/09/060920-lucy.html

http://www.youtube.com/watch?v=xT8Np0gI1dI

http://kids.britannica.com/elementary/art-172658/A-map-shows-five-great-ice-caps-or-centers-from

http://www.kidspast.com/world-history/0001-prehistoric-humans.php

http://earlyhumans.mrdonn.org/

http://www.watchknowlearn.org/Category.aspx?CategoryID=6669

http://www.factmonster.com/ipka/A0932663.html

Chapter 2: Mesopotamia, Egypt, and Kush

Mesopotamia

The land of Mesopotamia was the home of one of humanity's earliest civilizations; so early, in fact, that modern historians often claim that that Mesopotamia is the "Cradle of Civilization," meaning that it gave way to future communities and empires.

Mesopotamia sat in what today is called the Middle East, in modern-day Iraq, Turkey, Syria, and Iran. The name "Mesopotamia" means "the land between the rivers" in Ancient Greek, because the land rests between two major rivers in the Middle East: the Tigris River and the Euphrates River. These rivers make the land there lush and fertile, and excellent for farming. For this reason, the land is also called "the fertile crescent."

Because the land is so fertile, it was a perfect spot for early humans for settle down. The green and far-reaching land was ideal for farming; there was easy access to water; naturally, it was a great place to live. As the early humans made their communities, the population grew. With the newfound ability to build homes, communities, villages, towns, and even great cities were built. Here we see the rise of civilization, growing in the fertile crescent of Ancient Mesopotamia.

Now that humanity had drifted away from a hunting-centric society and more towards one that leaned toward farming in the aftermath of the Agricultural Revolution, farming was the main reason that people decided to settle Mesopotamia. Water was plenty, and the seasons were perfect for growing crops.

The agriculture of Mesopotamia was abundant and plentiful. Farmers grew wheat and barley for grains, and there were onions and cucumbers, apples and spices, and even more. Cattle was popular, along with sheep and goats. With such a flourishing beginning, Mesopotamia easily rose to greatness.

As was discussed in the last section, people that settle down eventually search for leaderships. Mesopotamia is one of the first civilizations with a strong sense of leadership, especially one for historians to study today. Mesopotamia was led by a single king; beneath the king were *nobles*, royal men who discussed politics and made decisions at the king's discretion. The nobles had the ability to declare war on other civilizations, and they also had their hand in Mesopotamia's religion. You could almost compare Mesopotamia's nobles to the current United States Congress; they are not exactly similar, but the idea is the same.

The people of Mesopotamia recognized that there was a fragile relationship between the king and his people. If the king made laws and did things that the people did not want, then the people would get angry and rise against the king. Because of this, the best kings listened very closely to their people and knew what they wanted—especially if they wanted to stay in power.

Mesopotamia was a very diverse place, and modern historians often divide it into three different sections: Sumer, Babylon, and Assyria. Sumer was very religious; it was one of the first recorded religions in history, and has given historians a lot to examine. Sumerians did everything in the name of the gods; if something good happened to them, they believed it was a reward; if something bad happened, they believed it was a punishment. Bablylonians and Assyrians worshipped the same gods and worked equally hard to please them.

In the land of Assyria, there was an enormous library called the Library of Ninevah, and it is from these archives that historians and archeologists have received the most ancient texts. One of them, named *Gilgamesh* was found inscribed on a stone tablet. It tells the tale of a man named Gilgamesh as he battles monsters and deals with the concept of death. It is the first story ever recorded by human beings.

Another stone tablet was engraved with the writing of *Hammurabi's Code.* The code was named after a Babylonian king, who tried to write down the laws of his people, in an effort to have more order. Hammurabi was upset that people wanted to change laws and some rich people thought they were above the law; his code made sure that the laws were set in stone.

Everyone is Mesopotamia belonged to one of four classes; each class had a spot in the hierarchy, meaning that some classes were above others. At the top of the social ladder sat the Priests, who instructed people on how to please the gods, and also healed the sick and injured. Below the Priests was the Upper Class, rich men and women who could afford jewelry, land, and other luxuries. Below the Upper Class was the Lower Class, who could afford some things but not at the level of the Upper Class. At the bottom rung of the ladder were the Slaves, people who had been captured in war and forced to do labor.

Egypt

To the east sat Ancient Egypt, which rested beside its own river. The Nile River, a popular tourist spot today, was an ideal spot for people to settle in Egypt. Egypt is in the northeastern corner of Africa, and it is surrounded by deserts. This made the Nile River a paradise for farmers and people who wanted a fresh water supply. People could also follow the Nile River north, right to the Mediterranean Sea. Because this area of Egypt was luckily lush and fertile, perfect for farmers to build crops, it was often called the "Gift of the Nile" by the Ancient Egyptians. The Nile River is the longest river in the world, at an astounding four thousand miles long.

When historians look at Ancient Egypt today, they look at Egypt in terms of three different eras, referred to as "kingdoms." The first era, called the Old Kingdom, Egypt was ruled by men called "pharaohs," their version of a king. When a pharaoh died, he was buried in a pyramid, which required months of slave labor to build. Even today, architects are astounded by how men thousands of years ago were able to build monuments of such great magnitude. Each pharaoh was buried with gifts, which people believed they took with them into the afterlife. It was considered horrible luck to steal from a pharaoh's tomb, but graverobbers still tried.

In the next era, the Middle Kingdom, pyramids were not used as often, mainly because of how expensive and laborious it was to build them. Instead, pharaohs wished to be buried in secret places, in hidden underground tombs. This way, graverobbers would not find them and their riches would be safe forever.

In the final era, the New Kingdom, all pharaohs were buried in the same area, called the Valley of Kings.

Each pharaoh controlled the army, the enforcers of the law, and relied on many people in the Egyptian government to help him rule. Each pharaoh also had someone called a *vizier*, or the "right hand man." Consider that the vizier might be the "vice-president" to the president today. The vizier took care of a lot of the pharaoh's duties, such as listening to cases in court and making reports on things that were happening far and wide across the civilization.

The Egyptians were very devoted to their gods; historians today count that the ancient Egyptians worshipped over two thousand gods, each one original and special. The Egyptians believed that their gods were twisted versions of animals, with parts that were mixed and matched between different species. While many of the people in Mesopotamia feared their gods, the Egyptians did not. They believed that the gods supported them in everything they did; if they were punished, they did not believe it was the gods' fault.

Egypt gave the world many new inventions, ideas, and technologies. Chief among them was papyrus, an early form of paper. It was taken from the plant called *papyrus*, which found be found in abundance around the Nile. Not only did the Egyptians use it to make paper, but also baskets, clothes, chairs, medicine, mattresses, boats, tables, and many other daily supplies. Egypt used walls and stone tablets to write still, but paper was one of their greatest inventions.

We can also thank Egypt for early conceptions of justice and courts. The vizier tried to weigh everything fairly in court; but besides their actual courts, the Egyptians believed that once you died, your whole life was weighed on a scale, something called "the weighing of the heart." While the Egyptians were not afraid of their gods, they were wary of one, which would come and get you if you did bad things. This goddess's name was Ammut, and she had the head of a crocodile, and the body of both a lion and a hippo (the lion, the hippo, and the crocodile posed dangers to ancient Egyptians, since these animals lived there too!).

When you died, you entered the Hall of Maat and met the god Anubis. It was there that Anubis weighed your heart, while the god Thoth wrote everything down. If you did good things during your life, you had a light heart. If you did bad things, you had a very heavy heart, and you would be punished by being eaten by Ammut. If you did good deeds during your life, Anubis would allow to pass safely on to the Afterlife.

Kush

To the south rested Ancient Kush, a smaller civilization. It was built around the bottom of the Nile, and also decided to settle there because of the great soil to grow crops. There was plenty of rain and healthy weather around the year, so the people of Kush could be prosperous. In addition to the crops in Kush, the people found other natural resources that could make their pockets fat. Chief among them was ivory from elephants, and mines from which they could reap gold and iron.

Naturally, since Kush was so rich, other civilizations tried to attack and conquer them. But in addition to a great economy, Kush also had an excellent military, made up of supreme archers. In fact, they were even known as the Land of the Bow because of this.

The Kush government was made up of nobles, much like the government in Mesopotamia. These nobles, along with the people of Kush, worshipped the exact same gods as the Egyptians; some of them even thought of themselves as Egyptians, although they did not live in the same area.

What separates Kush from Egypt is that they were not ruled by a pharaoh, but instead a queen. On the lower scale, each village of Kush was supported by a leader who had no authority; instead, this leader inspired discussions amongst the other village people.

These three lands (Mesopotamia, Egypt, and Kush) existed during the next age, the Iron Age. Now that the Stone Age had passed and technology had fast advanced, the Iron Age was ushered in with high civilizations. Tools were developed more than ever before in history, and even society and culture had a new face. Since stone was the popular element during the Stone Age, iron was now what everyone wanted. One of the reasons Kush was so successful as a civilization was because of its proximity to natural iron.

Kush sat on the eastern side of Africa, and these civilizations had had little to no communication with anyone on the western side of the continent. The people of Kush always wondered what was on the other side, across the vast and dangerous Sahara Desert. Eventually, people decided that they were going to make the trek across the arid desert land. Using camels to carry their belongings, a large group of traders from Kush made it across the desert and entered western Africa, discovering new lands and new people. This is significant in African history, because it represented the joining of different African peoples, and the introduction of a trade network that would further the African civilizations. This trade route was called the "Trans-Sahara Trade Route," "trans" meaning "across." We can thank Kush for this venture, which changed the face of Africa forever.

Mesopotamia, Egypt, and Kush: Discussion Questions

(1) Why are Mesopotamia and the Middle East often called the "Cradle of Civilization?" What does the word "cradle" imply?

(2) Why is being next to a river/lake/ocean advantageous for a civilization? What benefits can you reap from water?

(3) What did the transfer to a farming-centric society mean to humans? How was it different from their hunting-centric society?

(4) Who are the nobles in Mesopotamia, and what importance did they have to the government? Do you think Mesopotamia could have survived without them?

(5) What differences were there between the gods of the Mesopotamians and the Egyptians? Do any of these differences make sense, according to the culture?

(6) What was the Weighing of the Heart, and what importance did it have in Egyptian society? Did it affect the way people led their lives?

(7) What was the importance of the Nile River to the Egyptian economy?

(8) Why was Kush called "the Land of the Bow?"

(9) Now that the Stone Age had passed, why was the new era called the Iron Age? Why is this important in the overall development of humanity?

(10) Why might the Trans-Sahara Trade Route be beneficial for countries on both sides of Africa? How does trade help a country?

Mesopotamia, Egypt, and Kush: Activities

(1) Watch the following video about Mesopotamia, and write down five things that you learned afterwards. http://www.youtube.com/watch?v=X7A26no4np8

(2) Find a map of the Middle East, and research the exact boundaries of Mesopotamia. Color Mesopotamia in with RED marker. Draw important rivers, like the Tigris and the Euphrates.

(3) Take a look at this abridged for-kids version of the story of *Gilgamesh*, the first story ever recorded by humans. Create a storyline chart, where you define the following moments in the story: Introduction, Rising Action, Climax, Falling Action, and Resolution. http://www.mesopotamia.co.uk/geography/story/sto_set.html

(4) One of the lasting laws of Hammurabi's Code is "an eye for an eye." Write a short journal entry about what you think this means, and if you think that people should follow this rule.

(5) Watch the following video about the Great Pyramids, and write down two cool facts that you learned about them. http://www.history.com/topics/ancient-history/ancient-egypt/videos

(6) If your previous map of the Middle Eat contains Egypt within its boundaries, color in Egypt with a BLUE marker. Find the Nile River and draw that in. If you need to print out a new map, try to include Kush as well, and color that in GREEN.

(7) After learning about the Egyptian's version of the afterlife, pretend that you are an Egyptian who has just entered the afterlife. Describe what gods that you encounter, as well as what happens to you there. If you need to do additional research, the Internet and your local library are great resources.

(8) Visit the following crossword puzzle. In addition to finding the words, write a one-sentence definition of each term on another piece of paper. Again, use additional research if you need to. A dictionary, or an encyclopedia, would be of great use to you. http://www.activityvillage.co.uk/ancient-egypt-word-search

(9) The following video is very helpful in further understanding the Empire of Kush. Watch the short video, and then write down three new things that you learned about Kush. Also, write down a sentence or two about why it is lesser known that its Mesopotamian and Egyptian Empire counterparts.

(10) Religion is a very important part of life, and that is especially true for these empires. Create a three-circle Venn diagram (http://ndstudies.gov/sites/default/file/3_circle_venn_5.gif). Write about what the religions of these three empires have in common, and also what is different about them.

Mesopotamia, Egypt, and Kush: For Further Reading

Adamson, Heather. *Ancient Egypt: An Interactive History Adventure*. You Chose Books, 2009.

Alexander, Lloyd. *Time Cat: The Remarkable Journeys of Jason and Gareth*. Puffin, 1996.

Broida, Marian. *Ancient Egyptians and Their Neighbors: An Activity Guide*. Chicago Review Press, 1999.

Cobblestone Publishing. *If I Were a Kid in Ancient Egypt: Children of the Ancient World*. Cricket Books, 2007.

Hart, George. *Ancient Egypt*. DK CHILDREN, 2008.

Haskins, James. *African Beginnings*. Amistad, 1998.

Hunter, Erica. *Ancient Mesopotamia*. Chelsea House Publications, 2007.

Masiello, Ralph. *Ralph Masiello's Ancient Egypt Drawing Book*. Charlesbridge, 2008.

Mehta-Jones, Shilpa. *Life in Ancient Mesopotamia*. Crabtree Publishing Co., 2004.

Morley, Jacqueline. *How Would You Survive as an Ancient Egyptian?* Children's Press, 1996.

Moss, Carol. *Science in Ancient Mesopotamia*. Franklin Watts, 1998.

Nardo, Don. Mesopotamia: *Exploring the Ancient World*. CPB Grades 4-8, 2012

Shuter, Jane. *Mesopotamia: Excavating the Past*. NA-h, 2005.

Steele, Philip. *Mesopotamia*. DK CHILDREN, 2007.

Zamosky, Lisa. *Sub-Saharan Africa: World Cultures Through Time*. Teacher Created Materials, 2008.

Mesopotamia, Egypt, and Kush: Quiz

(1) Mesopotamia is often called the "_____ of Civilization."
  (A) Cradle
  (B) Birthplace
  (C) Origin
  (D) Catalyst

(2) What does "Mesopotamia" mean?
  (A) The Birthplace of Civilization
  (B) The Place of Royal Gods
  (C) The Land Between the Rivers
  (D) The City Beneath the Mountains

(3) How many kings did Mesopotamia have?
  (A) One
  (B) Two
  (C) Three
  (D) Four

(4) The Library of Ninevah was located in what area of Mesopotamia?
  (A) Babylon
  (B) Sumer
  (C) Assyria
  (D) Mesop

(5) Who was Gilgamesh?
  (A) One of Mesopotamia's famous kings, who led the people to success in war
  (B) One of Assyria's legendary scholars, who worked in the library of Ninevah
  (C) A character in an Ancient Mesopotamian story
  (D) A famous gladiator who fought in Mesopotamia's coliseum

(6) What was Hammurabi's Code?
  (A) A set of laws set down by King Hammurabi
  (B) The code that allowed people access into Hammurabi's Pyramid
  (C) The password that gave people permission to enter the Golden Gates of Egypt
  (D) A set of numbers and laws that gave Mesoptamia its library coding system

(7) Put the Mesopotamian class system in order, from *Highest Class* to *Lowest Class*.
  (A) Upper Class, Lower Class, Priests, Slaves
  (B) Slaves, Lower Class, Priests, Upper Class
  (C) Upper Class, Priests, Lower Class, Slaves
  (D) Priests, Upper Class, Lower Class, Slaves

(8) What river runs through Egypt?
  (A) Tigris

(B) Euphrates
(C) Amazon
(D) Nile

(9) What were the three kingdoms of Egypt called?
   (A) The Stone Kingdom, the Iron Kingdom, the Golden Kingdom
   (B) The First Kingdom, the Second Kingdom, the Third Kingdom
   (C) The Old Kingdom, the Middle Kingdom, the New Kingdom
   (D) The Left Kingdom, the Center Kingdom, the Right Kingdom

(10) Egypt was ruled by:
   (A) A pharaoh
   (B) A king
   (C) A group of nobles
   (D) The rich vizier

(11) Which society gave the world advanced justice systems?
   (A) Mesopotamia
   (B) Kush
   (C) Egypt
   (D) Assyria

(12) Which society sat between the Tigris and Euphrates Rivers?
   (A) Mesopotamia
   (B) Kush
   (C) Egypt
   (D) Babylon

(13) What is the longest river in the world?
   (A) Tigris
   (B) Euphrates
   (C) Amazon
   (D) Nile

(14) Kush was known as the "Land of the _____," because of _____.
   (A) Ivory, because of their abundant elephants.
   (B) Bow, because of their skilled archers.
   (C) Sword, because of their skilled knights.
   (D) Water, because of the Nile River.

(15) Kush was ruled by a:
   (A) Queen
   (B) Pharaoh
   (C) King
   (D) Group of nobles

(16) These civilizations took place during the Stone Age.
    (A) True
    (B) False

(17) Kush worshipped a singular God.
    (A) True
    (B) False

(18) A group of Mesopotamians traveled across the Sahara Desert and discovered other civilizations.
    (A) True
    (B) False

(19) The Egyptians gave us papyrus, and early form of paper.
    (A) True
    (B) False

(20) *Gilgamesh* is the first story recorded by humans.
    (A) True
    (B) False

Mesopotamia, Egypt, and Kush: Quiz Answers

(1) **A.** Mesopotamia is often called the Cradle of Civilization.
(2) **C.** Mesopotamia means "The Land Between the Rivers."
(3) **A.** Mesopotamia had one king.
(4) **C.** The Library of Ninevah was located in Assyria.
(5) **C.** Gilgamesh was a character in an Ancient Mesopotamian story.
(6) **A.** Hammurabi's Code was a set of laws set down by King Hammurabi.
(7) **D.** The class system, from highest to lowest, in Mesoptamia is: Priests, Upper Class, Lower Class, Slaves.
(8) **D.** The Nile River runs through Egypt.
(9) **C.** The three kingdoms of Egypt were the Old Kingdom, the Middle Kingdom, and the New Kingdom.
(10) **A.** Egypt was ruled by a pharaoh.
(11) **C.** Egypt gave the world advanced justice systems.
(12) **A.** Mesopotamia sat between the Tigris and Euphrates.
(13) **D.** The Nile is the longest river in the world.
(14) **B.** Kush was known as the Land of the Bow, because of the skilled archers.
(15) **A.** Kush was ruled by a queen.
(16) **False.** These civilizations took place during the Iron Age.
(17) **False.** Kush worshipped multiple gods, many of them Egyptian.
(18) **False.** Men from Kush traveled across the Sahara, not Mesopotamians.
(19) **True.** The Egyptians gave us papyrus.
(20) **True.** *Gilgamesh* is the first story recorded by humans.

Mesopotamia, Egypt, and Kush: Works Cited

http://mesopotamia.mrdonn.org/

http://www.ducksters.com/history/mesopotamia/ancient_mesopotamia.php

http://www.kidskonnect.com/subjectindex/16-educational/history/257-ancient-mesopotamia.html

http://egypt.mrdonn.org/

http://www.historyforkids.org/learn/egypt/

http://www.ducksters.com/history/ancient_egypt.php

http://africa.mrdonn.org/kush.html

http://www.kidspast.com/world-history/0095-kush.php

http://www.britishmuseum.org/pdf/KingdomOfKush_StudentsWorksheets.pdf

Chapter 3: Ancient Hebrews

Following the rise of ancient civilizations, there also rose many different religions. In Mesopotamia, we saw many different gods, and in Egypt we saw over two thousand gods, also followed by the people of Kush. These religions were *polytheistic*. "Poly" means "many," and "theistic" means having to do with religion. It basically means they believed in many gods. In Egypt, we also see the development of a *monotheistic* religion, the belief in a single god.

This monotheistic religion went against everything that the Egyptians had known. One of the pharaohs tried to convince his people to forget the other gods and worship only one: Aten, the sun god. Coincidentally, this pharoah's name was Akhenaten, and until his death everyone in Egypt followed only Aten. When Akhenaten died, the people of Egypt went back to their former religion.

Two hundred years later, historians believe, is when the seeds of Judaism were first planted. Judaism is a monotheistic religion, which originated in Israel, a country in the Middle East. Judaism is not the only city to call Israel its home: both Christianity and Islam also started here.

Sometimes it is hard for archeologists and anthropologists to trace back history through tools, so they also use scripts and books. Perhaps the most useful book for studying Ancient Israel has been the Bible, in which Ancient Israel is described in detail. The Bible credits the founding of Israel to a man named Abraham, who came from Mesopotamia. Abraham remains a very religious name to this day, and is studied in depth in the Jewish religion. The Bible states that God appeared to Abraham, promising him and his family prosperity—under one condition. Abraham and his family had to worship God, and forget all other gods. Abraham accepted God's offer.

Abraham and his family walked around the Middle Eastern desert, until they finally came to Canaan. They knew that this would be the place where they could finally settle, and worship their God.

Once Israel was founded, the fast-track to a worldwide religion had begun. There is the famous story of the drought, which forced the Israelites out of their land of Canaan. A *drought* occurs when a lack of rain causes the crops to dry up, resulting in no food and mass starvation. The Israelites traveled to Egypt; the Egyptians were more than happy to accept the Israelites.

This happiness did not last long, however. The Egyptians were soon uncomfortable with the rising power of Judaism. They did not like their monotheistic religion, and knew that their own gods would not like it. For this reason, the Egyptians attacked the Israelites. As was the custom at the time, the Egyptians forced their prisoners-of-war into slavery, where the Israelites would remain for *four hundred years*.

During this time, says the Bible, a number of plagues were brought down upon the Egyptians by God, for enslaving the Israelites. These plagues included frogs, flies, disease, meteors, locusts, eclipses of the sun and moon; the Nile River's water turned red with blood, and men, women, and children died. For all of the Egyptians that were affected with these many plagues, not one Hebrew was allegedly harmed.

The Bible describes in depth a man named Moses, who led the Israelites out of Israel. There is the story about how Moses parted the Red Sea in order to get his people across, and then he let the water rush over the Egyptians chasing them. While this parting may not be scientifically logical, it is likely that Moses did lead his people to safety. The Israelites made it to the land of Canaan, which they had fled hundreds of years ago. This journey is often called the "Exodus," which means a journey away from some place. Moses is also the Biblical figure who stood on Mt. Sinai and received the Ten Commandments from God, which are as follows:

(1) I am the Lord thy god, who brought thee out of the land of Egypt, out of the house of bondage.
(2) Thou shalt have no other gods before Me.
(3) Thou shalt not take the name of the Lord thy God in vain.
(4) Remember the Sabbath day to keep it holy.
(5) Honor thy father and thy mother.
(6) Thou shalt not murder.
(7) Thou shalt not commit adultery.
(8) Thou shalt not steal.
(9) Thou shalt not bear false witness against thy neighbor.
(10) Thou shalt not covet anything that belongs to thy neighbor.

These commandments can be found in the *Torah*, the religious book of Judaism. The Torah is to Judaism what the Bible is to Christianity. The Ten Commandments of Judaism may differ slightly from those in the Bible, but essentially convey the same meaning. In the Torah, these commandments are mentioned in both the Book of Exodus and the Book of Deuteronomy.

It is important to understand the Bible as a religious text; it is perfectly okay to recognize as everything as history, and equally okay to understand as a symbolic representation of what happened. Some people believe that Moses never *actually* parted the Red Sea, but instead see it as a tale representing him eluding the Egyptians; other people believe that Moses actually parted the Red Sea with the help of God. Both methods are okay, depending on your beliefs.

The Israelites were surprised when they arrived in Canaan, and found it settled by other people. The Israelites were not happy; this was their homeland! They believed that God had always wanted them to have this land, so they launched war against the usurpers of their homeland. This bloody war lasted for a total of two centuries. The Israelites eventually won, and they united under a single named King Saul.

After fighting their first war, a group of people named the Philistines attacked Israel for its land. King Saul, however, was not that great of a leader. He was quickly replaced by a man named King David. David is also known from ancient history as the man who fought and killed the monster Goliath. David's son Solomon followed in his rule. David and Solomon were excellent leaders, except where taxes and labors were concerned. They instituted forced labor upon their subjects and rose taxes to an uncomfortable point. Ten of the twelve Israelite tribes seceded and formed the official nation of Israel, which the other two named themselves Judah.

The formation of Israel was the highest point for the civilization. It was not soon after that the Assyrians rode down from Mesopotamia in the year 722 B.C. and swiftly conquered Israel. A little more than a hundred and fifty years later, the Israelites were ruled by the people of Persia, who told them they were allowed to return to Canaan and worship their god freely as they chose. But not everyone wanted to return to Canaan, in part because they had become attached to the lands they had lived in for nearly two or three generations. The Jews were scattered across the Middle East, from Egypt to Assyria to Babylon.

A new Empire soon had a large effect on the Jewish people: the epic Roman Empire. Beginning in the city of Rome, the empire soon eclipsed almost all of Europe, extended into Northern Africa, and reached the eastern Mediterranean, which included Israel. In the year 63 B.C.E., the Romans conquered Israel; their rule was forceful and stern, and soon the Jews realized they had no chance but to rebel against their new conquerors.

The Jewish forces were no match for the legions of Roman soldiers, however. The rebellion was easily crushed, and the Romans marched forth to destroy the Biblical city of Jerusalem. It was their hope that the Jews would no longer revolt once they saw the true might of Rome. The destruction of Jerusalem is a significant event in the history of Ancient Israel; many of the Jews fled and scattered once again. This event is known as the "Diaspora" which is Greek for "scattering."

In the year 0, Jesus Christ was born, who proclaimed himself a Jew. He declared himself a prophet of God, and sacrificed himself in order to absorb the sins of humanity. It is the current belief of Christianity that Jesus was the true Messiah, Jews believe that he was only a great teacher and prophet.

In the year 313 C.E., Emperor Constantine ruled Rome. He was swayed away from *pagan* beliefs, which means he did not believe in the main religions at the time. He became a faithful Christian, and he soon declared Christianity the official religion of the Roman Emperor. Only in the past two hundred years had Judaism revived in the Palestinian region.

An interesting artifact from these ancient times is called the Dead Sea Scrolls. They were discovered in the year 1947 by a man named Muhammad Adh Dhib. He was walking along the Dead Sea with a herd of goats, when he stumbled upon a cave in the cliffside. In this cave was a jar of scrolls, referred to today as the Dead Sea Scrolls. These ancient documents were from the year 100 B.C.E., describing the daily lives of the ancient Hebrews. Very few other Biblical writings have survived all these centuries, which make the Dead Sea Scrolls very unique and a marvel to modern historians. You can even view the Dead Sea Scrolls, which have been put on display at the Shrine of the Book, a section of the Israel Museum in the city of Jerusalem.

The land of Israel is significant; it sits in an ideal place in the Middle East, where it touches the Mediterranean Sea and the Dead Sea, and it rests between Egypt, the entrance to Africa, and the rest of the Middle East. This means that traders would have gone through Israel on their way from the Middle East to Egypt, making Israel an economic advantage as well as a religious home. It borders the countries of Egypt, Jordan, Syria, and Lebanon.

Today, the Dead Sea is one of the most-visited tourist spots in the world. The water is nine times saltier than any ocean; the salt is so dense that it often causes people to immediately float when they step in. Because it makes you look like you "dead," it is called the Dead Sea.

Jewish holidays are a way in which people can celebrate the ancient history of Israel. One of these holidays is *Rosh Hashanah*, the Jewish New Year. It is also called the Feast of Trumpets. Rosh Hashanah is supposed to celebrate God's formation of the world on the sixth day, described in the Bible. On Rosh Hashanah, it is believed, God opens two books in Heaven. One of them is called the Book of Life, and the other is called the Book of Death. Those who are good and righteous are recorded in the Book of Life, and those who have done evil are recorded in the Book of Death. It is interesting to compare this system of judgment to that reported by the Egyptian religion, when one's heart is weighed in the afterlife.

Another holiday is *Yom Kippur*, even more significant than *Rosh Hashanah*. *Yom Kippur* means "Day of Atonement" and in ancient times the day was used as a way for priests to atone for the sins of humanity. Yom Kippur was the only day on which priests were allowed the room called the Holy of Holies in a Jewish temple. The high priest of the temple would bring two goats with them: the first would be used for confession. The high priest would describe all of the sins of the Jewish people, and then let the goat run free. The second goat was killed in an act of sacrifice; its blood was put on the altar. The priests believed the blood of the goat would stand in for the sins of humanity as a sacrifice.

Even today, the Jewish religion has maintained its deep religious ties to the land of Israel. Each year, thousands upon thousands of people go to Israel to see the ancient lands described in the Bible and study the history of the Ancient Hebrews.

Ancient Hebrews: Discussion Questions

(1) What is the difference between *monotheistic* and *polytheistic*? In the world today, are most religions monotheistic or polytheistic?

(2) What major religions also started in the Middle East? Are there any connections between these three religions?

(3) What effect did a drought have on the Israelites? What factors does weather play in everyday life, especially when it comes to farming and feeding a society?

(4) Why did the Egyptians attack and enslave the Israelites? What factor did religion play in all of this? Can you connect these reasons to any modern-day historical events?

(5) What influence did the Ten Commandments have on Jewish life? Why might having a set of religious laws be advantageous, and are there reasons why it might be disadvantageous?

(6) What was the significance of the destruction of Jerusalem? What is the Diaspora, and what place does it have in Jewish history? Why is it often studied?

(7) Jesus played a very important part in the development of modern religion. What does Jesus have to do with Christianity, and does he play any part in modern Jewish religion?

(8) What were the Dead Sea Scrolls, why were they only discovered in the 1900s, and what importance do they have to our study of Ancient Hebrews?

(9) What is the importance of *Rosh Hashanah* and *Yom Kippur*? In general, what part do holidays play in religion?

(10) Location plays a key part in the land of Israel. Discuss what the significance of location is when it comes to religion and politics.

Ancient Hebrews: Activities

(1) Create three columns on a piece of paper. Label each column: Polytheistic, Monotheistic, and Other. Explore the following website, which details World Religions for kids. Put each religion into a category, according to how many gods they worship. http://www.uri.org/kids/world.htm

(2) Write a creative short story! This can either be in the first or third person. Pretend that you/your character is in Canaan during the drought. What is life like during the drought? Do you decide to travel to Egypt? What is the journey like? What is Egypt like? You can either write this from the perspective of a journal, or write a short story.

(3) Watch the following YouTube video, which depicts the conflict between the Egyptians and the Israelites, and the story of Moses. Write down the three things you find most interesting about this story. http://www.youtube.com/watch?v=PM5gO8hF1EA

(4) The Ten Commandments are a common link between Christianity and Judaism. Write a few sentences on the importance of the Ten Commandments. Think about the intersection of governing laws and religion. Should religion give people laws to follow? Or should that strictly be the government's job? Give your opinion on paper.

(5) The Bible and Torah are sprinkled with some stories that are, some people think, imaginative, such as Moses parting the Red Sea, plagues being sent down to the Egyptians, and David fighting Goliath. Think about each story, and what it means to its historical context. For example, Moses parting the Red Sea signifies his victory over the Egyptians. Think about the other two examples, and write down they mean to the story's history.

(6) The history of Israel and the Hebrews is a long one. Watch the following informational video that describes Israel's history. Write down three new things that you learned during the video. http://www.dailymotion.com/video/xxhuoi_kid-s-animated-history-with-pipo-the-ancient-israelites-part-1_lifestyle

(7) Look at the following links concerning the Dead Sea Scrolls.
http://channel.nationalgeographic.com/channel/the-truth-behind/videos/dead-sea-scrolls/
http://www.socialstudiesforkids.com/articles/religions/deadseascrolls.htm

Write a paragraph about the importance of archaeology when it comes to discovering ancient artifacts. Do you think it would be fun to be an archaeologist? What would be something fun about having this job, and what might be some challenges to the people who look into the past?

(8) Find a map of Europe and the Middle East. In BLUE, color in the areas that were owned by the Roman Empire. In RED, color in the areas owned by Mesopotamia. In GREEN, color in Egypt. Draw in key rivers like the Tigris, the Euphrates, and the Nile, as well as seas such as the Mediterranean and the Dead Sea. Mark down Canaan, Cairo, and Rome on your map. In another color of your choosing, draw the

modern boundary lines of Israel. Draw a line from Canaan to Cairo, indicating the Israelites' Exodus. Also acknowledge how large the Roman Empire grew.

(9) Create a Venn diagram. One circle will be *Rosh Hashanah,* and the other will be *Yom Kippur.* Compare and contrast the two holidays and their significance to the Jewish religion.

(10) Create a timeline, although specific dates will not be necessary. Simply create a chronology of the journey of the Israelites, from Abraham receiving the word of God to the absorption of Israel by the Romans. Include all important historical events; again, dates are not incredibly important here.

Ancient Hebrews: For Further Reading

Abrahams, Israel. *Judaism*. 2012.

Annett, Leanne. *Hanukkah for Kids! A Children's Book on Hanukkah Lights, Hanukkah History, Traditions & Much More*. 2013.

Broida, Marian. Ancient Israelites and Their Neighbors: An Activity Guide. Chicago Review Press, 2003.

Church, Alfred J,. *The Story of Last Days of Jerusalem*. Redhen, 2012.

Connolly, Peter. *The Holy Land*. Oxford University Press, 1999.

Cooper, Ilene. *The Dead Sea Scrolls*. Harper Collins, 1997.

Green, Robert. *Herod the Great*. Franklin Watts, 1996.

Greene, Jacqueline Dembar. *Slavery in Ancient Egypt*. Franklin Watts, 2000.

Herbst, Eva. *Tales and Customs of the Ancient Hebrews*. Yesterday's Classics, 2008.

Kimmel, Eric. *Hershel and the Hanukkah Goblins*. Holiday House, 1989.

Mann, Kenny. *The Ancient Hebrews: Cultures of the Past*. Cavendish Square Publishing, 1999.

Marx, David. *Rosh Hashana and Yom Kippur*. Children's Press, 2000.

Morrison, W.D.. *The Jews Under Roman Rule*. Didactic Press, 2013.

Reece, Katherine. *The Israelites: The Children of Israel*. Rourke Educational Media, 2005.

Sherman, Josepha. *Your Travel Guide to Ancient Israel: Passport to History*. Lerner Publications, 2004.

Waldman, Neil. *Masada*. Boyds Mills Press, 2003.

Ancient Hebrews: Quiz

(1) What form of religion worships more than one god?
   (A) Monotheistic
   (B) Polytheistic
   (C) Christianity
   (D) Islam

(2) What form of religion worships only one god?
   (A) Monotheistic
   (B) Polytheistic
   (C) Pentistic
   (D) Mesopotamian

(3) To what country do Christianity, Judaism, and Islam have historical ties?
   (A) Turkey
   (B) Israel
   (C) Russia
   (D) Egypt

(4) Why did the Israelites leave Canaan?
   (A) They were attacked by Egyptian slavers
   (B) God brought many plagues down upon them
   (C) They suffered a terrible drought
   (D) God commanded them to leave

(5) What country took in the Israelite refugees, and then enslaved them later?
   (A) Egypt
   (B) Mesopotamia
   (C) Kush
   (D) Canaan

(6) Which of the following was NOT one of the plagues that, according to the Bible, God brought down upon the Egyptians?
   (A) Locusts
   (B) River of blood
   (C) Eclipse of the sun and moon
   (D) Termites

(7) What was the "Exodus?"
   (A) The Israelite journey from Canaan to Egypt, to escape the drought
   (B) The Israelite journey out of Egypt, led by Moses
   (C) The Egyptian journey to Canaan, to enslave the Israelites
   (D) The Israelite journey from Egypt to Kush, to find a new homeland

(8) What is the religious book of Judaism?

    (A) The Bible
    (B) The Quran
    (C) The Torah
    (D) The Book of Good and Evil

(9) What famous empire stretched across Europe, into northern Africa, and reached the eastern Mediterranean?
    (A) Mesopotamian
    (B) Greek
    (C) Roman
    (D) Egyptian

(10) What was the Diaspora?
    (A) The Israelite journey from Canaan to Egypt
    (B) The destruction of the Library of Ninevah
    (C) The destruction of Jerusalem
    (D) The destruction of the Roman capital by the Israelites

(11) In 1947, a set of scrolls were found that are called the _____ Scrolls.
    (A) Red Sea
    (B) Dead Sea
    (C) Mediterranean Sea
    (D) Narrow Sea

(12) The Dead Sea is called such, because _____.
    (A) Bodies often turn up on shore, some of them decades old.
    (B) The salt level allows people to float, often making them appear "dead."
    (C) The salt level is so high that no fish or aquatic creature can survive there.
    (D) It was the sea upon which King David of Israel was pronounced dead.

(13) What holiday celebrates the Jewish New Year?
    (A) *Rosh Hashanah*
    (B) Torah Day
    (C) The Day of Judgment
    (D) *Yom Kippur*

(14) What Jewish holiday is the "Day of Atonement?"
    (A) *Rosh Hashanah*
    (B) The Day of the Book of Good and Evil
    (C) The Day of Judgment
    (D) *Yom Kippur*

(15) Israel sits in what part of the world?
    (A) Europe
    (B) Middle East
    (C) Greater Asia
    (D) Minor Eurasia

(16) According to the Bible, King David of Israel previously killed a monster named Goliath.
    (A) True
    (B) False

(17) Egyptians believed in a religious system of monotheism.
    (A) True
    (B) False

(18) Today, Jews believe that Jesus Christ was the messiah.
    (A) True
    (B) False

(19) Emperor Constantine of Rome declared that Christianity would be Rome's official religion.
    (A) True
    (B) False

(20) The Ten Commandments were received by King Solomon at the peak of Mount Olympus.
    (A) True
    (B) False

Ancient Hebrews: Quiz Answers

(1) **B.** Polytheism means the worship of more than one god.
(2) **A.** Monotheism means the worship of only one god.
(3) **B.** Christianity, Judaism, and Islam have historical ties to Israel.
(4) **C.** The Israelites left Canaan because they suffered a terrible drought.
(5) **A.** The Egyptians took in Israelite refugees and enslaved them later.
(6) **D.** Termites was NOT one of the plagues that, according to the Bible, God brought down upon the Egyptians.
(7) **B.** The "Exodus" was the Israelite journey out of Egypt, led by Moses.
(8) **C.** The religious book of Judaism is the Torah.
(9) **C.** The Roman Empire stretched across Europe, into northern Africa, and reached the eastern Mediterranean.
(10) **C.** The Diaspora was the destruction of Jerusalem.
(11) **B.** In 1947, the Dead Sea Scrolls were found.
(12) **B.** The Dead Sea was named after the fact that the salt levels allow people to float, often making them appear "dead."
(13) **A.** *Rosh Hashanah* celebrates the Jewish New Year.
(14) **D.** *Yom Kippur* celebrates the Day of Atonement.
(15) **B.** Israel sits in the Middle Easts.
(16) **True.** According to the Bible, King David of Israel previously killed a monster named Goliath.
(17) **False.** Egyptians believed in a polytheistic system, not monotheistic.
(18) **False.** Today, Jews do not believe that Jesus was the messiah.
(19) **True.** Emperor Constantine declared that Rome's official religion would be Christianity.
(20) **False.** The Ten Commandments were received by Moses on Mt. Sinai, not King Solomon on Olympus.

Ancient Hebrews: Works Cited

http://ancienthistory.mrdonn.org/hebrews.html

http://www.historyforkids.org/learn/religion/jews/

http://score.rims.k12.ca.us/activity/ancient_hebrews/

http://www.penn.museum/long-term-exhibits/canaan-and-israel-gallery.html

http://www.pbs.org/wnet/heritage/index.html

http://www.historyguide.org/ancient/lecture4b.html

http://www.kidspast.com/world-history/0047-Israels-beginnings.php

http://ancienthistory.pppst.com/hebrews.html

http://www.socialstudiesforkids.com/articles/worldhistory/ancientmiddleeastreligion2.htm

http://www.education.com/study-help/article/ancient-history-middle-east-israel/

Chapter 4: Ancient Greece

Of all the great ancient empires, Greece is perhaps only second to Rome. Ancient Greece gave the world many gifts, some of them objects and some of them ideas. In fact, Greece is known for its advanced manner of thinking, and many of their ideas gave birth to our modern forms of thought and democracy. When the founding fathers discussed the formation of the United States of America, they borrowed many ideas from Ancient Greece. There is a reason that this ancient civilization is still studied today; mainly because, if you want to understand the world we live in, you need to also understand the people and the world that came before us. The men and women of Greece had a large part in forming the past, and even the present.

First, let's start with the geography of Ancient Greece. As you can deduct, it was centralized around the modern country of Greece. Greece rests on the Mediterranean Sea. It is composed of a mainland, and dozens of islands. One of these islands is Crete, which today is a popular tourist destination. However, Greece also extended into the land of *Asia Minor*, or modern day Turkey and Middle East. The civilization was composed of many different areas: there was Crete, of course, and a larger area called Peloponnesus. North of that was Thessaly, Illyria, Paeonia, and Macedonia; east of that was Thrace. Phrygia, Aeolis, Lydia, and Lycia were all areas that could be found in Asia Minor. Memorizing these names is not that important, but it can help you out if you decided to examine a map of Greece, to study its history.

In terms of a historical timeline, Greece was at the height of its power before the Roman Empire began. The Grecian Empire emerged around 800 BCE and ended around 146 BC. We will explore the significance of these dates in a moment, as we push through the rich history and culture of Ancient Greece.

Historians and scholars look at Greece is terms of three periods, very similar to the three kingdoms of Ancient Egypt. The first period is called the *Archaic Period*, which began in 800 BCE and ended in 508 BCE. The Archaic Period was significant because it solidified Greece's culture. For one, the Olympic Games began during this time period. That means that the Olympics have been held for over 2500 years! Each couple years when you watch the world Olympics, keep in mind the exciting history behind the event.

The Archaic Period also gave birth to Greece's most lasting pieces of literature. They were two books written by a blind man named Homer; the books, written in a poetic form, were called *The Iliad* and the *Odyssey*. *The Iliad* tells the tale of the Trojan War, and *The Odyssey* recounts the journey of a Greek soldier home following the battles. These two pieces are essential in understanding Greek culture and literature; more than that, they are fun reads with beautiful language. Today, most students will read one of the two in high school literature classes.

Another famous piece of literature is a collection of stories called *Aesop's Fables*, which mainly feature talking-animal characters. Each story, likely no more than a paragraph or two, has a very specific message in mind, often called a moral. Today, as in the past, they are used in order to teach children to behave well.

The second period is called the *Classical Period.* This is often considered the height of Ancient Greece, mostly because this is when most of its prominent philosophers lived. Socrates, Plato, and Aristotle were Greece's biggest thinkers; they gave us the idea of *democracy*, the voice of the people, along with advanced ways of thinking that were almost unknown before that time period. Socrates was the first of them, and he taught Plato everything he knew; Plato then took on Aristotle as a student. Socrates was known for never writing anything down, so it was the job of Plato and Aristotle to take down these revolutionary ideas. Many of their texts can be read today, from books in the bookstore or even online.

The Classical Period also witnessed the brutal fighting between Athens and Sparta, two *city-states*. A city-state is a city that acts independently; Athens and Sparta essentially ruled a great portion of Ancient Greece. Having two large powers controlling the same empire was sure to breed conflict, especially since each Grecian city-state had its own army and navy, its own government, and its own rules. While Athens and Sparta were the biggest of the Grecian city-states, there was also Corinth, Megara, and Argos that tried to stay out of conflict. It was difficult to keep Athens and Sparta away from each other's throats, however.

Athens was known for being greedy, and tried to conquer the other city-states. Athens was a center for education and thought. Sparta would not stand for it; being a military power, whose entire way of life was based on warfare, they certainly had the manpower to take down Athens. Sparta created an alliance with Corinth, and they teamed up to take Athens down. This was the start of the *Peloponnesian War*.

While the Spartans had the manpower, Athens had the money and a better navy. The Spartans could never reach the Athenians, who were hiding behind the great walls—until a horrible plague struck Athens, likely due to so many people being stuck inside the city. Athens decided to move out and take the Athenians head-on, but it did work out in there favor. In a huge battle over the Spartan-controlled city of Sicily, the Athenian soldiers were wiped out. Those who did not die were taken prisoner and enslaved, and that was the end of Athens's warmongering.

Also during the Classical Period rose a name famous in history: Alexander the Great. He originated from Macedonia, and was made a king at a very young age after the death of his father. The philosopher Aristotle was one of Alexander's tutors, and they got along well. But more than philosophy, Alexander was trained well in the art of warfare. He had dreamed of conquering the world, and that was what he set out to do.

Alexander the Great is known for never losing a single battle. From the Grecian Peninsula, he set out across Asia Minor, the Middle East, and even northern Africa, bent on conquering them. But he was not a cruel ruler; he taught his new subjects about Greek culture. Many people wanted to live under Alexander the Great and surrendered to him immediately; others fought back, but they never held out long against one of the greatest commander's in history. Some cities were too poor and deprived by themselves that they openly welcomed Alexander to come; being part of the rich Greek Empire had its advantages! By the time he was thirty-two years old, he had earned his empire. But the spritely young commander, never defeated in battle, was finally defeated by sickness. He died at that age, leaving behind a vast swath of conquered lands.

More than conquering lands, however, Alexander spread Greek culture to new parts of the world. Democracy spread, as did the Greek gods and other forms of culture, such as theatre, poetry, and even fashion. Today, in the Middle East, some archaeologists have unearthed artifacts very similar to those found in Ancient Greece; likely, ideas were spread by Alexander that had a lasting impact on other parts of the globe.

It was the death of Alexander the Great that ended the Classical Period, in the year 323 BCE. This also signified the beginning of the final period, the *Hellenistic Period*. The word "hellen" is a term that the Greeks used to identify themselves. To us, they are Ancient Greeks, but to them, they were *hellens*. The Hellenistic Period ended when the budding empire of Ancient Rome conquered Greece. Eventually, all of Greece's citizens, far and wide, became members of the Ancient Roman Empire, soon to become the greatest empire the world had ever seen.

A popular area of study today is the Greek gods, which are a fun area to study. They even laid the basis for the kids' series, *Percy Jackson and the Olympians*. Here is a helpful section that details the Greek gods and their areas of power.

Zeus – God of Lightning, Thunder, and the Sky.

Hera – Goddess of Families and Marriage

Poseidon – God of the Sea

Hestia – Goddess of the Hearth

Ares – God of War

Athena – Goddess of Wisdom

Apollo – God of Archery

Artemis – Goddess of the Moon

Hephaestus – God of Fire and Blacksmiths

Aphrodite – Goddess of Love and Beauty

Hermes – God of the Travelers, Thieves, and Merchants

Hades – God of the Underworld

These were the main twelve gods, referred to as the Olympians. There are a number of minor gods, which also form parts of Greek mythology. Mythology is one of the lasting memories of Ancient Greece; each story had a message. Because Ancient Greece was a society that believed in many gods, many of their stories attempted to explain the way the world works with the gods; some attempted to strike fear into people's hearts, to tell them to fear the gods, while others tried to explain why the gods are good and benevolent. Other myths involved creatures, such as the minotaur.

The story of Theseus and the Minotaur is one of the most interesting stories, and it will feature a part in the Activities section. What is important to understand, however, is that each story had a purpose: it was created and told, and retold and retold and told again, to convey a message. Even today, that is the purpose of many books: to teach, to show, to explain. Next time you read a book, try to think of a *message*. What is the author trying to tell you? Is there anything the characters are doing that have terrible consequences, perhaps acting as warning to you Is there anything for which your characters are rewarded, perhaps acting as an encouragement to you?

You can thank the Ancient Greeks for a lot of things; more than just the Olympics, they gave us good ideas, such as Trial by Jury. This means that if someone gets sent to court, a set of jurors, ordinary citizens, can decide whether you are innocent or guilty, based on information presented by the lawyers. This was something first exercised in Ancient Greece, and it is commonly used in the United States justice system today. In modern America, you need to be eighteen years or older to serve on a jury, and it likely a judge that will mediate the courtroom and decide upon a punishment.

Have you ever seen columns outside a building, perhaps a library or a city hall? Well, these were first invented by the Greeks! The columns were often ornate; they symbolized power and beauty. For over 2500 years, people have been inspired by the Ancient Greeks to construct buildings with columns. They help support the building as well; they're not just for decoration! The Ancient Greeks also made large leaps in architecture. Without them, the Romans would have had much to learn.

The Greek columns are perhaps most emblematic in their use in the Parthenon. The Parthenon is also called the Temple of Athena, because it was a holy place. It is still standing today; 2500 years later! That goes to show how excellent the Greek architecture truly was. It was one of the most popular European tourist destinations. It is built upon a land called an acropolis, which just means an elevated area. High ground is easier to defend than low ground, so the Greeks often put the most important buildings on hills, such as the Parthenon. The Parthenon sits in Athens.

The Ancient Greeks were a fascinating people. They led a nation of thought and arts, of war and fighting; a nation that, though it was conquered by the Romans, endures today. While Rome no longer controls Greece, the

Grecians have maintained a rich history. Though the country has suffered economic troubles in recent years, it remains one of Europe's most-visited countries. And for anyone who cannot visit a country as far away as Greece, you need only to open a copy of *The Iliad* or *The Odyssey* to jump into Greece's history and live the world as its people did.

Ancient Greece: Discussion Questions

(1) Many of the greatest European empires have been based around the Mediterranean Sea (French, Roman, Greek, Egyptian). What significance does the Mediterranean Sea have, and what advantages might it offer?

(2) Similarly, other empires are also broken up into different time periods (Archaic, Classical, and Hellenistic were three period of Greece). To both historians and students, what are the advantages of studying an empire in different parts? Does it help or hurt the way you look at history?

(3) What do you gain from reading literature from a specific time period? Although you may have not read *The Odyssey* or *The Iliad* yet, what do you think is important about reading Ancient Greek literature or mythology? What educational opportunities does it offer you?

(4) What happened during the Classical Period of Ancient Greece that makes it the height of the empire? Why might people call it the greatest period of Greece?

(5) There were more *polytheistic* religions in the past than there are now, and historians say that this is because past civilizations used each god to explain the world around them (for example, Zeus explained thunder and lightning, while Ares guided warfare and Athena gave people wisdom). Why did past civilizations need to explain these things, and why did they turn to religion to explain it? Think about how technology and science has developed across the past two thousand years.

(6) What is your opinion of a trial by jury? Is it a good thing to have, or should the United States get rid of it? Explain your answer.

(7) Why did some people want to be conquered by Alexander the Great? What did he do to his subjects that helped them? Why might someone want to be part of a larger empire, than a small city?

(8) After learning about Ancient Greece, discuss three ways that you can access the past. How can you learn about Ancient Greece in our modern age?

(9) Sparta and Athens were part of Greece, but still they fought each other. This is likely because each one was a city-state with its own independent resources. Discuss the advantages and disadvantages of being a city-state.

(10) To you, what is the most obvious evidence that Ancient Greece existed? The way we think? Literature? Architecture? Why do you think this?

Ancient Greece: Activities

(1) Print out a map of Europe, the Mediterranean, the Middle East, and northern Africa. Using some additional research, highlight Ancient Greece at the height of its power. Include the various areas of Greece that were detailed earlier in the lesson, as well as Asia Minor.

(2) Watch the following YouTube series on Alexander the Great. It will detail why he rose to power so quickly, and also his conquest around Europe and Asia. For each video, write down *three* interesting facts about Alexander the Great. When you've finished watching them, write a paragraph about how Alexander the Great impacted the rest of the world and why we still study him today. In contrast, discuss how Alexander was impacted by Persian culture.
Part One: https://www.youtube.com/watch?v=9ykNUugV3vw

Part Two: https://www.youtube.com/watch?v=v6jmffoxdU0

Part Three: https://www.youtube.com/watch?v=G0Ezo6iHvg4

(3) Listen and read to the following story about Theseus and the Minotaur. When you have finished, write down three lessons, messages, or morals that readers can learn from the story.
http://myths.e2bn.org/mythsandlegends/playstory563-theseus-and-the-minotaur.html

(4) Listen to the following story; this is an interesting activity, because this is how stories were often told. Before writing was very popular, it was told *orally* – or by mouth. Listen to the story of the Trojan Horse, and at the end write down what you thought about listening to a story, rather than reading it. Are there any advantages or disadvantages? After you've written this, put your ideas into a Venn diagram. One circle will be "Listening to a Story" and the other will be "Reading a Story." The space in the middle will be used to describe what happens when you read and listen to a story at the same time.
http://ec.libsyn.com/p/d/1/0/d107129f0eba8b99/woodenhorse.mp3?d13a76d516d9dec20c3d276ce028ed5089ab1ce3dae902ea1d06c88137d4ce5e6e0e&c_id=1306912

(5) Create three columns on a piece of paper. The first column will be "Archaic Period," then "Classical Period," then "Hellenistic Period." Write down at least two important events that happened in each period, as well as the dates. If you need to look up additional information online, feel free to do so.

(6) Pick three of the twelve main Olympic gods and goddesses. Write *three paragraphs* about each one; include what that person is the god or goddess of, research any Greek myths that involve him or her, and also include why the people of Greece might need that Olympian. What makes them so special?

(7) Create your own Greek god/goddess and myth! Imagine that you are someone living in the Archaic Period in Ancient Greece. You are wondering how the world works; embody the reasons into your own god or goddess. Name your new Olympian, and then write your very own myth. If you have trouble thinking of an idea, you can either use one of the Olympians' domains (sky, wisdom, love, war) and create your new god, or write a new myth about one of the existing Olympians.

(8) Read the following article on the way in which Socrates has impacted today's education system, and how teachers use his methods in the classroom and everyday life. When you are finished, define the following terms:

Socratic Method

Socratic Circle

Socratic Seminar

After that, imagine that you are a teacher in a classroom. Would you, or would you not, use the Socratic Method/Circle/Seminar in your classroom? Would you use just one or two? All three? None at all? Explain.

(9) The Seven Wonders of the Ancient World were largely decided upon by Greece. Use the following link to read about each wonder. After that, create a scrapbook about the seven wonders. Include a picture of each place (either drawn or printed out), write about its history, and finish with a section about *why* it deserves to be a wonder of the world. Have fun with this activity! http://www.learnnc.org/lp/pages/4994

(10) The home life of Ancient Greece was largely attended to by women. Studying the daily life can reveal a lot about the women of Ancient Greece, who had a large impact on the civilization. Read the following article, and then write down five interesting facts about the role or daily activities that women had in Ancient Greece. http://www.metmuseum.org/toah/hd/wmna/hd_wmna.htm

Ancient Greece: For Further Reading

Bordessa, Kris. *TOOLS OF THE ANCIENT GREEKS: A Kid's Guide to the History & Science of Life in Ancient Greece.* Nomad Press, 2006.

Caper, William. *Ancient Greece: An Interactive History Adventure.* You Chose Books, 2010.

Cobblestone Publishing. *If I Were a Kid in Ancient Greece: Children of the Ancient World.* Cricket Books, 2007.

Factly, IP. *101 Facts, Amazing Facts, Photos & Videos.* IP Factly, 2014.

Green, John. *Life in Ancient Greece Coloring Book.* Dover Publications, 1993.

Hatt, Christina. *Ancient Greece: Excavating the Past.* NA-h, 2004.

Lassieur, Allison. *The Ancient Greece: People of the Ancient World.* Childrens Press, 2004.

MacDonald, Fiona. *Wonder Why Greeks Built Temples: and Other Questions about Ancient Greece.* Kingfisher, 2012.

MacDonald, Fiona. *You Wouldn't Want to Be a Slave in Ancient Greece!* Franklin Watts, 2013.

Osborne, Mary Pope. *Magic Tree House Fact Tracker #10: Ancient Greece and the Olympics: A Nonfiction Companion to Magic Tree House #16: Hour of the Olympics.* Random House Books, 2004.

Pearson, Anne. *Ancient Greece.* DK CHILDREN, 2007.

Riordan, Rick. *Percy Jackson and the Olympians.* Disney-Hiperion, 2006.

Solway, Andrew. *Ancient Greece.* Oxford University Press, 2001.

Steele, Philip. *Navigators: Ancient Greece.* Kingfisher, 2011.

Van Vleet, Carmella. *Explore Ancient Greece!* Nomad Press, 2008.

Ancient Greece: Quiz

(1) Ancient Greece rested on what major European sea?
   (A) Baltic
   (B) Black
   (C) Ural
   (D) Mediterranean

(2) The first period of Ancient Greece was the _____.
   (A) Classical Period
   (B) Hellenistic Period
   (C) Archaic Period
   (D) Alexandrian Period

(3) *The Odyssey* and *The Iliad* were about what war?
   (A) The Spartan Wars
   (B) The Peloponnesian War
   (C) The Trojan War
   (D) The War of Greek Conquest

(4) The second period of Ancient Greece was the _____.
   (A) Classical Period
   (B) Hellenistic Period
   (C) Archaic Period
   (D) Middle Period

(5) Choose the option with the Greek philosophers in which they first appeared. Who taught who?
   (A) Plato→Socrates→Aristotle
   (B) Socrates→Plato→Aristotle
   (C) Aristotle→Plato→Socrates
   (D) Aristotle→Socrates→Plato

(6) What war was fought between Athens and Sparta because Athens tried to conquer other city-states?
   (A) The Trojan War
   (B) The War of Spartan Defense
   (C) The War of the Five Kings
   (D) The Peloponnesian War

(7) Whose death ended the Classical Period?
   (A) Alexander the Great
   (B) Homer
   (C) Jesus Christ
   (D) Socrates

(8) The third and final period of Ancient Greece was called the _____.
   (A) Archaic Period

(B) Classical Period
(C) Hellenistic Period
(D) New Period

(9) How many *Olympians* were there in Greek mythology?
 (A) Over one hundred
 (B) Twelve
 (C) Ten
 (D) Fifteen

(10) Who wrote *The Odyssey* and *The Iliad*?
 (A) Socrates
 (B) Homer
 (C) Plato
 (D) Alexander the Great

(11) What impact did the Greeks have on our modern court system?
 (A) Trial by jury
 (B) A judge to preside over the trial
 (C) Allowing citizens to watch the trial
 (D) Limiting jail sentences to thirty-five years for minor crimes

(12) What did the Greeks call themselves?
 (A) Greeks
 (B) Grecians
 (C) Hellens
 (D) Hellenistics

(13) Who was the ruler of the Greek gods?
 (A) Hades
 (B) Zeus
 (C) Hero
 (D) Ares

(14) What is an *acropolis*?
 (A) A temple to worship the gods
 (B) An elevated area of land
 (C) A city hall in Ancient Greece
 (D) A mountain where the Grecians believed the gods lived

(15) What form of religion did the Ancient Grecians follow?
 (A) Monotheistic
 (B) Polytheistic
 (C) They had no form of religion
 (D) Everyone followed a different belief system

(16) Alexander the Great was from Macedonia.
 (A) True
 (B) False

(17) The Ancient Grecians used gods and goddesses to explain the way the world worked around them.
 (A) True
 (B) False

(18) Athens won the Peloponnesian War.
 (A) True
 (B) False

(19) Alexander the Great failed to spread Greek culture during his conquests throughout Eurasia.
 (A) True
 (B) False

(20) The Ancient Greeks conquered the Roman Empire.
 (A) True
 (B) False

Ancient Greece: Quiz Answers

(1) **D.** Ancient Greece rested on the Mediterranean Sea.
(2) **C.** The first period of Ancient Greece was the Archaic Period.
(3) **C.** *The Odyssey* and *The Iliad* were about the Trojan War.
(4) **A.** The second period of Ancient Greece was the Classical Period.
(5) **B.** Socrates→Plato→Aristotle
(6) **D.** The Peloponnesian War was fought when Athens tried to take over other city-states.
(7) **A.** Alexander the Great's death ended the Classical Period.
(8) **C.** The third and final period of Ancient Greece was the Hellenistic Period.
(9) **B.** There were twelve Olympians in Greek mythology.
(10) **B.** Homer wrote *The Odyssey* and *The Iliad*.
(11) **A.** The Greeks came up with trial by jury.
(12) **C.** The Greeks called themselves *hellens*.
(13) **B.** The ruler of the Greek gods was Zeus.
(14) **B.** An *acropolis* is an elevated area of land.
(15) **B.** The Ancient Greeks were polytheistic.
(16) **True.** Alexander the Great was from Macedonia.
(17) **True.** The Ancient Greeks used gods and goddesses to explain the way the world worked around them.
(18) **False.** Athens did not win the Peloponnesian War; Sparta did.
(19) **False.** Alexander the Great succeeded in spreading Greek culture during his conquests throughout Eurasia.
(20) **False.** The Ancient Greeks did not conquer the Roman Empire; it was the other way around.

Ancient Greece: Works Cited

http://greece.mrdonn.org/

http://greece.mrdonn.org/lessonplans.html

http://www.bbc.co.uk/schools/primaryhistory/ancient_greeks/

http://www.historyforkids.org/learn/greeks/

http://www.ducksters.com/history/ancient_greece.php

http://www.activityvillage.co.uk/ancient-greece

http://www.learnnc.org/lp/pages/4994

http://www.kidspast.com/world-history/0071-socrates.php

Chapter 5: Ancient India

Of the many powerful Asian empires, Ancient India is perhaps one of the most fascinating – both because of its rich history, and because of the incredible culture it gave the world. Like many eastern empires, it is often overlooked because of its thousands of years of complicated history, but that will be simplified into an engaging timeline and examination of Ancient Indian life. If we want to understand what Indian culture means to the world today, we must first understand what it meant to the world centuries ago.

Earlier, we discussed the *Out-of-Africa theory*, the idea that humans originated in Africa and left through Egypt, entering the Middle East; and from there, they spread to Europe and Asia, and from Asia they spread to North and South America. Well, India was one of the first places, according to archaeologists, that ancient humans went, considering how close it is to the Middle East. Along with its proximity to the Arabian Sea, the Bengal Sea, and the Indian Ocean, it is a perfect location.

India is home to some of the biggest mountains in the world, the Himalayas, which stretch along the northeastern edge. It borders Pakistan, Nepal, China, and Bangladesh, which offered it a great variety of trading options. The fact that it was close to the sea was also a big plus – people there could trade very easily! If there's anything that we've learned so far, it's that any form of water (lakes, mountains, rivers, oceans) makes a perfect spot for civilization.

It is estimated that humans first set foot in India around fifty thousand years ago. As it did everywhere, it took a while for civilization to start up. During the Bronze Age, Indian civilization finally kicked off, under a rule known as the Harappan Empire. The people of this empire traded with people to the west – in the lands currently known as Pakistan, Afghanistan, and even Iran.

But if there's anything *else* that we've learned, it's that empires do not stick around forever. After one thousand years, the Harappan Empire finally collapsed. While no one is exactly sure why it fell, some scholars are unearthing new information—but you'll read more about that in the Activities section.

Next began a period of time in which many people wanted to conquer the Indus Valley (which covers parts of Iran, Pakistan, Afghanistan, and eastern India), as well as the rest of India. The first of these people came from central Asia, likely China. With them came horses, disease, new languages, and a new religion. The blending of the Indian and Eastern Asian people created a civilization known now as Vedic.

It was not long, however, around 550 BCE, before a new conqueror entered the playing field. His name was Cyrus of Persia, and he was on a quest to take over northern India—or what is *now* known as Pakistan. Northern India eventually became territory of the Persian Empire, until someone set out to conquer the Persians.

His name was Alexander the Great of Macedonia, and on his conquest of the Middle East, he also found himself in Northern India. It did not take long for him to introduce Greek culture to the Indians, before he set off on more battles.

Alexander the Great departed from India in the year 324 BCE, on his way to Babylon. In his absence, someone called Chandragupta staged a coup of the government, meaning that he took it over. Chandragupta rallied soldiers together, and they took back their land from Alexander. This was the start of the Mauryan Empire. It lasted just over a hundred years due to incompetent rulers. In the year 231 BCE, the Mauryan Empire fell about, setting the stage for new leadership.

Until the year 320 CE, there was not a significant form of empire in Indian civilization. Many small kingdoms, like the Mauryan Empire, attempted to seize power, most of them failing rather quickly.

A man named Chandragupta II, in the year 319 CE, lived up to his namesake and decided to create a new empire of the Indian kingdoms. His focus was in northern India, but his conquests did take him into the south. His rule was called the Guptan Empire, and it was an immediate success. The people of India wanted to be ruled. They wanted some form of powerful government. Under Chandragupta II, money flowed through the hands of Indian subjects. Soldiers deflected attacks from all angles and kept the people safe. The government strengthened trade with other Indian kingdoms, and also with China, the giant neighbor to the north.

Because the Guptan Empire flourished, so did its technology and science. Sugar became very popular during this period, and became one of Indian's chief exports, especially to China. But it was not long before the Guptan Empire would be brought to its knees. It was the Huns, who rode from Mongolia, which brought down the Guptan government.

The Huns were led by the infamous Genghis Khan, one of the world's strongest conquerors. If there was anyone who could bring down an empire, it was him. Ruler of the Mongols, he had no mercy and took the Guptan Empire mercilessly. His grandson, Kublai Khan, went on to take over China, and it was ruled by the Mongols for approximately one hundred years.

After its collapse, the Indian people once again divided into many different, smaller kingdoms. The Guptan Empire lasted about 180 years.

For the next *one thousand years*, India was the subject of numerous attacks from both China, the Muslims of the Middle East, and the Huns once again. It seemed that, after so many generations of submission, India would never be able to unite once again.

In the 1400s, Muslims had control of India. They attempted to defend their land against the Mongolians (also called *Mongols*). However, the Mongols were too powerful. They had an unbelievably coordinated cavalry that could break almost any army; uniquely, the Mongolians were trained in the ability to shoot arrows backwards, so they could fire at people behind them if attacked.

The Mongols took control of India, and they were called *Mughals* by the Indian people. At the start of the 1400s, the Mughal Empire began in India. A man named Babur took the helm as the first Mughal ruler of India. He made an effort to capture the Indian city of Delhi, something that had been very difficult to previous Muslim rulers. The reason that Babur was successful was because of the invention of *gunpowder* and *guns*, technology that originated in Asia and was quickly spreading.

Babur's son Humayun succeeded him as ruler of the Mughal Empire, but the Indian people had had enough of other people ruling them. They staged a revolution, and Humayan quickly fled. Once he gathered his strength, he launched attacks against the Indian rebels, but he did not live long enough to see any results. He died in the year 1545 CE. He left behind a thirteen-year old son named Akbar, that was unfit to rule an empire because of his age.

Before he died, Humayun decreed that the military general Bairam Khan and his wife Hamida Banu would rule, until Akbar came of age. But Khan and Banu were not eager to give up their power. Akbar did not fully acquire power of the Mughal Empire until he was twenty-eight years old. Under his rule, the Mughal Empire grew powerfully.

At the time, there was an intricate network of roads that veined across Asia and the Middle East. It was called the Silk Road, and a small portion of it was controlled by the Mughal Empire. We'll explore the Silk Road more in the section about China, but for now it's important to understand that it was a very significant tool for trade. There were not only goods (like silk) that were exchanged across the Silk Road, but also ideas (like religion and philosophy). More on that fascinating topic later.

Even more than warfare, religion has played a very significant part in India's history. To understand India's religious history, you must understand three major religions: Islam, Hinduism, and Buddhism.

Islam is practiced by Muslims. It is a *monotheistic* religion; Muslims believe in a single God, like Jews and Christians, except they call this one god Allah. Muslims recognize the teachings of Jesus and Moses, but they also worship the prophet Mohammed, who stands above the others in Islamic teachings. The Islam religion worked to serve Allah; the people believed that everything they did was in service of Allah, and if you followed his laws, you would be rewarded well in the afterlife. The divide in Islam today (between two groups called the Sunnis and Shiites) has created endless problems for hundreds of years, and continues to spark war in the Middle East to this day. But when you think of the time period in which India was ruled the Muslims, *this* is the religion that they instituted above all others.

Hindu is one the world's most ancient religions. It is very similar to what the early Indians practiced, in the days of the Harappan Empire. The word "*Hindu*" is derived from the word *Indus*, as in the Indus Valley. Like many religions, Hinduism evolved over time. When East Asian cultures blended with Indian culture, new gods were added, some were taken out, some changed forever. But it eventually melded into the Hindi religion. Hinduism is a *polytheistic* religion, but it is hard to tell exactly what the Harappan people named their gods; their writing is so old, that it is difficult to historians and cryptographers to decipher it. Hindus believe in the idea of reincarnation: that when you die, your soul is transferred to a new body and you live again and again. If you have behaved well, you will be blessed a good next life. If you have been, you will be put into a nasty body, perhaps even an animal (like a rat). While Hinduism began as a religion that practiced animal sacrifice in order to appease the gods, the Hindi people eventually changed to give nice gifts to the gods, such as flowers. They would play music and have feasts in the gods honor, and cite nice prayers. The two gods, Vishnu and Shiva, were now benign gods, as opposed to the old, malevolent gods Indra and Varuna. Hinduism was one of India's earliest religions, and led to the formation of much of the rich Indian history.

Buddhism is similar to Hinduism. Instead of being reincarnated again and again, a man named Siddhartha Gautama Buddha thought that if a person were good enough during his or her life, that person would not be reincarnated again, and instead move on to the afterlife. Buddha gathered thousands of followers, and eventually millions. He taught his followers to be moral and pure, to treat one another with respect. There were two different types of Buddhists – the everyday people, who attempted to live their lives (working, getting married, climbing the social ladder) while also following these practices. There was the more extreme group, the monks who decided to devote their life to the teachings of Buddhism.

It was during the Mauryan Empire in India that one of the kings converted to Buddhism. This instance made many of his subjects do the same; essentially, it helped Buddhism spread across the Indian region. During the Guptan Empire, many Buddhist monks travelled across Asia, some even using the Silk Road to do so. They went west and east, bringing the teachings of Buddhism with them. In China especially, Buddhism became a powerful form of religion, and it still is today (although the Chinese government made recent headlines by declaring that reincarnation would be illegal).

No matter what you believe in, it is important to understand that religion and warfare are two key factors in Indian history. Warfare ripped apart the Indian people for hundreds of years, while religion simultaneously united them. The diverse Indian geography, as well as its culture, is worth studying if we want to understand Asia and its effect on the rest of the world.

Ancient India: Discussion Questions

(1) In Ancient India's history, its land trade was more profitable than its sea trade. Why is this? What countries are near India that made offer valuable resources?

(2) China is one of India's most important neighbors. Explain why this is. What advantages and disadvantages come with having such a powerful neighbor, and how did this affect India's history?

(3) Throughout the centuries, India saw many different rulers, often from the time it came into existence. Why was India so easy to conquer? How could other people so easily take over the government?

(4) What does the *Out-of-Africa* theory have to do with the settlement of India? Explain the relationship between the two.

(5) In what ways is Islam similar or different to other religions you've learned about, such as Judaism, Christianity, Hinduism, and Buddhism?

(6) What do Hinduism and Buddhism have in common? According to history, *why* do they have so much in common (who got ideas from who)?

(7) Do you think that warfare or religion had a more profound impact on India's history? Explain your answer.

(8) Although you have not learned much about the Silk Road yet, discuss why you think a single road might be a great idea. What pros and cons might the Silk Road have, connecting both Asia and the Middle East? Think about the following: disease, violence, goods, religion, philosophy, and technology.

(9) It has been said that "History repeats itself," and that can be supported by the many cycles of Indian leadership. But think about the following quote: History does not repeat itself, but it rhymes with itself." What does this mean? And why this it apply to Indian history? What does the word "rhyme" mean here?

(10) The arrival of Alexander in the Indus Valley is an important moment in history, because it means that people from different continents are traveling further from their homes and entering new territory. What other implications does Alexander the Great's explorations have on the history of India, as well as the world? What impact did he have on India?

Ancient India: Activities

(1) Print out a map of India (it can be a modern one). Label the following: Himalayas, Pakistan, Nepal, Bangladesh, China, Iran, Afghanistan, Saudi Arabia, Egypt, Arabian Sea, Bengal Sea, Indian Ocean.

(2) Read the following article that attempts to explain why the Harappan Empire collapsed. Write down three different ways in which scientists are discovering the truth of the past, as well as your three favorite facts from the article. http://www.sci-news.com/archaeology/science-collapse-harappan-civilization-01705.html

(3) On a piece of paper, draw a line; this will be your timeline! Using dates found here, as well as any online research you wish to do, create a timeline of India, beginning with the Out-of-Africa theory and ending with the Mughal Empire. You may design the timeline in any fashion that you like.

(4) Watch the following video on the Guptan Empire, which also includes information about their fall at the hands of the Huns. Write down three facts that you did not know before watching this video, in addition to three facts that you find interesting. https://www.youtube.com/watch?v=5upeOZHzSyw

(5) Create your own journal! Imagine that you are living in the Indus Valley under the Guptan Empire. Imagine what it would be like to have the Huns invade and take over; what was the invasion like? Is there any form of order or government when the Huns leave? Why did they come in the first place? Feel free to do additional research for your journal entry.

(6) John Green, as well as the bestselling author of *The Fault in Our Stars*, teaches world history for free online. Watch his video on Buddhism, and answer the following questions.
    (1) What was the Indian caste system based on?
    (2) What are the Four Noble Truths?
    (3) What are the elements of the Eightfold Path?
    (4) To be a Buddhist monk, what do you have to give up?
    (5) Why was Buddhism so attractive to Hindus? Why did they convert?
    (6) Under what two dynasties did India experience unity?
    (7) Who was Ashoka and what relationship did he have to Buddhism?
https://www.youtube.com/watch?v=8Nn5uqE3C9w

(7) Create a three-circled Venn diagram; each circle will represent one of the following religions: Islam, Buddhism, and Hinduism. Compare and contrast each one, according to what you have learned.

(8) John Green has also made an excellent video about the Mongols, which are an important people to understand, since they had a big hand in forming Indian government, as well as that of the rest of Asia and Europe; the video also includes information about Alexander the Great's empire. During the video, write down *five* ways in which the Mongol Empire impacted the world around them. Try to make at least one of them relate to India. https://www.youtube.com/watch?v=szxPar0BcMo

(9) Outside rulers had an enormous effect on India. Choose one of the following people, and write a five-paragraph biography on that person: Babur, Buddha, Alexander the Great, Genghis Khan, or Humayan.

(10) To wrap up study of the Indus Valley, here is one final John Green video that details the history of the Indus Valley, essential to an understanding of the development of India. Watch the video, and write a one-paragraph essay about something that you liked or did not like about the video. Was it easy to understand? Were there any things that could have been made clearer? https://www.youtube.com/watch?v=n7ndRwqJYDM

Ancient India: For Further Reading

Bankston, John. *Ancient India/ Maurya Empire.* Mitchell Lane Publishers, 2012.

Barr, Marilynn. *India: Exploring Ancient Civilizations.* Teaching & Learning Company, 2003.

Cohn, Jessica. *The Ancient Indians.* Gareth Stevens Publishing, 2012.

Conkle, Nancy. *Coloring Book of Ancient India.* Bellerophon Books, 1989.

Daud, Ali. *Ancient India: Hands-On History!* Armadillo, 2014.

Gassos, Dolores. *India.* Chelsea House Publications, 2005.

Gedney, Mona. *The Life and Times of Buddha.* Mitchell Lane Publications, 2005.

Holm, Kirsten. *Everyday Life in Ancient India.* Powerkids, 2012.

Julia, Nelson. *India.* Heinemann Library, 2001.

Kenoyer, Jonathan. *The Ancient South Asian World.* Oxford University Press, 2005.

Nardo, Don. *Ancient India.* Lucent, 2007.

Schmop, Virginia. *Ancient India.* Children's Press, 2005.

Sundermann, Elke. Discover Ancient Civilizations in History: India, China, and Japan: Big Picture and Key Facts. CreateSpace Independent Publishing Platform, 2010.

Sundermann, Elke. *A Walk Through Ancient India, China and Japan: Time Travels.* CreateSpace Independent Publishing Platform, 2010.

Zamosky, Lisa. *India: World Cultures Through Time.* Teacher Created Materials, 2008.

Ancient India: Quiz

(1) What theory says that humans came and traveled through Egypt and the Middle East, and spread across the world?
 (A) Human Travel Theory
 (B) Out-of-Africa Theory
 (C) Egyptian Tunnel Theory
 (D) Early Human Travel Theory

(2) What continent is India part of?
 (A) Europe
 (B) Asia
 (C) Eastern Europe
 (D) Middle East

(3) What mountains tower over the northeastern part of India?
 (A) The Rocky Mountains
 (B) The Misty Mountains
 (C) The Himalayan Mountains
 (D) The Alpian Mountains

(4) What was the *first* significant Indian empire?
 (A) Mughal
 (B) Guptan
 (C) Harappan
 (D) Buddhist

(5) What country is *not* included in the Indus Valley?
 (A) India
 (B) Pakistan
 (C) Iran
 (D) Turkey

(6) Which of the following empires did *not* conquer India?
 (A) Mongolian

(B) Persian
(C) Greek
(D) Egyptian

(7) The Persians conquered India—who then conquered the Persians?
(A) Alexander the Great
(B) Babur
(C) Buddha
(D) Genghis Khan

(8) Who staged an Indian revolution and took Indian lands back from Greece?
(A) Buddha
(B) Genghis Khan
(C) Chandragupta II
(D) Chandragupta

(9) Chandragupta II started *what* empire in India?
(A) Mauryan
(B) Guptan
(C) Mugal
(D) Guptianian

(10) Who led the Mongols against India?
(A) Buddha
(B) Genghis Khan
(C) Chandragupta
(D) Alexander the Great

(11) What network of roads connected Asia and the Middle East?
(A) The Kingsroad
(B) The Egyptian Road
(C) The Silk Road
(D) The Iron Road

(12) What does the word *Mughal* mean?
(A) It was the name of the Indian rebel-ruled empire
(B) It was the Indian word for *Mongol*
(C) It was what the Indians called themselves
(D) It was the main Indian export to China

(13) What importance did sugar have to India?
(A) It was used during their religious services
(B) It served as the basis of *all* India's popular foods
(C) It was a main Indian export to China
(D) A lack of sugar eventually led to the fall of the Mauryan Empire

(14) Which of the following was *not* one of India's central religions at one point?
(A) Judaism
(B) Hinduism
(C) Islam
(D) Buddhism

(15) What do the Muslims call their god?

(A) Mughal
(B) God
(C) Allah
(D) Babur

(16) Both Hindus and Buddhists believe in reincarnation.
(A) True
(B) False

(17) India endured almost a thousand of years of foreign rule.
(A) True
(B) False

(18) India was never ruled by its own people.
(A) True
(B) False

(19) Gunpowder and guns were invented in England, and spread to Asia.
(A) True
(B) False

(20) Sugar was used primarily in India, and spread to other places.
(A) True
(B) False

Ancient India: Quiz Answers

(1) **B.** The Out-of-Africa theory says that humans traveled through Egypt and the Middle East and spread throughout the world.
(2) **B.** India is part of the Asian continent.
(3) **C.** The Himalayan Mountains are in northeastern India.
(4) **C.** The Harappan Empire was the first significant Indian empire.
(5) **D.** Turkey is not included in the Indus Valley.
(6) **D.** The Egyptians did not conquer India.
(7) **A.** Alexander the Great conquered the Persians.
(8) **D.** Chandragupta staged an Indian revolution and took lands back from Greece.
(9) **C.** Chandragupta started the Guptan Empire in India.
(10) **B.** Genghis Khan led the Mongols against India.
(11) **C.** The Silk Road connected Asia and the Middle East.
(12) **B.** *Mughal* is the Indian word for Mongol.
(13) **C.** Sugar was a main Indian export to China.
(14) **A.** Judaism was not a central religion in India.
(15) **C.** Muslims call their god Allah.
(16) **True.** Both Hindus and Muslims believe in reincarnation.
(17) **True.** India endured about a thousand years of foreign rule.
(18) **False.** India was indeed ruled by its own people on occasion.
(19) **False.** Gunpowder and guns were invented in Asia.
(20) **True.** Sugar was perfected in India, and spread elsewhere.

Ancient India: Works Cited

http://www.historyforkids.org/learn/india/

http://india.mrdonn.org/

https://sites.google.com/site/1ancientcivilizationsforkids/ancient-india

http://www.socialstudiesforkids.com/subjects/ancientindia.htm

http://www.timeforkids.com/destination/india/history-timeline

Chapter 6: Ancient China

Of the Asian countries, China is second biggest, only dwarfed by Russia's massive expanse. China also holds one of the most impressive empires ever seen; for hundreds upon hundreds of years they ruled the east. They created technological marvels, both in science and medicine, in architecture in archaeology, and in many other fields. In order to understand today's large world, it is crucial to have an understanding of one of the largest empires the world has ever seen. China has a rich and flourishing history that spans generations of some of humanity's most interesting personalities. China also helped give mankind great structures, such as the Great Wall and the Silk Road.

China sits in eastern Asia. To the north rests Mongolia; to the east are the lands of Korea and Japan; to the south are Myanmar, Thailand, Vietnam, and India; to the west are Afghanistan, Pakistan, Uzbekistan, and Kazakhstan. It touches one body of water on its southeastern shore: the East China Sea, a large body of water that gives it access to trade with countries like Korea and Japan, as well as access to the Pacific Ocean. Meanwhile, the Yellow Sea is on the northeastern shore.

But in the early days of Chinese civilization, the people of China did not know that all of this existed. They were confined to their fields and their villages, although they did not know that the Mongolians Huns were in the north. The Huns were made infamous by their raiding and their pillaging. The border between China and Mongolia is stricken with hot deserts, while the east of the country has a more coastal climate. The southern border of China, its border with India, is marked by the Himalayan Mountains

The Himalayan Mountains are a marvel of the natural world; they hold the record of ten of the tallest mountains in the world, which includes Mount Everest, *the* tallest above-water mountain. The Himalayas can be seen as both a blessing and a curse. Firstly, they helped protect China against possible invaders on the other side (as we know, India had a long history of being occupied by foreign conquerors who would have loved to access China). Secondly, the Himalayas are hard to cross; they are treacherous terrain for any traveler.

In northern China, along its border with Mongolia, are two important deserts. The first is the Gobi Desert, one of the most dangerous deserts in the world. This is because of its almost complete lack of water. The other desert is the Taklamakan Desert, which holds the record for the world's second-largest desert, next to the Sahara. The Taklamakan has been named by many the "Sea of Death," for all the travelers that don't make it out alive. The sun rises in the morning and casts an infernal heat upon the sands; during the day, sand storms can strike at any minute, along with venomous snakes; when the sun falls, the nights turn to debilitatingly cold temperatures. There's a chance of death almost any time. Just like the Himalayas, the Taklamakan Desert stops other people from coming in and invading.

China has two major rivers that are important to know. The first is the Yangtze River, which was surrounded by high banks. This meant that people could live near the river and not be in danger of the water overflowing and flooding their house—something that was common in China, to people who lived near the rivers. The second river is called the Huang He, also named the Yellow River. Its banks are much lower, so the houses on its sides are elevated.

People have populated China for thousands of years; they first reached there when humans left Africa and populated Asia. But the ancient civilization of China was not founded for hundreds of years after that. Today, historians say that Ancient China began in the year 2,000 BCE, by a group of people called the Lungshan. The Lungshan lived along the Huang He River, and they had been doing so for over a thousand years. Eventually, the Lungshan grew tremendously, both in population and intellect. This birthed a period known as the *Xia Dynasty*, the first dynasty in Chinese history.

Chinese history is divided into sections called *dynasties*, each one a different part of the overall hereditary rule. The throne would be passed on to the next person in line in the family.

The people of the Xia Dynasty were, according to scientists, advanced compared to other people around the world at the time. The Xia people knew how to build structures well; they used plaster as floors, instead of dirt; they made jewelry and pottery; and their clothes were exquisitely designed from silk, a very valuable material.

The Xia Dynasty was host to a polytheistic religion, as most religions were at the dawning of mass civilization. They believed that there was a god for rivers, a god for rain, a god for the earth, and so on; and there was one god, T'ien, that, like Zeus, ruled all of the other gods and stood above any king.

The Xia Dynasty lasted for about three hundred years, until the Shang Dynasty took up the reins of Ancient China. The Shang Dynasty was also the first family to rule during the Bronze Age. They did not follow the typical laws that said the son would inherit rule from his father; instead, the throne was exchanged between brothers, and then to nephews. As with any society, there will be people who do not like their ruler; to protect themselves against this, the Shang Dynasty created something called the Mandate of Heaven, which stated that the gods gave them the right to rule; hence, anyone who questioned their rule would also be questioning the gods.

The next dynasty was the Chou Dynasty, who wanted to rule while the Shang were still in power. But because the Shang invoked the Mandate of Heaven, it was tough for the Chou to overthrow them. The Chou then did something unthinkable; they claimed their own Mandate of Heaven, that the gods wanted the Shang to step down and the Chou to rise up. The Chou believed that their own Mandate of Heaven could only be in effect if they were good rulers; they recognized that the Shang were corrupt, and they did not want to become like them.

When this conflict arose, the people of China rose up in rebellion against the Shang Dynasty; it was quickly brought down, and the Chou rose to power. They were good rulers, focusing on fixing China's broken roads. They wanted their merchants to travel safely, since this would help the economy. They also gave money to science, so that people could study the night sky, the stars, and the planets. With money flowing and science booming, so too did literature. Books and texts were written feverishly.

The Chou eventually fell out of power, though, and the Qin Dynasty replaced it. Emperor Qin only stayed in power for fifteen years; despite this short time, however, the Qin Dynasty remains one of the most influential. First of all, Emperor Qin was strict and harsh. He believed that his subjects were born evil, and for that reason, they needed to be controlled tightly. He controlled the government and the country with an iron fist, but he also gave the order to build one of the world's greatest inventions: the Great Wall of China.

The Great Wall was originally built to protect China from the Huns, who would come down from the north and raid Chinese villages, killing innocent citizens and stealing goods. Qin ordered several different types on people to work on the wall, including prisoners and criminals—but normal Chinese citizens and laborers worked on it too. It was a very difficult job; the days were long, there was not much food, and many of the workers ended up dying from exhaustion.

It was not finished in Emperor Qin's lifetime, though; in fact, it was continuously built for 1700 years; each emperor after Qin added a little more to the wall, in the hopes of fortifying it. Today, the Great Wall of China is one of the most visited tourist destinations in the world; technically, you can walk its entire length, but it would be very difficult, considering the wall is 3700 miles long.

After the Qin Dynasty, the Han Dynasty took power, and it was during this time period that the Silk Road became popular. Rather than being one single road, the Silk Road was a whole network of paths that led from China across Asia, across the Middle East, into Arabia and Asia Minor, to Byzantium and the Black Sea. The Silk Road is significant because many goods, like silk, reached new parts of the world. People in Rome could purchase Asian goods they had never seen before. But, even though it's called the Silk Road, silk was not the most important thing that was traded.

Ideas, such as religion and philosophy, made their way across the world with unprecedented speed. For the first time, the world's best thinkers in Asia and the Middle East and Europe could collaborate. It affected the way people wrote books and the way people thought. Someone in China could listen to tales of Greek conquests and Greek gods, while someone in Russia might learn of the Indian culture. It was a method for expanding human knowledge.

The distance from Rome to China is about 4,000 miles, something that could hardly be trekked, especially with all of the deserts and mountains in the way. But with official roads connecting the two countries, things became easier. The paths lining the Silk Road became abundant with cities of mixed peoples and cultures; temples of many religions could be found, as well as trading posts and even oases.

China offered Rome its silk (Rome had only seen silk during their conquests; they had no idea where it originally came from), while Rome gave China gold.

Next came the Tang Dynasty, but there was period of warfare between the Han and the Tang. It is called the Age of Division, when the numerous Chinese kingdoms fought each other for power and wealth; most people became horribly poor and excitedly rich during this time, but most people were in crippling debt.

When the Tang Dynasty came out on top, China entered its Golden Age, experiencing peace after its many wars. Gunpowder had just been invented, which made it easy to hunt. Tea was made popular in China, and it quickly spread around the world. It was also a sort of renaissance for China, which made leaps in the areas of art, music, and literature. In terms of religion, Buddhism became the predominant religion, spreading ideas of peace and enlightenment.

After the Tang Dynasty came the Song Dynasty, which was almost a period of success, then followed by the Ming Dynasty, around the middle of the 1000s. It was during this time period that many humans, the Chinese included, were traveling across the world in search of other lands. The Chinese were famous for their enormous boats. Because most of the land around them was already mapped out and known, the Chinese adventurers sought to map the Pacific Ocean.

The Ming Dynasty ruled from a place called the Forbidden City; starting in 1406, it took fourteen years to complete. The Forbidden City is composed of eight hundred buildings, and is also one of the world's most popular tourist destinations. While the Forbidden City was the place where the Ming Dynasty ruled, it is now available as a museum, allowing tourists to view China's rich and elaborate history.

Hopefully this serves as a helpful basis for studying Chinese history and culture; more aspects of Ancient China, such as the Zodiac and Confucius, will be detailed in the Activities section. For now, it's important to know that China was ruled by a series of dynasties, and that the transition between these dynasties was not always peaceful; the fighting would often bankrupt its citizens and send the country into complete chaos. But when peace was achieved and China united, they made enormous bounds in arts and science that contributed to today's world.

Ancient China: Discussion Questions

(1) Do you think China's size has anything to do with the numerous civil wars it experienced over the centuries? If China were smaller, would there have been as much fighting? Explain your answer.

(2) What stopped the Chinese people from knowing what lay beyond their borders? Did nature come into play? Was it because the land was so large, it seemed fruitless to travel anywhere? Come up with at least two answers.

(3) What is the *advantage* of having dynastic rule (rule by inheritance)? What are the disadvantages of this? Your opinion here will shape your understanding of China's complex history, especially where succession is concerned.

(4) Many early civilizations were polytheistic when it came to religion. Do you think there is a reason behind this? Explain why this might be.

(5) What were some of the problems with the Mandate of Heaven? Did it eventually succeed or fail? (This is your opinion.)

(6) How did fixing China's roads help its economy? What is the relationship between the construction of roads and trading?

(7) The Chou Dynasty fought the Shang Dynasty for control of China. What reasons did they give for wanting to take down the Shang? Were these reasons just, and can you think of any historical moments or even movies/books that might be similar?

(8) The Great Wall of China was built to keep out the invading Mongolians. In today's world, do you think it has any military importance? Or is it just a monument of the past, used to understand China's history?

(9) What was more important on the Silk Road: goods or ideas? Explain your answer.

(10) Do you think China's entry into the Golden Age has anything to do with the rise of Buddhism? Based on your knowledge of Buddhism and Chinese history, explain the relationship between the two.

Ancient China: Activities

(1) Print out a blank map of Asia and the Middle East. You may use whatever colors you wish to code the following items:

China, Mongolia, North Korea, South Korea, Japan, Thailand, Vietnam, India, Nepal, Cambodia, Russia, Pakistan, Afghanistan, Uzbekistan, Kazakhstan, Iran, Turkey, Iraq, Saudi Arabia, and Egypt

Gobi Desert, Taklamakan Desert

Yangtze River, Huang He (Yellow) River

Yellow Sea, Sea of Japan, East China Sea, South China Sea, Pacific Ocean, Bay of Bengal, Arabian Sea

Understanding this map will give you a good understanding of Asia's vast expanse, as well as the various lands that could be reached because of the Silk Road and new exploring.

(2) Using this cool website, explore some areas along the Great Wall of China with both pictures and a 3D tour. Read the descriptions as well, and then write down two interesting facts about the Great Wall. http://www.thechinaguide.com/index.php?action=activity/greatWallOfChina

(3) On a piece of paper, draw a line (this will be your timeline!). Use the dates given here, as well as some additional online research, to create a timeline of the various dynasties in Ancient China, starting with the Xia and ending with the Ming.

(4) Here's another 3D tour, this one of the Forbidden City. Read the description, and then take a tour. Write down your initial impressions of the Forbidden City, and what you think it must have been like to live there. http://www.thechinaguide.com/index.php?action=activity/view&activity_id=2

(5) In Ancient China, many people followed the "Three Teachings:" Confucianism, Taoism, and Buddhism. Create a small journal about these three philosophies, based off research from the library or online. Include at least five paragraphs about each teaching. Here are some ideas to help you get started: How did the teaching start? What did people think about it at first? Were there any significant people that started or helped spread the thought? Was this teaching only used in China? Did it spread? If you'd like, you may also compile pictures for your journal.

(6) Read the following story about the Chinese zodiac—essentially, each year is correlated to a specific animal. If you are born during that year, then that is your animal, and it gives you a prediction for your personality. There are western zodiac signs too (such as Scorpius, Gemini, Taurus, and so on). When you're finished, write a paragraph on how the Zodiac relates to Chinese history, as well as what the Zodiac is used for. http://www.logoi.com/notes/chinese_zodiac.html

(7) Read the following Chinese folk story about Nian, the Horrible Monster. When you've finished, draw a picture of what you think Nian looks like, and then write down the relationship between Nian and the Chinese New Year. http://china.mrdonn.org/newyear.html

(8) Choose one of the Ancient Chinese dynasties, from Xia to Ming. You will focus on that dynasty and create a portfolio for it. In your portfolio you will detail who ruled during that dynasty, their greatest successes, their greatest failures, how they rose to power, how they fell to power, and the overall impact on Chinese culture and the world. You may use the library or the Internet for this exercise.

(9) Gunpowder is one of China's most significant inventions. Read the following article on the creation of gunpowder, and then write three ways in which it changed the world, not just China, forever.
http://kaleidoscope.cultural-china.com/en/136Kaleidoscope1.html

(10) Watch the following video about the tomb of Emperor Qin; it is quite an amazing video to watch. Write down three interesting facts, as well as what you think the significance of the Terra-Cotta Warriors is.
http://video.nationalgeographic.com/video/exploreorg/china-terra-cotta-warriors-eorg

Ancient China: For Further Reading

Beshore, George W. *Science in Ancient China (Science of the Past)*. Children's Press, 1

Challen, Paul. *Life in Ancient China*. Crabtree Publishing Company, 2004.

Collins, Terry. *Ancient China: An Interactive History Adventure*. You Chose Books, 2012.

Conkle, Nancy. *A Coloring Book of Ancient China*. Bellerophon Books, 1984.

Cotterell, Arthur. *Ancient China*. DK CHILDREN, 2005.

Deady, Kathleen W. *Ancient China: Beyond the Great Wall (Great Civilizations)*. Fact Finders, 2011.

Friedman, Mel. *Ancient China*. Scholastic, 2010.

Kramer, Lance. *GREAT ANCIENT CHINA PROJECTS: 25 GREAT PROJECTS YOU CAN BUILD YOURSELF*. Nomad Press, 2008.

Lee, Gisela. *China: World Cultures Through Time (Primary Source Readers)*. Teacher Created Materials, 2008.

Mann, Elizabeth. *The Great Wall: The story of thousands of miles of earth and stone that turned a nation into a fortress (Wonders of the World Book)*. Mikaya Press, 2006.

Morley, Jacqueline. *You Wouldn't Want to Work on the Great Wall of China!* Children's Press, 2006.

O'Connor, Jane. *Hidden Army: Clay Soldiers of Ancient China*. Grosset and Dunlap, 201

Osborn, Mary Pope. *Magic Tree House Fact Tracker #31: China: Land of the Emperor's Great Wall: A Nonfiction Companion to Magic Tree House #14: Day of the Dragon King (A Stepping Stone Book(TM))*.

Random House, 2014.

Ross, Stewart. *Ancient China (TALES OF THE DEAD)*. DK CHILDREN, 2006.

Sherman, Josepha. *Your Travel Guide to Ancient China (Passport to History)*. Lerner Publishing Group, 2004.

Ancient China: Quiz

(1) What Asian country is bigger than China?
    (A) Korea
    (B) Russia
    (C) Mongolia
    (D) India

(2) Which of the following bodies of water does NOT border China?
    (A) Yellow Sea
    (B) East China Sea
    (C) South China Sea
    (D) Bay of Bengal

(3) What mountain range sits on the border between India and China?
    (A) The Alps
    (B) The Mountains of the Moon
    (C) The Himalayas
    (D) The Gobi Mountains

(4) Who were the Lungshan?
    (A) The warriors from Mongolia that repeatedly invaded China
    (B) The people who existed in Chinese lands before the Xia Dynasty
    (C) The group of scholars who invented gunpowder
    (D) The builders who worked on the Great Wall of China and the Forbidden City

(5) Which dynasty *first* created the Mandate of Heaven, which decreed the gods gave them the right to rule?
    (A) Xia
    (B) Qin
    (C) Chou
    (D) Shang

(6) Construction of the Great Wall of China began during what dynasty?
    (A) Xia
    (B) Qin
    (C) Chou
    (D) Shang

(7) Why was the Great Wall of China built?
    (A) To stop the Chinese people from emigrating to Mongolia
    (B) To stop the Chinese people from dying in the Gobi Desert
    (C) To create a walkway connecting the Yellow Sea and central China
    (D) To create a barricade, keeping the Mongolian invaders out

(8) During what dynasty did the Silk Road bloom?
    (A) Han

    (B) Ming
    (C) Song
    (D) Chou

(9) What major European empire desired China's abundance of silk and spices?
    (A) Greek
    (B) Egyptian
    (C) Taklamakan
    (D) Roman

(10) What was the Age of Division?
    (A) A period during which many people were torn between supporting the Xia or the Ming Dynasty
    (B) A period during which China almost split into two different countries, Gobi and Taklamakan
    (C) A period during which the Chinese kingdoms fought each other for power
    (D) A period during which the Chinese and Mongolian kingdoms battled for control of the Korean Peninsula

(11) When the Tang Dynasty rose to power, China entered the _____.
    (A) Age of Division
    (B) Era of Good Feeling
    (C) Age of Heroes
    (D) Golden Age

(12) What two inventions became popular as China moved into the Golden Age?
    (A) Gunpowder and tea
    (B) Scrolls and coffee
    (C) Sugar and silk
    (D) Bows and arrows

(13) What was the Forbidden City initially used for?
    (A) A secret training center for Chinese soldiers
    (B) A hideout for Chinese royalty during times of war
    (C) The place from where Chinese royalty ruled
    (D) The place where China centered all of their riches and wealth, to stop the Mongolians from stealing it; hence, the "Forbidden" City

(14) During what dynasty did the Forbidden City come about?
    (A) Xia
    (B) Tang
    (C) Chou
    (D) Ming

(15) What people to the north continually invaded Chinese lands?
    (A) The Russians
    (B) The Mongolians
    (C) The Gobis
    (D) The Koreans

(16) The Great Wall of China was completed during the Qin Dynasty.
   (A) True
   (B) False

(17) The Himalayas were easily passable to Chinese travelers.
   (A) True
   (B) False

(18) The Chinese kingdoms were often at odds with each other, especially during the Age of Division.
   (A) True
   (B) False

(19) The Silk Road is called so, because China only wished to trade silk with Rome.
   (A) True
   (B) False

(20) The Xia Dynasty was China's first dynasty.
   (A) True
   (B) False

Ancient China: Quiz Answers

(1) **B.** Russia is bigger than China.
(2) **D.** The Bay of Bengal does not border China.
(3) **C.** The Himalayas sit on the border between India and China.
(4) **B.** The Lungshan were the people who existed on Chinese lands before the Xia Dynasty.
(5) **D.** The Shang Dynasty *first* created the Mandate to Heaven, and the Chou used it after them.
(6) **B.** Construction of the Great Wall of China began during the Qin Dynasty.
(7) **D.** The Great Wall was built to keep Mongolian invaders out.
(8) **A.** The Silk Road bloomed during the Han Dynasty.
(9) **D.** The Roman Empire desired China's abundance of silk and spices.
(10) **C.** The Age of Division was a period during which the Chinese kingdoms fought each other for power.
(11) **D.** When the Tang Dynasty rose to power, China entered the Golden Age.
(12) **A.** As China moved into the Golden Age, gunpowder and tea became popular.
(13) **C.** The Forbidden City was initially the city from where Chinese royalty ruled.
(14) **D.** The Forbidden City came about during the Ming Dynasty.
(15) **B.** The Mongolians continually invaded Chinese lands.
(16) **False.** The Great Wall was not built during the Qin Dynasty; it took 1700 years to build.
(17) **False.** The Himalayas were not easy to pass for Chinese travelers.
(18) **True.** The Chinese kingdoms were often at odds with each other, especially during the Age of Division.
(19) **False.** The Silk Road was not given that name because China only wanted to trade silk with Rome.
(20) **True.** The Xia Dynasty was China's first dynasty.

Ancient China: Works Cited

http://www.china.mrdonn.org/

http://www.historyforkids.org/learn/china/

http://www.ducksters.com/history/china/ancient_china.php

https://sites.google.com/site/1ancientcivilizationsforkids/ancient-china

http://www.historyforkids.net/ancient-china.html

http://www.neok12.com/History-of-China.htm

http://www.kidskonnect.com/subjectindex/16-educational/history/252-ancient-china.html

Chapter 7: Ancient Rome

As the saying goes, "The bigger they are, the harder they fall." Rome, one of the biggest and most impressive empires the world has ever seen, rose to enormous heights and experienced a tragic and inevitable downfall. Rome was a city that rested on the Italian peninsula, near the Tiber River. But of course, history and myth twisted the founding of the city into something much more extraordinary.

The Romans believed that two boys, Romulus and Remus, had been abandoned by their parents (one of whom was Mars, the god of war) and then found by a female wolf. The female wolf raised them until they were found by an old shepherd. Eventually, Romulus and Remus grew and built their own city. They contested for power, to see who would come out as king. Romulus killed his brother Remus, and crowned himself King of Rome. The Romans believed that, since Romulus was the son of Mars, that Rome was blessed by the gods and shined in their eyes.

Rome started as a city, grew into a kingdom, and then into an empire. It existed primarily in modern-day Italy, which is surrounded on three sides by water—the Mediterranean Sea, which gave the Romans trading access to numerous other European and African countries. Italy is pockmarked with mountains, including the mighty Alps. Italy is also surrounded by numerous islands, which helped serve as outposts.

As Rome's power steadily grew out of Italy and across Europe, it became a *republic*. A republic is a government in which the officials are elected and can only serve for a certain amount of time. This contrasted previous kingdoms, where rulers were given the throne by blood and served until they died or resigned. Men wrote Rome's laws, and even penned a state constitution. Historians call the first period in Rome's history the *republic*, since that's what it was. It would soon grow into an expansive empire.

But before it could do that, Rome did have trouble becoming a republic. First of all, it was ruled by a king named King Tarquin the Proud, who was upsetting the people of Rome. He refused to listen to their complaints, however; the people called for justice and equality, they wanted to rule themselves, and not a tyrannical king. They wanted to give power to the people. They wanted to elect people who would actually listen to them. The people of Rome overthrew Tarquin the Proud, and created their new government.

The Roman Republic was run by a group called the Senate (did you ever wonder where the United States Senate got its name?). It was the Senate's duty to pass laws, as well as gather taxes from the Roman citizens. Members of the Senate were selected, and were typically wealthy. The Senate was led by two men called the Consuls, who chose the senators. Once a consul chose a senator, that man stayed in the Senate for the rest of his life. It was considered an honor and a sacred duty. The Consuls were elected by the people of Rome.

Religion was an enormous part of daily Roman life. Like Ancient Greece, the Romans had twelve major gods, and a series of minor gods. Historians can directly correlate the Greek and Roman gods. Here is a small section that will identify the similarities.

Roman	Title	Greek
Jupiter	Supreme Ruler of the Gods	Zeus
Neptune	Ruler of the Sea	Poseidon
Pluto	Ruler of the Underworld	Hades
Vesta	Goddess of the Hearth	Hestia
Juno	Goddess of Marriage	Hera
Mars	God of War	Ares
Minerva	Goddess of Wisdom	Athena
Apollo	God of the Sun and Archery	Apollo
Venus	Goddess of Love and Beauty	Aphrodite
Mercury	Messenger God	Hermes
Diana	Goddess of the Moon	Artemis
Vulcan	God of Fire	Hephaestus

As you can see, there is a correlation between the two. However, you can also see that many of the Roman gods share the name of planets, and that is because by the time the Romans rose to power, astronomy had taken the world by storm. The Romans studied the sky and related the planets to their gods and goddesses.

Though they both revered the gods, two different classes of people lived apart in Rome. The lower class was called the *plebeians* (plee-bee-ins), or plebs for short. The upper class was called the patricians, who could afford jewelry and fancy clothes and large feasts. They often lived in better houses. It was not usual for plebeians and patricians to get together, and even rarer for them to marry each other. It was a social divide that transcended even the mighty Roman Empire.

Romans also loved entertainment. One of their favorite sports was chariot racing, during which horses would pull a man on a two-wheeled cart. The chariots raced in a placed called the *Circus Maximus*, which started in around the sixth century BCE.

As the Roman Republic grew, so too did its need for an army. The Romans were coming into contact with people all across Europe and the Middle East, and even northern Africa. One such African city called Carthage had ventured into the Mediterranean Sea and captured three Italian islands—this upset Rome, who believed the unoccupied islands should belong to them. Rome and Carthage never settled upon any agreement, except total war.

Thus began a series of war called the Punic Wars. Carthage had the advantage of a supreme naval force and an okay army, while Rome's army was excellent and navy was subpar. The twenty-year war ended in a draw; Carthage decided to give Rome only one of the original three islands that they conquered. But the Romans did not give up; they desperately wanted the other two.

Carthage decided to conquer some areas in Spain (also called Iberia), some areas that were allied with the Roman Republic. Rome reacted drastically and declared war once again on Carthage. Instead of attacking the Carthaginian forces in Spain, Rome instead attacked Carthage itself. Hannibal, a Carthaginian general in Spain, decided he would then attack Rome directly. He crossed the Alps, something said couldn't be done, and approached Rome.

Hannibal raged across Italy for fifteen years, while the Roman legions slowly defended their territory. Carthage, worried about Hannibal's safety, ordered him to retreat to northern Africa. Before he could though, Rome surrounded Carthage and Carthage surrendered. They agreed to stay away rom Spain and Italy and to size down its army. However, as soon as Hannibal returned to Carthage, they soon went back on their deal; the rebellion was put down quicker than it had started. Rome had them surrounded.

Once again, months later, Carthage rose up against Rome. They sent Hannibal into Spain. They tried to attack Italy. Rome had had enough. They invaded Carthage and burned the city down. They ruined the fields and sold its people into slavery. Carthage had been entirely destroyed, and the Punic Wars were over.

Rome was now falling apart—not from external forces, but from within. Firstly, there was a lack of money. It takes a lot of money to run a country! The buildings and bridges and roads were out of shape and dangerous, the sewer system was outdated, the soldiers needed to be paid, the poor needed to be fed—it was a financial disaster. Secondly, as with most governments, the politicians fell into corruption. Most of the time, rich people would pay others to vote for them. Hence, money won over the voters (many of whom were poor), not their philosophies. Thirdly, crime was a huge problem. There was no official police in the Roman Republic; if you were rich you could hire guards to protect you, and the soldiers were often fighting in other places.

There was one man who claimed he could solve everyone's problems, though—his name was Julius Caesar (the month July is named after him!). He first served as both a general in the Roman army, and a government official. He was a man of the people; he listened to their complaints and did something about them. Crime was up in Rome; he vowed to stop it. Taxes were rising; he vowed to lower them. Over time, the Romans became so infatuated with Julius Caesar that the other government officials feared that Caesar would crown himself king.

After many of the politicians disagreed with him, a brief Roman civil war followed. Caesar defeated all of his enemies and declared that he would be the dictator of Rome—but at the time, dictator was not seen as a horrible position. It was seen as an honor, and many people viewed Caesar as a man who seized power in order to fix Rome's problems. He solved the economy problem, fixed roads and buildings, gave more power to the Senate, and even changed the yearly calendar. Roman rules said that if someone became a dictator, they could only do so temporarily; otherwise, they were taking on the power of a king, something the Romans resented. Caesar, however, declared that he would be dictator until he died.

The senators of Rome stood in stark opposition to their new dictator, and they decided to do something about it. Two men, Cassius and Brutus, plotted an assassination against Caesar. On March 15th, 44 BCE, Julius Caesar was stabbed several times. His nephew Octavian then took the rule and changed his name to Augustus.

Under Augustus, Rome officially became an empire, mostly due to all of the changes that Caesar had made. Anyway, Augustus was crowned the first *emperor* of Rome. The Senate was now mostly powerless; their job was to advise the emperor, who created Rome's laws. Little did anyone know that the Roman Empire would last another five hundred years, before it would hopelessly crumble.

It was during the Empire that gladiators became popular. A gladiator was someone who willingly fought in the Roman Coliseum; sometimes they would fight animals, sometimes other people. Many people from across Rome would come to watch these fights; it was a source of great entertainment. To relate it to modern pop culture, the Roman coliseum was a huge inspiration behind Suzanne Collins's *The Hunger Games* trilogy.

It was also during the Empire that Christianity rose to power. Today, Italy has one of the biggest Christian and Catholic populations on the planet; originally, however, the Romans never wanted to move away from their twelve gods and convert to a monotheistic religion. It was in 313 CE that Emperor Constantine made a drastic move; amidst the growing popularity of Christianity, he declared it to be the empire's central religion. He converted to Christianity himself, and he ordered the Romans to stop harassing those who were Christian.

As Christianity grew, so too did the Empire. Eventually, Rome stretched from England to the Middle East, from Africa to northern Europe. It was massive! It was too much for a single emperor to control, so in later years, Emperor Diocletian decided to split Rome in two. One emperor would rule from Rome, and the other from

Byzantium. Each emperor would control his own part of the empire, and work together to make sure Rome worked efficiently.

In terms of Rome's enemies, there were many barbarian tribes throughout Europe that all despised Rome—because of their power and prowess in the world. They often assaulted Rome's borders, becoming more of a nuisance than anything. In order to stop the attacks, Emperor Valens decided to extend an allyship to the Visigoth barbarian tribe. He would be their friend and pay them money, if they stopped attacking and turned on the other tribes. But there was one problem—Rome could afford to pay these barbarians.

The Visigoths, when they realized Rome had no intention of paying them, were furious and turned on the Roman Empire. Thus began the fall of the greatest empire the world had ever seen. All at once, everything seemed to fall apart. Two emperors were not enough to keep everything under control; a lack of money caused soldiers to quit the army, depleting the Roman forces; the barbarians saw these weaknesses and attacked; the corrupt and rich in Rome turned their backs on the lower classes, who fought each other wildly over money and philosophies; the economy sank, while the population did too. Death skyrocketed, as did taxes.

With all of the chaos, the Visigoths invaded. They battled their way to Rome and attacked the city. What remained of the once-powerful Roman legions was not enough to hold them back, and the city was eventually sacked. The Visigoths killed and enslaved the Romans they found there.

The Fall of Rome invited a period of turmoil for Europe, who had been ruled by a strong and powerful government for so long. This period is now called the Dark Ages, and is marked by failures in education, government, population, and a rise in disease and death.

While the end of the Roman Empire is depressing, it is important also to understand what the Roman Empire gave the world. The Romans were responsible for new building techniques, which they improved from the Greeks; they initially gave money to the poor, setting this precedent across the world; they helped Christianity spread; they created the idea of "innocent until proven guilty," one of the backbones of the United States justice system; and much more. They also gave us a rich history to study, and one that will not easily be forgotten.

Ancient Rome: Discussion Questions

(1) How might the phrase "The bigger they are, the harder they fall" apply to Rome? What happened in the aftermath of Rome's fall?

(2) What advantage did Rome have by being situated on the Mediterranean Sea? Were there any disadvantages?

(3) Why did the Roman people dislike being ruled by a king, and why did they overthrow King Tarquin? How did they replace him?

(4) What are some the similarities and dissimilarities between the Greek and Roman gods? Do you think the Romans "stole" the Greek gods, or created an entirely new religion that is coincidentally similar?

(5) Do you think the Punic Wars could have been avoided? How? Were they important to Rome's history?

(6) Julius Caesar solved Rome's problems, but he also went against the rules and claimed to be a dictator for life. In your eyes, is he a hero or a villain? Did he deserve the death he received?

(7) What do you think the difference is between a *republic* and an *empire*? Who ruled the republic, and who ruled the empire?

(8) Do you think Christianity would have spread if Emperor Constantine had not embraced it?

(9) Was it a wise decision to split Rome into two empires?

(10) What do you think is the *most significant* reason for the fall of Rome?

Ancient Rome: Activities

(1) Watch the following John Green video that discusses Julius Caesar and the relationship between the Roman Republic and Empire. After you've finished the video, answer the following question: Did Caesar's death bring about the fall of the Republic, or had Rome become an Empire far before then? https://www.youtube.com/watch?v=oPf27gAup9U

(2) Choose one of the Roman/Greek gods, and then write three paragraphs about that god/goddess. In your short essay, compare and contrast the different versions of the deity, and what he or she meant to the Greek or Roman people. Feel free to use the library or the Internet for this activity.

(3) When the Carthaginian general Hannibal crossed the Alps, he had several dozen elephants in tow. Watch the following video about how he managed such a feat, and when you have finished write down three problems that Hannibal faced on his journey. http://www.history.com/topics/ancient-history/ancient-rome/videos/hannibals-war-elephants

(4) Create three columns on a piece of paper. The first one will be "Roman Kingdom," the second will be "Roman Republic," and the third will be "Roman Empire." Write down important events that occurred during each section in Rome's long history.

(5) Explore this cool 3D gallery, depicting what Rome looked like. Can you point out any buildings that you recognize? http://news.nationalgeographic.com/news/2007/08/photogalleries/rome-reborn/index.html

(6) The Punic Wars were defined by three different "wars." Reread the section, or do additional research, and outline each different explosion of conflict between Rome and Carthage. Then, create a timeline that details the Punic Wars. You do not need to include dates, just the order of events.

(7) Listen to the following song about the fall of Rome. When you've finished, write down an answer to the following question: Do you think it is helpful to learn about history through art and music, as in this video? Explain your answer. http://www.history.com/topics/ancient-history/ancient-rome/videos/the-fall-of-rome?m=528e394da93ae&s=undefined&f=1&free=false

(8) Print out a map of Europe, the Middle East, and northern Africa. Mark the following places: Rome, Carthage, Italy, Greece, Turkey, Byzantium, Spain, England, the Alps, the Rubicon River, the Mediterranean Sea, the Black Sea, the Caspian Sea, the Atlantic Ocean. Use a red marker or colored pencil to color in the areas that Rome reached in its height. Use additional online maps for help!

(9) Watch the following video about the Roman games. After you've finished, write down three interesting facts about the Coliseum and Roman forms of entertainment. http://www.history.com/topics/ancient-history/ancient-rome/videos/games-in-the-coliseum?m=528e394da93ae&s=undefined&f=1&free=false

(10) Imagine that you are Julius Caesar. You have enacted many reforms to help your people, but still the senators are angry that you are taking too much power. Write a journal entry, detailing how Julius Caesar

might have felt at this time. Was he trying to gain more and more power? Was he innocently trying to help his country? You decide.

Ancient Rome: For Further Reading

Brooks, Philip. *Hannibal: Rome's Worst Nightmare (Wicked History)*. Franklin Watts, 2009.

Cobblestone Publishing. *If I Were a Kid in Ancient Rome: Children of the Ancient World*. Cricket Books, 2007.

Conkle, Nancy. *A Coloring Book of Rome*. Bellerophon Books, 1988.

Connolly, Peter. *The Ancient City: Life in Classical Athens and Rome*. Oxford University Press, 2000.

Daynes, Katie. *See Inside Ancient Rome (See Inside Board Books)*. Usborne Pub Ltd., 2006.

Dickinson, Rachel. *TOOLS OF THE ANCIENT ROMANS: A Kid's Guide to the History & Science of Life in Ancient Rome (Build It Yourself)*. Nomad Press, 2006.

Dubois, Muriel L. *Ancient Rome: A Mighty Empire (Great Civilizations)*. Fact Finders, 2011.

Green, John. *Life in Ancient Rome (Dover History Coloring Book)*. Dover Publications, 1997.

Hanel, Rachael. *Ancient Rome: An Interactive History Adventure (You Choose: Historical Eras)*. You Choose Books, 2010.

Honan, Linda. *Spend a Day in Ancient Rome: Projects and Activities that Bring the Past to Life*. Wiley, 1998.

James, Simon. *Ancient Rome (DK Eyewitness Books)*. DK CHILDREN, 2008.

Murrell, Deborah. *The Best Book of Ancient Rome*. Kingfisher, 2004.

Osborne, Mary Pope. *Magic Tree House Fact Tracker #14: Ancient Rome and Pompeii: A Nonfiction Companion to Magic Tree House #13: Vacation Under the Volcano.* Random House, 2006.

Solway, Andrew. *Rome.* Scholastic Reference, 2003.

Ancient Rome: Quiz

(1) The city of Rome exists in what modern-day country?
    (A) England
    (B) Spain
    (C) Greece
    (D) Italy

(2) Which of the following was one of the names of Rome's mythical founders?
    (A) Lupin
    (B) Nero
    (C) Caesar
    (D) Romulus

(3) What happened to King Tarquin the Proud?
    (A) He was overthrown by the Roman people.
    (B) He was put into power by the Roman people, following a rebellion.
    (C) He was assassinated by Julius Caesar.
    (D) He was killed in the Coliseum by a gladiator.

(4) What group ruled the Roman Republic?
    (A) The Roman Congress
    (B) The Roman Empire
    (C) The Roman Senate
    (D) The Roman Patricians

(5) Who was the leader of the Roman gods?
    (A) Zeus
    (B) Poseidon
    (C) Ares
    (D) Jupiter

(6) What was the Roman lower class called?
    (A) Plebeians
    (B) Patricians
    (C) Consuls
    (D) Hobos

(7) The Punic Wars were fought between Rome and _____.
    (A) Gaul
    (B) The Visigoths
    (C) Julius Caesar
    (D) Carthage

(8) What Carthaginian general led his soldiers and dozens of elephants through the dangerous Alps?
    (A) Julius Caesar

(B) Tarquin the Proud
(C) Hannibal
(D) Romulus

(9) What was Julius Caesar's fate?
(A) He was sent into the Coliseum to face a lion.
(B) He was stabbed repeatedly by Roman senators.
(C) He died of old age after successfully turning Rome into an empire.
(D) He was murdered by his nephew Octavian, who wanted the throne.

(10) According to historians, which Roman leader was the first true *emperor*?
(A) Julius Caesar
(B) Tarquin the Proud
(C) Romulus
(D) Augustus

(11) What religion did Emperor Constantine adopt?
(A) Judaism
(B) Buddhism
(C) Christianity
(D) Islam

(12) In what structure did the Roman gladiators battle?
(A) The Coliseum
(B) The Senate
(C) The Fighting Pit
(D) The Plebeian

(13) To which tribe did Emperor Valens extend an allyship?
(A) The Visigoths
(B) The Gauls
(C) The French
(D) The Vikings

(14) Why did this tribe eventually turn on the Romans?
(A) The Romans tried to slaughter them.
(B) The Romans could not pay them money.
(C) The Romans insulted them at a feast.
(D) The Romans were planning to annihilate their leader at a wedding.

(15) Which was NOT one of the reasons that the Roman Empire fell?
(A) Corrupt politicians
(B) Failing economy
(C) Invading barbarians
(D) The discovery of the New World

(16) Rome was an Empire, and then a Republic.
(A) True

(B) False

(17) The Romans had twelve main gods, as did the Greeks.
   (A) True
   (B) False

(18) The Carthaginians overcame the Romans during the Punic Wars.
   (A) True
   (B) False

(19) Julius Caesar was viewed by all as a great leader.
   (A) True
   (B) False

(20) The Visigoths sacked the city of Rome.
   (A) True
   (B) False

Ancient Rome: Quiz Answers

(1) **D.** The city of Rome exists in modern-day Italy.
(2) **D.** Romulus was one of Rome's mythical founders.
(3) **A.** Tarquin the Proud was overthrown by the Roman people.
(4) **C.** The Roman Senate ruled the Republic.
(5) **D.** Jupiter led the Roman gods.
(6) **A.** The Roman lower class was called plebeians.
(7) **D.** The Punic Wars were fought between Rome and Carthage.
(8) **C.** Hannibal led his soldiers across the Alps.
(9) **B.** Julius Caesar was stabbed repeatedly by Roman senators.
(10) **D.** Augustus was the first true emperor of Rome.
(11) **C.** Emperor Constantine adopted Christianity.
(12) **A.** Roman gladiators battled in the Coliseum.
(13) **A.** Emperor Valens extended an allyship to the Visigoths.
(14) **B.** The Visigoths turned on the Romans because the Romans could not pay them money.
(15) **D.** The discovery of the New World did not affect the fall of the Roman Empire.
(16) **False.** Rome was a Republic, then an Empire.
(17) **True.** The Romans had twelve main gods.
(18) **False.** The Carthaginians did not overcome the Romans during the Punic Wars.
(19) **False.** Julius Caesar was not viewed as a great leader by all.
(20) **True.** The Visigoths sacked the city of Rome.

Ancient Rome: Works Cited

http://www.rome.mrdonn.org/

http://www.bbc.co.uk/schools/primaryhistory/romans/

http://www.historyforkids.org/learn/romans/

http://www.ducksters.com/history/ancient_rome.php

http://www.socialstudiesforkids.com/subjects/ancientrome.htm

http://www.roman-empire.net/children/

http://www.historyforkids.net/ancient-rome.html

CPSIA information can be obtained at www.ICGtesting.com
Printed in the USA
BVOW09s1022220916

462973BV00008B/10/P